Law and Philosophy Subversive of Democracy

San Francisco State University Series in Philosophy

Anatole Anton
General Editor

Vol. 4

PETER LANG
New York • Washington, D.C./Baltimore • Bern
Frankfurt am Main • Berlin • Brussels • Vienna • Oxford

James W. Syfers

Law and Philosophy Subversive of Democracy

PETER LANG
New York • Washington, D.C./Baltimore • Bern
Frankfurt am Main • Berlin • Brussels • Vienna • Oxford

Library of Congress Cataloging-in-Publication Data

Syfers, James W.
Law and Philosophy Subversive of Democracy / James W. Syfers.
p. cm. — (San Francisco State University series in philosophy; vol. 4)
Includes bibliographical references and index.
1. Antitrust law—United States. 2. Industrial concentration—United States.
3. Economic liberties (U. S. Constitution). 4. Democracy—United States.
5. Law—Philosophy. I. Title. II. Series.
KF1649 .S98 343.73'0721—dc21 00-064768
ISBN 0-8204-2887-6
ISSN 1067-0017

Die Deutsche Bibliothek-CIP-Einheitsaufnahme

Syfers, James W.:
Law and Philosophy Subversive of Democracy / James W. Syfers.
–New York; Washington, D.C./Baltimore; Bern;
Frankfurt am Main; Berlin; Brussels; Vienna; Oxford: Lang.
(San Francisco State University series in philosophy; Vol. 4)
ISBN 0-8204-2887-6

Cover design by Lisa Barfield

The paper in this book meets the guidelines for permanence and durability
of the Committee on Production Guidelines for Book Longevity
of the Council of Library Resources.

275 Seventh Avenue, 28th Floor, New York, NY 10001
www.peterlangusa.com

Printed in the United States of America

This book is dedicated to Oliver C. Cox
in appreciation of his extraordinary
work, *The Foundations of Capitalism*,
and to Gustav Bergman,
an extraordinary teacher.

Contents

The San Francisco State University Series in Philosophy

Anatole Anton

This series is designed to encourage philosophers to explore new directions in research, particularly directions that may lead to a re-integration of philosophy with the sciences, the arts and/or the humanities. The series is guided by three premises: (1) The intellectual division of labor into distinct academic disciplines is a product of changing historical circumstances and conditions (including developments within the disciplines themselves); (2) The current intellectual division of labor has outlived its usefulness in many ways; (3) There is a pressing need to reintegrate the metaphysical and evaluative concerns of philosophy with current work in the sciences and their associated technologies, the humanities and the arts. Works in this series are intended to challenge social and philosophical preconceptions that block the reintegration of philosophy with other disciplines and at the same time to maintain unquestionably high standards of scholarship. The fourth volume in our series, *Law and Philosophy Subversive of Democracy* by Jim Syfers, exemplifies our intentions. Metaphysics, political philosophy, social science and legal theory are rarely studied in their intimate connection. For this reason, political philosophers have tended to ignore the ways in which legal doctrine both stands in contradiction to democratic political philosophy and depends upon an obsolete metaphysics. Yet, as Jim Syfers notes in his essay on the right of association, "...there is nothing in the Constitution or Bill of Rights that requires the United States of America to be a democracy. Indeed, as historians have made clear, the Constitution was not drafted with the intent of establishing democracy or a democratic society; it was intended to be a representative government controlled by a property holding elite."

The eighteenth century foundations of our Constitution are liberal but not democratic. The aim of that document was to create a state which would protect and promote both property rights and, as an afterthought with the Bill of Rights, civil liberties. Resulting from popular pressure and, ultimately, a Civil War, this liberalism was progressively democratized. The expansion of the franchise is the most dramatic example of such democratization. At the same time, however, what is called "democracy" was liberalized to the point of rendering problematic that word's original meaning, rule of the demos. Syfers argues that part of the explanation of the Court's ability to dilute democracy is that "the legal system itself was and is based on an eighteenth century metaphysical premise that is not compatible with an industrialized Society." The general process of the "liberalization" of democracy has been discussed by political theorists, including, for example, C. B. Macpherson and Noam Chomsky, but relatively little attention has been paid to the role of the Supreme Court in the process of anti-democratic "liberalization." (Professor Kurt Nutting's analysis of election law, which is attached to this volume as an appendix, is extra-ordinarily illuminating in this regard.) Syfers' work is thus addressed to a lacuna in democratic theory. Indeed, as Syfers argues, the Supreme Court has consistently interpreted the law, especially the Constitution, without regard to the nation's professions of democracy. The result is a deeply anti-democratic system of law as it bearson such matters as dynastic trusts, patents, the nature of corporations, labor unions, human rights and elections. In the same period as the suffrage was expanded, the Supreme Court undermined the potentially democratic implications of this development by creating a body of law that makes substantive democracy impossible and substitutes for it "a government by and for corporations." To justify this development, social scientists, following the lead of Joseph Schumpeter, Walter Lippman and, more recently, Robert Dahl, re-defined the concept of liberal democracy "realistically" so as to make it consistent with those features of society that democratic theorists from the time of Gerard Winstanley to John Dewey and today Noam Chomsky have critiqued as undemocratic. In the hands of such "realistic" social scientists, democracy has been reduced to the method of selecting rulers among elites by means of electoral competition. In opposition to this re-definition, Syfers notes that:

> "After the American Revolution virtually all of the states abolished laws providing for primogeniture and entail, either by statute or by constitutional provision. These were laws that made dynastic wealth possible in the form of land holdings, land being the principal form of wealth in the early states. It was believed by many that there was no place in a democratic society for an aristocracy perpetuated by wealth. The form of wealth has shifted in the last one hundred years, land having given way to securities, but the belief is just as valid."

Thus, Syfers work forces us to consider the extent to which our nation's present re-definition of the concept of democracy rules out of consideration the very possibility of a democratic alternative to the undemocratic legal system which has been constructed in the United States in the last century. Syfers work also suggests the ways in which the present legal system can be rectified by the addition of a democracy amendment to the U.S. Constitution (see "The Right of Association: The Shameful History of a Right Essential to Democracy") and by insisting that the Supreme Court take to heart the deeply democratic implications of international law as the supreme law of the land (see "Human Rights vs. Classical Liberalism: A Study of Metaphysics and the Theory of Value"). The democracy amendment to the Constitution proposed by Professor Syfers is simple and straightforward. "No article or amendment of the Constitution shall be interpreted as authorizing a decision, act, policy, rule or law by any branch of government or any part thereof that limits or is detrimental to the preservation of democracy or a democratic society." Some of the profundity of this amendment emerges in the words of the 1993 Vienna Declaration on Human Rights: "...democracy, development and respect for human rights and fundamental freedoms are independent and mutually reinforcing. "Syfers case for substantial democracy turns on a point of metaphysics. Philosophic individualism, the view that "only individual things have ultimate reality," is an obstacle to democratic interpretations of the Constitution. Once this metaphysics is recognized as inadequate, the plausibility of a democratic interpretation becomes plain. Thus, as Syfers explains, the Constitutional framework allows individual rights but prohibits group rights. "There is ... no group right of the minority to have, proportionately as many doctors, nurses, teachers, airline pilots, or what have you as the white population." The import of this point becomes clear by way of contrast. "Every woman who qualifies has the right to run for the office of United States Senator; women as a class, however, have no right of representation in that body." Similarly, as Nutting argues with respect to the law of elections, though individual candidates are seen as having rights, the electorate as a whole has no rights, e.g., to a serious, many-sided debate prior to an important election. Indeed, Syfers breaks new ground when, in discussing these and related matters, he postulates the existence of a "cultural a priori."

> "Explanations of this type [philosophical individualist] will be what people hear, what they read, what are given at home and in schools, and what they will therefore make use of themselves, since explanations that depart from the social standard (for example, one of the structural type) would not be apt to be taken seriously. In these circumstances one could say that the proposition that only individual things exist has the status of an a priori truth in that society, a cultural a priori."

To put the point differently, like any foundational myth, it is simply presupposed by a society's network of institutions and is thus immune to questions or challenges that might stem from conflicting evidence. There is no area of law in which the undemocratic implications of philosophical individualism assert themselves more clearly than in the law as it concerns corporations. This body of law protects a veritable profit making army, constituted by a complex, hierarchical system of internal relations, as though it were an individual person. As Syfers tells us, the need for Federal law to gain democratic control over corporations was noted, in retrospect, by Justice Brandeis:

> "The removal by the leading industrial States of the limitations upon the size and owners of business corporations appears to have been due, not to their conviction that maintenance of the restrictions were undesirable in itself, but to the conviction that it was futile to insist upon them; because local restriction would be circumvented by foreign incorporation. Indeed, local restriction seemed worse than futile. Lesser states, eager for revenue derived from the traffic in charters, had removed safeguards from their own incorporation laws. Companies were early formed to provide charters for corporations in sites where the cost was lowest and the laws least restrictive. The states joined in advertising their wares. The race was not one of diligence but of laxity...

Democracy might have been served in this situation had the Federal government acted appropriately. As the democratic controls on corporations inherent in state charters were progressively eroded, only Federal law might have reversed this process. Syfers cites a statement made by Justice Harlan in 1894 to this effect.

> "Suppose another combination, organized for private gain and to control prices, should obtain possession of all the large flour mills in the United States; another, of all the grain elevators; another of all the oil territory; another of all the cotton mills; and another of all the great establishments for slaughtering animals, and the preparation of meats. What power is competent to protect the people of the United States against such dangers except a national power - one that is capable of exerting its sovereign authority throughout every part of the territory and over all the people of the nation?"

Having watered down state charters and failed to enact Federal law to allow for democratic controls on corporate behavior, the devolution of democracy, as Syfers recounts, took place in three additional steps. In 1886, in Santa Clara County v. Southern Pacific Railroad Co., the Court decided without argument that corporations were to be counted as persons under the equal protection clause of the fourteenth Amendment. Corporations were thus implausibly assimilated into the framework of philosophical individualism, our cultural a priori. By so doing, the Court altered the very meaning of the Constitution, for surely, when the founders in the Preamble to the Constitution, referred to "We, the people...," they did not have entities such as Chevron or Texaco in mind. Nor could they have imagined the second step in the devolution of the Constitution: that in giving the Congress power to regulate commerce, they were denying Congress the power to regulate manufacturing. But this is what the Court decided in "the Sugar Trust case," making, as Professor Syfers explains, "most of the trusts beyond the grasp" of the Anti-Trust Acts. Nor finally, to consider the third step in the devolution of democracy, would they have had any truck with the so-called "Rule of Reason," the notion that Congress only had the power to regulate "unreasonable monopolies, trusts, and cartels, "as decided in the great Oil and Tobacco Trust cases of 1911. Thus, for all intents and purposes, the Supreme Court, in positing that corporations were to be treated as persons under the fourteenth amendment, initiated the process by means of which the business corporation was placed outside the purview of democratic control. To regard a corporation as an individual person of any kind strains credulity. In fact, as Syfers argues, to begin to get an adequate grasp of the reality of corporations, we need to see them as complexes or systems (within larger systems). The notion of a simple individual will not do. Since our thinking is dominated by our cultural a priori, Syfers tells us, we lack the capacity for plausible self-representation and thus the capacity to transform ourselves in the direction of our democratic ideals. The implications of Syfers' line of reasoning are clearly that our democratic convictions fall victim to false consciousness. The reason is that, given philosophical individualism, we cannot see that our social system as a whole is the primary source of value. It is simply wrong headed to exclusively reward individuals, corporate or ordinary, for the creation of value, when their contributions would be unthinkable without an entire system of socialized results as well as the socialization of costs on which private production, particularly corporate production, depends.

The internet, for example, derives from the socialization of much research and development carried on by the Department of Defense and given over to corporations together with an educated labor force and a whole history of ideas and theories of computation, algorithms (an arabic word) and so forth. More generally still, In Professor Syfers' words, "...recognition of the existence of systems as such would make possible their protection in law and their modification by law. Thus an ecosystem could be protected in its own right, rather than as a byproduct of the protection of individual members of an endangered species. "At any rate, a realistic look at the economy makes a mockery of the doctrine of philosophic individualism. What Syfers argues instead is that the concept of "system" forces itself upon us. We have developed an economic system of extraordinary technical complexity; its fundamental units of production, the corporations or corporate conglomerates, are themselves organized in a complex mosaic of trade associations and national and international policy making bodies, and these organizations have in turn developed symbiotic relationships with quasi-sovereign governmental agencies. At the same time legal title to this system of production has been shifting slowly over this century from individuals to financial and nonfinancial corporations, further removing the control of the economy from a moral and political community of persons that alone makes civilized society possible. None of this accords with the Classical Liberal political and economic theory that continues to be put forward as its moral and theoretical foundation. Democratic convictions are further strained when it is seen that one part of this system is political. To take Syfers' example, The Committee for Economic Development (CED), "an organization originally formed in 1942 to work out plans for shifting from a wartime to a peacetime economy," is made up of 200 of the largest corporations of the country. In 1962, the CED determined, in a model of pure private sector planning, that there ought to be "a reduction of the farm labor force on the order of one third in a period of not more than five years." Though it seems that the CED implemented its plan successfully, Syfers underscores the implications for democracy of such a result. Clearly the place for deciding on a national farm policy in a democratic society is its elected legislative body, and the Congress of the United States has never adopted a policy of eliminating small farms in favor of large corporate farms. In fact, the Agricultural Act of 1961 adopted a policy of acting "to encourage, promote and strengthen" the small farm. However, far more federal law and policy is created by unelected federal department and agency bureaucracies than by the U.S. Congress (the ratio is 18 to 1). In this case, the relevant bureaucracy, the Department of Agriculture, has long favored the agribusiness corporation over the small farmer, through the policies and regulations of its Agricultural Stabilization and Conservation Service, its Extension Service, and its Agricultural Research Service. The corporate political system as exemplified by the CED is, in fact, an unacknowledged part of the corporate economic system. The negative implications for democracy of this absence of acknowledgment are obvious. If Syfers is right, another unacknowledged part of the corporate system are the ideas of philosophical individualism themselves. If the corporate system has an unacknowledged political part, it has an unacknowledged intellectual part as well. In this way, the doctrine of philosophical individualism becomes part of a larger system. It allows corporations as persons to own patents, despite the fact that such ownership often conflicts with anti-trust laws. Scandalously, as Syfers reports, these ideas are used selectively—as in the failure of the Court to recognize the personhood of labor unions (in contrast to corporations)—but the ideas do undergird the very concept of a dynastic trust, a legally constructed individual the main purpose of which is to prevent the redistribution of wealth from one generation to the next. On the other hand, as Syfers shows, with the rejection of philosophic individualism and the recognition of social systems as sources of value, human rights law, as reflected in the Covenant on Civil and Political Rights and the Covenant on Economic, Social and Cultural Rights taken together, implies at least two things: (1) Private property in the income producing category would be a public trust to be managed for the common good; (2) Every member of the social system would have a rightful claim to the social product, meaning in practical terms a decent standard of living, including medical care, security in old age and disability, education, and meaningful participation in the social, cultural and political life of the society. The democratic implications of a serious commitment to human rights have never been stated more clearly. Furthermore, if Professor Syfers is correct, democracy ultimately requires "the collective ownership of the social system and its product." We might call this the substantive, fullblooded conception of democracy in contrast to the notion of democracy that is now current.

Preface

LAURENCE H. SHOUP

YOU HOLD IN YOUR HANDS an unusual and important book. Its very title, *Law Subversive of Democracy* stimulates thought. How could law, which is supposed to ensure democracy, somehow subvert it? By bringing together insights from several social scientific fields, this book presents the answers, logically, step by step, fact upon fact, until conclusions vital for our collective future are evident. The resulting usable history and analysis develops several key points. Over the last century and a half, inheritance laws have been codified which have facilitated the development of vast dynastic wealth on a scale unheard of in prior human history. At the same time, patent laws encouraging the monopolization of industry have been put on the law books. Finally, court cases have successfully given the corporation so many unfettered rights that it has become more powerful than any other institution in this or almost any other country. This has made the capitalistic corporation, which is a narrow and shortsighted organization, virtually all powerful. Its purpose has evolved almost solely into a money-making machine for its biggest owners, not beneficial to the people or society at large. While this was being done, other laws and violent government actions were severely undercutting, even destroying, the very countervailing powers—labor unions and peoples' movements—which could limit the unchecked power of the developing plutocracy and their corporations. The result has been not only untold suffering by millions and millions of people, but also the loss of much of our democracy to a privileged class. The open buying of our government at all levels, through large campaign contributions, massive lobbying and other less subtle forms of political payoffs and corruption, is obvious even in the limited reporting characteristic of the corporate media. Government-corporate collusion against the peoples' interests has thus become endemic. At the root of the problem all along has been and still is big money in politics along with the winner take all political system (instead of proportional representation or forms of direct democracy). And behind the big money is a totalitarian aristocracy of inherited wealth largely created by the laws that have usurped our democracy.

One of the beauties of this book is that it expresses faith in the process of renewal and change. It goes beyond mere description and offers us a thoughtful antidote for the hegemony of the corporate rich. In this respect it follows an old adage: a writer's duty is to instruct, set a moral tone and try to make the world better. The better in this case is to implement the proper goal of society, namely the full, all sided development of every member of the human family and the community/collectivity, not a life denying and obscene commitment to unlimited wealth and unlimited power of the few over others. Collective ownership of the socioeconomic system is properly seen as necessary, creating a public trust with environmental protections and equal access to the social product for everyone. If such a system of equality, social justice and environmental protections is not implemented, and the corporate forces which now dominate the development of life on earth continue to do so, then we will lose not only what is left of our freedom but eventually the entire fabric of life. The earth with its finite resources will not be able to take many more decades of the kind of intense exploitation it has suffered at corporate hands for the past century. But the promise of humanity resides within itself, and trend is not destiny.

We can take the future into our hands. As the author points out, international treaty law, specifically the Covenant on Civil and Political Rights and the Covenant on Economic, Social, and Cultural Rights, can be used as rallying points for the struggle to create a new society which is both just and sane.

The insights of the book you now hold are an excellent place to begin the intellectual journey that is a necessary prelude to higher consciousness and bolder action.

Oakland, California
October, 1999

Acknowledgments

I WISH TO THANK THE MEMBERS of *Group San Francisco* for their critical comments on my work and for their support: Anatole Anton, Kostas Bagakis, Ann Ginger, Kurt Nutting, and Roberto Rivera. Special thanks to Anatole Anton, editor of this series, without whose help and encouragement this book would never have come into being.

Introduction

AS WE ENTER THE TWENTY-FIRST CENTURY it is not at all clear that American democracy will survive in a form acceptable to the majority of its citizens; what was established as a government of, by, and for the people has increasingly become a government by and for corporations. How this state of affairs came about is one of the questions that led to these essays. Hopefully they will point the way toward some of the things that must be done if we are to realize our democratic heritage.

Around the turn of the previous century, prompted by the democratic Populist Movement and subsequently by the Socialist and Progressive Movements, Congress passed a number of laws that could have curtailed to a considerable degree the growing power of corporations and the massing of wealth in the hands of a relative few. Some of the principal laws passed were the Interstate Commerce Act (1887), the Sherman Anti-Trust Act (1890), an inheritance tax (1898), an act prohibiting corporate contributions to federal elections (1907), and an anti-bribery statute (1909). Whatever were the purposes that have ultimately been served by this legislation, however, the democratic purpose of preventing the further concentration of wealth and power has turned out not to be one of them.

There were undoubtedly many reasons for this failure to stop the concentration of wealth and power, but three of those reasons were as follows: first, the Courts independently developed bodies of law that served the interests of some individuals, yet were in direct conflict with the goal of developing or maintaining a democratic society; second, the Supreme Court made a series of decisions without regard to their consequences for the further development or preservation of a democratic society, and lastly, the legal system itself was and is based on an eighteenth century metaphysical premise that is not compatible with a modern democratic industrial society. Most of the essays in this volume are occupied with one or more of these reasons for what is in effect the present usurpation of the sovereignty of the people by a very small upper class holding or controlling most of the nation's wealth through the legal instrumentality of the corporation.

The first essay deals with a body of law that permitted the creation of a new form of dynastic wealth in the United States, any form of which is necessarily antagonistic to democracy. It also considers a body of law that has permitted the creation of extensive legalized monopolies, ultimately placing control of the nature and direction of the economy of the country in hands unaccountable to the public. The second essay, on the history of the right of association, details the process by which the Supreme Court turned what should have been a constitutional right of association into what amounted to a privilege exercisable by the few to the detriment of the many; it also contains a proposal as to what might be done about this situation. These two essays go a certain distance toward explaining how it has been possible in recent years for a small minority of the population to devastate a considerable part of the middle class, treat a large part of the working class like feudal serfs rather than American citizens, and plunge hundreds of thousands into homelessness.

The third of the three reasons given above is more complicated than ill-considered or unfortunate decisions of the judiciary. We have inherited a legal system based upon an *a priori* metaphysical premise that was once revolutionary and did much to advance moral and scientific progress; it has since become a foundation stone of reactionary politics. This is the premise I have called *Philosophic Individualism*. How this premise now stands in the way of the implementation of the International Bill of Human Rights and of a democratic reconstruction of the economy is the subject of the third essay; a significant part of this opposition stems from the general theory of value that is a corollary of Philosophic Individualism. Why this theory is no longer reasonable and what ought to replace it is a further subject of that essay. The fourth essay considers a series of legal and moral consequences of Philosophic Individualism, as well as the manner in which such metaphysical premises function in human society. Another consequence of Philosophic Individualism as a cultural premise is the subject of the fifth essay, examining the way in which the premise has functioned as the principal intellectual basis for Western racism. The sixth is an attempt to get some bearings on the present crisis in Western civilization, included because it touches upon many of the above themes.

And now a disclaimer and an apology. The disclaimer is in connection with the title of this book. There is nothing in any of these essays endorsing or suggesting the view that either government or law is *per se* an evil, or that less government and less law is in some way better than more of the same. The problem is that of establishing democratic control over the government and forging a legal system that is supportive of it.

The apology is for the fact that there is occasional repetition of some points from one essay to another, as I explore different aspects of some of the main subjects and their interconnections, particularly the subjects of Classical Liberalism, Philosophic Individualism, and the International Bill of Human Rights.

I have included a part of the International Bill of Human Rights—the International Covenant on Social, Economic and Cultural Rights—as an appendix. Together with the Covenant on Civil and Political Rights it constitutes a rough blueprint for a human civilization in the ethical sense of the term, and it is a blueprint now officially accepted by virtually all of the governments on earth. If there is any hope of our creating a decent civilization in the next century, however, people the world over will have to become familiar with the rights they possess under this body of international law; for otherwise they cannot demand that it be implemented by their governments. Such a mass international democratic movement is now possible with the technology of the internet and the growing number of non-governmental organizations dedicated to human rights.

Law Subversive of Democracy

Introduction

WHETHER A BODY OF LAW IS subversive of democracy depends in part on what is meant by democracy. It is only in the last half of this century that the term has come to mean a form of government in which everyone is to be given equal treatment under the law; in which everyone is to be treated equally by the law (no so-called separate but equal facilities), and in which everyone is to have equal opportunity for advancement, intellectually, socially, and economically.

This meaning of democracy has been the result of both popular struggles and enlightened acts of governments and states. The forty or so nations that founded the United Nations developed a Universal Declaration of Human Rights in 1948; in the 50's and 60's the Warren Court—continuing the process begun by an earlier court—applied much of the Bill of Rights to the States through the 14th Amendment. In the 60's our Congress passed the Civil Rights and Voting acts, and the now one hundred and sixty or so members of the United Nations made two great covenants on human rights a part of international law in 1976. One is the Covenant on Civil and Political Rights, the other the Covenant on Economic, Social, and Cultural Rights. And very recently, in April of 1992 our Senate consented to the ratification of the first of these two Covenants.[1] If you study these international conventions closely you will find that most of the rights of the one are presupposed by those of the other and vice versa. By this I mean that it is impossible to fully enjoy the rights in the one document without having and enjoying those in the other. For example, it is impossible to fully enjoy the right of freedom of speech and/or the press, if indeed one can enjoy them at all, if one is illiterate, unhoused, and without security of one's person. By 'enjoying a right' I mean being able to exercise the right without interference, or, if there is interference, being able to secure the appropriate remedy.[2] So the two Covenants form a closely interlocked whole.

Another interesting fact about these two Covenants is that it would be extremely difficult if not impossible for a nation to implement the Covenants—and all are pledged to do so—without becoming a democracy. I will not argue that here, but what I will mean by 'democracy' is more than the idea that all citizens have the right to vote and periodically elect those who will govern them for the next stipulated period of years. I will use the term in the deeper sense in which it refers to a form of political life in which every person enjoys all the rights to which they are now entitled under international law. This includes a minimum standard of living that insures health, health care, safety, individual development, and participation in the political life of the society.

Now the preceding is a subject that deserves an extensive treatment of its own, spelling out all the whys and wherefores, but it will have to suffice as a prelude to the main subject of this essay. And that subject is two bodies of law that are subversive of democracy in the sense of 'democracy' I have indicated. So what I will be arguing is that in order to have democracy in the sense it has come to have in the second half of the this century, there are two bodies of law that need to be radically altered or eliminated because they are subversive of this result. They are not, I believe, the only bodies of law of that kind, but they are two of the most important.

The bodies of law I will be considering have to do with the economic life of the country; one has to do with the creation and perpetuation of a privileged class, and the other has to do with the control of the fundamental economy of the nation by that class.

Part I: A Curious Result

In November of 1973 Senators Lee Medcalf and Edmund Muskie submitted a report to Senator Sam Ervin, Chair of the U.S. Senate Committee on Government Operations. The report detailed the results of an investigation concerning the ownership of corporate stock in the largest financial and non-financial corporations in the United States.[3] The results of the study were very curious indeed. Senators Medcalf and Muskie were Chairs of two Government Operations Subcommittees; they had requested each of the nation's largest corporations to provide them with a list of their thirty largest stockholders. Over half submitted full or partial replies. The replies were rather mysterious; here, for example, is the beginning of the report on the thirty largest stockholders for Travelers, the insurance company:

1. Cede & Co. 789,684 shares
2. Barnett & Co. 224,500 shares

3. Kane & Co. 1, 041,487 shares
4. Cudd & Co. 295,028 shares
5. Stuart & Co. 903,196 shares
6. Sigler & Co. 347,307 shares
7. Carson & Co. 839,620 shares
8. Schmidt & Co. 783,104 shares
9. Reing & Co. 490,500 shares
10. Ince & Co. 347,106 shares
11. Lynn & Co. 225,000 shares[4]

And each of the largest corporations provided, in the main, the same "X and Co." sort of list, frequently with some of the same names. These turned out to be the same stockholder lists that the corporations provided to the Securities Exchange Commission, the Interstate Commerce Commission, and to the other four Federal regulatory commissions that required some stockholder reporting. But what did they mean? Or perhaps better, who were they?

The answer was found in another list, privately held by the American Society of Corporate Secretaries until it was made public for the first time in the Congressional Record (June 24, 1971); called the Nominee List, it revealed the real legal owners behind the "nominees" or "street names" that were reported as being the stockholders. And the Nominee List revealed something that was quite startling. Extrapolating from the data provided by the corporations that replied, it appeared that virtually all the largest stockholders of virtually all the largest corporations in the United States were banks, and not very many banks at that. In the above list the real owners were a subsidiary of the New York Stock Exchange followed by seven of the largest New York banks. Numbers (3) and (4), for example, were Chase Manhattan, and numbers (7)—(11) were Morgan Guaranty. And this proved to be true for the largest banks themselves—their 30 largest stockholders were the other large banks!

There had developed, in other words, a situation in which the most powerful economic institutions of the country were the legal owners of each other! More accurately, the controlling interest in the largest 300 or more corporations in the country appears to be held collectively by the banks in trust accounts, and the banks collectively hold the controlling interest in each other in the same way. Evidently, after a century, the nightmare of Karl Marx had finally come to pass; the process of the concentration of the ownership of capital had reached its final stage. However, it was not human beings who legally owned it all, it was fictional corporate beings, creatures of the legal system, mutually owning each other!

What the Subcommittee report revealed, then, is surely the most significant alteration in the institution of private property since the creation of the corporation itself.[5] An increasing share of the productive wealth of the nation has, beginning especially after World War I, been placed in trust accounts in banks, a very large part of which is protected and preserved in dynastic trusts. It is the law of dynastic trusts that is the first of the two bodies of law that I will argue are subversive of democracy.

It will be helpful to begin with two distinctions. The first is a distinction between *productive* and *unproductive* wealth. Productive wealth produces income; unproductive wealth consumes income. Owning a three hundred thousand dollar house in which you live (looked at from this standpoint) is an unproductive form of wealth, since you have to pay for repairs, painting, insurance, and so forth. Having the same three hundred thousand in stocks would be productive wealth since there is no cost (save broker's fees and perhaps a safe deposit box), and there are periodic dividends.

The second distinction is that between *transient* and *permanent* wealth; a great fortune amassed by an individual in one lifetime very easily flies off in a dozen different directions on its owner's death; call this transient wealth, since it lasts no longer than one lifetime. Permanent wealth will then mean wealth that is protected from division and dissipation over generations. If it is productive wealth and it is substantial, it is likely to grow larger with time rather than smaller.

Now the creation of a permanent upper class requires the development of permanent forms of productive wealth. In feudal times such wealth took the form of title to land. With the coming of industrial capitalism, productive wealth assumed the form of stocks and bonds, and in the United States this was turned into permanent wealth by the development of dynastic trusts. Trusts of this dynastic type are the outcome of court decisions going back into the late 19th century, and while the law is constantly changing there are three main components to such a trust:

1. Our constitution prohibits taxing wealth directly (Article I, Section 9); barring a constitutional amendment—like the 16th, that allowed the income tax—we can only tax personal wealth when it is transferred from one party to another or others. Either taxing the estate of the deceased or taxing those who inherit. Permanent wealth must find some means of escaping these transfer taxes. The problem is resolved by the generation skipping feature of the dynastic trust.

   The testator assigns the legal ownership of the wealth to a trustee, typically a bank; the beneficial ownership is assigned to the heirs. Since the bank is an "immortal," the legal owner of the wealth does not change until the termination of the trust (which may be in the fourth generation but no longer, according to the rule against perpetuities).
2. But there is a second protective shield needed to establish a dynastic

trust. What if the heirs, enjoying their beneficial interests, decide it would be better still if they controlled the principal? In the case *Clafin v. Clafin*, 1889, a Massachusetts court decided this should not be allowed, and this Clafin doctrine has become the standard in 41 states.

3. Finally, the full-fledged dynastic trust contains a *Spendthrift Clause*, a clause that prevents the beneficiary from anticipating income from the trust for the purpose, for example, of assigning it to a creditor, and in some cases prevents the assignment of future income even by a court action. This feature is surely beneficial in the case of pension funds in trust or an incompetent heir, but dynastic trusts are not pension funds nor are their beneficiaries necessarily incompetent.

It is interesting that neither the Clafin doctrine nor the Spendthrift Clause (save in a very restricted form) is part of trust law in England. In fact, the United States seems to be the only country that has developed a body of trust law that so honors the will of the testator, or looked at from a somewhat different angle, a body of law that is so helpful in creating a permanent upper class.[6]

Now what does this mean in practical terms? First of all it is very difficult to get an accurate idea of how much wealth is buried in dynastic type trusts. We know that it has increased every year since World War I, and one close student of the subject estimates that while it was around 800 billion in 1972, it is probably 1.6 trillion now. In 1972 the IRS estimated that 6.1% of the population held 629 billion dollars worth of the total stock held in the United States. That total was, in 1972, 870.9 billion.[7] Clearly a very large part of the total stock as well as the bonds is being held in trusts. And a very large percentage of these trusts are thought to be dynastic.

Now what does this phenomenon mean in relation to a democratic society? The dividends and interest that flow into the trust accounts come primarily from the profits of corporations. And these profits are generated by the organized labor of hundreds or thousands of individuals, from managers to clerks, from officers to security guards. All of these people are contributing a part of their labor to the creation of the profits that flow into the trusts (1.5 billion if we assume a 10% return on a trillion and a half). And on the other side, the privileged beneficiaries are receiving their shares of those profits. So you have a society where some are born to contribute a part of the fruits of their labor to unknown others, and some are born with the privilege of receiving the product of the work of unknown others.

That such a state of affairs is directly contrary to the principle of equal treatment under the law is a point that has been made many times previously. It is still a valid point to my mind, and I want to explore it for a moment. In the 19th century and earlier the doctrine was widespread that all value is created by individuals. That is still the definition of `Individualism' in most dictionaries. It never meant "by each and every one of us"; it meant something more like "by unusual, specially endowed, particularly vigorous, and/or creative individuals." Yet I think it is clear that the doctrine greatly distorts reality. Let us confine the question to economic value only. Not only is economic value not created by individuals, it is not even created by organizations or institutions. It is created, in our world, by the functioning of an extraordinarily complex social system in which these organizations and institutions are deeply and inextricably embedded, and without which they could neither function nor exist.

So economic value is not created individually, it is created systemically. It is the product of a vast social system made up of many interlocked subsystems at many levels, both mental and physical. To put this in another way, the primary agency of production in our time is no longer the extended family of the late 18th and early 19th century, nor the corporation of the late 19th and early 20th century. It is the entire social system with the State as its "chief executive officer." And this fact provides the fundamental ground for the entitlement rights, economic and social, of all our citizens. It is the material basis for the philosophy of democracy that has developed in this century and is now part of international law.

As value is produced by the social system it should be distributed equitably to all citizens, both those fortunate enough to find a productive place within a society with fewer and fewer such places, and those who are not so fortunate. All should be treated equally under the law and that is the law, domestically and internationally.

But this is not the only law, and it is deeply opposed by those who have the view very nicely expressed by the Attorney General of the United States under President Cleveland. That was Richard Olney, former attorney for the Whiskey Trust. In his message to Congress in 1893 he made the following observations on the fate of the Sherman Anti-Trust Act:

1. Congress cannot limit the right of state corporations or of citizens in the acquisition, accumulation and control of property;
2. Congress cannot prescribe the prices at which such property shall be sold by the owner, whether a corporation or an individual;
3. Congress cannot make criminal the intents and purposes of persons in the acquisition and control of property which the states of their residence or creation sanction...[8]

I assume that the Whiskey Trust was gracious enough to provide Attorney General Olney with a lifetime supply of his favorite beverage in return for these edifying points concerning our constitutional law. On this view, then, there can be no limit on the acquisition of property. Evidently there has been very little limit so far, as evidenced by the Du Pont family. They are estimated to own or control some 211 billion dollars worth of property, here and abroad.[9] This is wealth beyond the wildest dreams of avarice, far beyond the capacity of the family to spend, even if each member of the family were prodigality incarnate. At this level, wealth has only one principal value—economic and political power over others.

So one of the two bodies of law that I want to say are subversive of democracy is the law that helped to create and helps to preserve this upper class. The second body of law has to do with the private control of the economy through the control of technology.

Part II: A Fundamental Contradiction in the Law

I turn now to the second body of law (the creation in part by Congress and in part by the Courts) a body of law that constitutes the legal machinery for the creation and preservation of the great industrial monopolies that produce the profits that go out to the beneficiaries of the trusts.

The body of law I refer to is United States patent law. The Constitution empowered Congress (Article I, Section 8) "to promote the progress of science and useful arts, by securing for limited times to authors and inventors, the exclusive right to their respective writings and discoveries." And Congress passed the first patent act in 1790; the law as it now stands can be found in the USCA Title 35 Section 101 and following. It grants to the patent holder a legal monopoly for 17 years. But the Founders never imagined the corporate form of business enterprise, nor the extraordinary decision of the Supreme Court in 1886 (*Santa Clara Cty. v. Southern Pacific RR Co.*, 118 US 394) that made corporations individuals under the law. And when corporations began to take over the basic economy of the United States, as the primary agency of economic production, it was not long before they realized the beneficial aspects of being included in the Constitution as individuals, with the rights of individuals, including the holding of patents.

What happened in the early part of this century—which I want to illustrate by considering three great industrial monopolies—what happened was that while we enacted a body of law to make monopolies illegal, the Sherman Act in 1890 and the Clayton Act in 1914, at the very same time we continued to develop another body of law that made monopolies perfectly legal and even strengthened their position.

I have constructed a somewhat oversimplified diagram (Diagram 1) that may make what follows easier to follow. It is not a snapshot taken at some specifiable moment in time; it is, rather, a rough portrait of the connections between three great industries over a period of decades, the nineteen tens, twenties, and

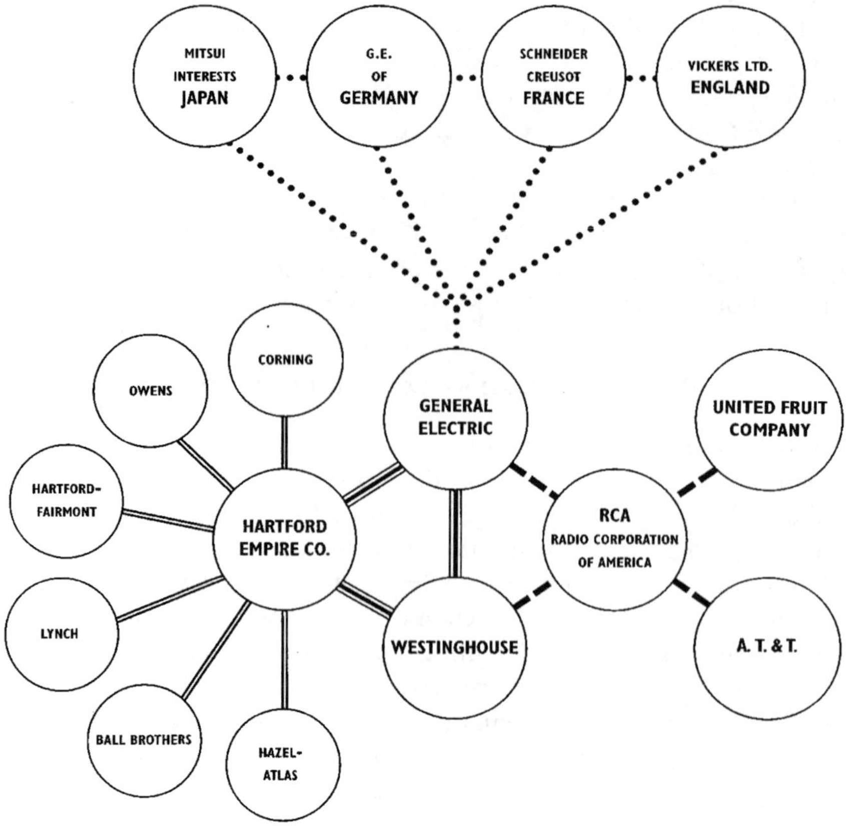

DIAGRAM I

FOUR TYPES OF PATENT MONOPOLIES

CROSS LICENSING
PATENT POOLING
PATENT TRUST
PRIVATE GOVERNMENT

thirties. Not all the participants are shown; not all of those shown are equally nefarious, and not all of the various lines from one to another were permanent or unwavering.

Now those of you familiar with the theories of Adam Smith will know that in his "Free Market" system, the competition of a multitude of sellers is supposed to have the result of keeping the price of commodities down to the lowest feasible level, keeping the quality of the goods high, and producing a somewhat fair distribution of wealth among the citizenry. The purpose of monopolies is not to do this. That is one way of putting it.

When you have monopolies you get an excess share of what-there-is-to-be-had flowing upward where some of it can be put to very good use; that is, some of it can be spent on insuring the continued existence of the monopoly in question by bribing public officials, taking judges to lunch, filing lawsuits, lobbying congress in the best professional and scientific fashion, and so on. This political fallout of monopolies is extensive and is as or more important over the long haul than the economic consequences; so it should be studied along with the textbooks on monopoly by economists if you want to get a clear picture of what monopolization actually means.

And when you have this situation where there is a fundamental contradiction in the law, along with the fundamental division of outlook in the governing class I spoke of earlier—one side holding views similar to Attorney General Richard Olney and the other side having to some extent honest democratic and/or free market sentiments—then the Justice Department has real problems in trying to quash these monopolistic growths on the economy—even when you have a Justice Department that actually wants to do something about them. The Courts may be entirely unsympathetic; and since we have two antithetical bodies of law co-existing with each other the Court is often free to move in either direction at will. Congress is also divided. Early in the century, for example, bills were introduced into Congress year after year and continuing sporadically thereafter to make patents void if they were used to bring about violations of the Sherman or Clayton Acts. But none of these bills were ever successful.

Turning now to the three great domestic monopolies in the diagram, I will begin with the left side of the page and the monopoly in the glass container industry. Here you have seven companies who held patents in this industry at the beginning of the mechanization of production stage and decided to pool them in order to control virtually the entire developing industry. The story of this conspiracy which began around 1916 is spelled out in great detail in the federal case *Hartford Empire Co. et al v. United States*, 323 US 386, 1944.

Very briefly, Corning created Empire Co. to hold around 100 patents, many dealing with its suction method of glass container production; Hartford-Fairmont held a large number of patents on a rival method called the suspended gob feeder method; Owens had around 60 patents, Hazel-Atlas around 70, and so on. They all agreed, though not at the same time, to assign these patents to Hartford-Empire in return for various considerations. This is the method called patent pooling. And up to 1933 they controlled 82% of glass container production in the United States, and after 1933 they controlled 92%. If you tried to manufacture glass containers anywhere in the United States without the permission of Hartford-Empire and without acceding to their terms, you would very likely be bankrupted by legal fees for violating patent rights.

Now these arrangements in the glass container field were of no little interest to those manufacturing light bulbs. Here you had further collections of very valuable patents in the hands of General Electric Co. (formed in part out of the Thomas Edison Co.) and Westinghouse. In this case, however, the patents were not pooled; rather the three companies involved—now in the middle of the diagram—cross-licensed each other. In so doing they were able to control 94% of the production of light bulbs, and the 37 companies they licensed in turn had to pay royalties to the monopoly and had to sell the product at a price set by G.E. Even Westinghouse was forced to do this by the U.S. Supreme Court in 1926, in the case *U.S. v. G.E.* 272 US 476, which approved cross-licensing and approved the private property right of the main patent holder to fix prices for all licensees.

Finally on the right side of the diagram you have the response to the invention of radio which began with big glass radio tubes; in this case the complete domination of the industry was secured by the formation of RCA in 1919. I show four companies participating, but there were more like seven; one of the others was Marconi Wireless of Britain. Marconi had demonstrated the feasibility of transatlantic radio transmission in 1901. (The feasibility of radio transmission as such was demonstrated and patented in 1888 by the lesser known Nathan Stubblefield of Murray, Kentucky; a model of his quaint apparatus is kept there at the Murray State Teacher's College.) The seven companies, however, turned ownership of their patents over to RCA in exchange for stock, so that RCA became sole owner of around 4000 patents. If you wanted to manufacture radios you had to guarantee to RCA that you could produce $100,000 a year in royalties, and you had to pay a fee of 7.5% of the value of each set sold. By 1954 RCA was holding around 10,000 patents.[10] So you have here three different ways of monopolizing a market: through patent pooling, through cross-licensing, and through the creation of a patent trust.

This tale can be carried on into various other interconnecting industries. Indeed, given the physical interrelatedness of modern industrial production it is likely that you would find a great web of legal interconnections between all the industries. But the general picture is clear; by amassing hundreds and then thousands of patents corporations are able to dominate industries, forcing citizens, other companies, and the government to pay more than should be paid for nearly everything we use in a modern economy. And it does not end there. As the top of the diagram illustrates, you also have the formation of international monopolies, such as the Electric Light Bulb Cartel. The Constitution of the Cartel established a complex government characterized—in keeping with modern political theory—by the separation of powers. Who can produce what kinds of bulbs anywhere in the world and who can sell how many of any given type was set by the legislative branch of the Cartel. Its' rulings were carried out by the executive branch; appeals were made to a judicial branch.[11] How many of the international cartels are organized in this particular fashion I do not know. However organized they pose a difficult problem for newer countries that are trying to develop their own industrial base; if they want to participate in the international economy they must agree to obey international law. And this means they must respect international patent agreements. Hence manufacturing milk bottles in Ghana could be as problematic as in Texas.

But let us come back to the domestic economy. The developments I have been discussing that occurred at the beginning of the century are still occurring. As new technologies are developed, patents are inevitably applied for; as patents are taken out, the process of consolidating inevitably begins. So the monopolizing process is underway now in the most advanced areas of technological development such as biotechnology, and it is being aided by the courts and the U.S. Patent Office. The Patent Office allowed the first patent on seeds in 1970, on microbes in 1980, and on animals in 1988. So this new industry will surely follow in the footsteps of the glass container industry and so many others.

What we have, then, is a body of law regarding patents which provides a legal basis for monopoly. And as long as we have this in place and it is supported by the philosophy of unlimited ownership and control of property, we are prevented from actualizing the modern conception of democracy. What needs to be done is in one sense not that complicated; we need to change the tax laws to eliminate dynastic trusts, and we need to change the patent law to either prohibit corporations from holding patents or severely limit what they can do with them. Politically, of course, both changes would be very difficult. Yet both will have to be done sooner or later.

The Right of Association

The Shameful History of a Right Fundamental to Democracy

The Right of Association has been relatively neglected in the literature on rights, at least in comparison with the rights of the first, fifth, and sixth amendments. Yet as I will argue the Right of Association is not only a necessary condition for a democratic society, it is also one of the keys to reestablishing American democracy in the twenty-first century. The overall argument of the paper will be divided into three parts. Part I presents the argument for the Right of Association as a necessary condition for a democratic society, along with a closely related argument for the absence of such a right as a sufficient condition for regarding a society as totalitarian.

If the right of association is a necessary condition for a democratic society, however, it can also be an important cause of its dissolution if the right is not appropriately regulated. Part II reviews the legal history of the right of association with respect to some species of economic associations (namely the corporation, the trust, and the cartel) and the failure of the Supreme Court or Congress to develop regulatory principles appropriate to the preservation of democracy in relation to these species. Part III reviews the right of association in relation to labor unions, a history that is a dark chapter in American law and particularly in the record of the Supreme Court of the United States.

Part I begins with a few preliminary points that will be useful later on. The first separates the distinction between democracy and totalitarianism from that between capitalism and socialism. The second compares the legal status of the right of association in the U.S. and U.S.S.R. (prior to the end of the Cold War). That is followed by the argument for the right of association as a necessary condition for democracy and its absence as a sufficient condition for regarding a society as being totalitarian.

Part I

The first thing that should be noted in connection with the right of association as a necessary condition for democracy is the point that the distinction between a democratic society and a totalitarian one is independent of that between a capitalistic society and a socialistic one. By a capitalistic society I mean a society in which the principal means of production are by and large privately owned or controlled, and by a socialistic society one in which they are publicly owned or controlled. It should be noted that the means of production include banks and other financial institutions, since much production is as dependent on financing as it is on physical plant and raw materials; and the means of production also includes human labor power, for without the ability to organize labor power production is also impossible.

How the means of production are owned or controlled, however, whether publicly or privately, is a matter that is logically distinct from the further issue as to whether the society is democratic, totalitarian, or somewhere in between the two. Thus while a legally enforceable right of association is a necessary condition for a democratic society, and while its presence rules out a society being totalitarian (both of which points will be argued below), it is not a necessary condition for either capitalism or socialism. The "free market" system as outlined by Adam Smith, for example, ideally excludes any kind of economic association, whether of "masters" or "workmen". That there have been examples of socialistic societies as defined above that do not include a right of association probably need not be argued. To put this in another way, capitalism and socialism in the sense given are evidently neutral with respect to democracy or totalitarianism, i.e., either one could be of either sort. There can be democratic capitalism and democratic socialism, but there can also be totalitarian capitalism and totalitarian socialism; the right of association would thus be a necessary condition for the former two, and its presence would be sufficient to rule out both of the latter.

It may be objected, however, that while a right of association would not be a necessary condition for the classical capitalism of the Smith vintage, it is a necessary condition for the type of capitalism in the United States of the present day, considering its dependence on such economic associations as corporations and trade associations. This point is undoubtedly true, but it also raises exactly the problem to be considered later on, namely the extent to which the capitalism of the present day, with its relatively unrestricted right of economic associations on the side of capital, is itself compatible with a democratic society.

The second preliminary point concerns an apparent paradox in the history of the right of association in relation to the United States and the former Union of Soviet Socialist Republics. The United States is famous for, among other things, a climate of free association; De Tocqueville (writing in the early 19th century) is quoted often on the subject:

> In no country of the world has the principle of association been more successfully used, or more unsparingly applied to a multitude of different objects, than in America.[1]

Yet the Constitution of the United States does not contain an explicit right of association either in its main body or the Bill of Rights. On the other hand the U.S.S.R. before the end of the Cold War was widely regarded as a society in which the freedom of association was virtually non-existent, although the Constitution of the Union of Soviet Socialist Republics, adopted October 7, 1977, under Leonid Brezhnev, contained a clear statement of the right:

> Article 51. In accordance with the aims of building communism citizens of the USSR have the right to associate in public organizations that promote their political activity and initiative and satisfaction of their various interests.
>
> Public organizations are guaranteed conditions for successfully performing the functions defined in their rules.[2]

Whatever may have been the official interpretation of the phrase 'public organization,' in practice it was interpreted in such a way as to exclude any and all private organizations. Thus while there was a rich infrastructure of associations in the USSR, they were all creatures of the State, and organizations that were not part of or allied with the State bureaucracy—such as independent labor unions, private human rights organizations, private peace organizations and the like—generally had a history of State harassment to the point of dissolution.[3]

In the case of U.S. law the situation is more complicated. Despite a strong tradition of freedom of association there is as noted above no explicit statement of the right of association in the Constitution, Bill of Rights, or subsequent amendments. And as will be seen in Part III, the working people of the United States have suffered for that lack. It may be argued that the right is entailed by other rights, especially those provided by the First Amendment, and that argument will be presented below. In this century the Supreme Court has found the right to be implicit in the Fourteenth Amendment, and in the case of at least one category of activity, trade unionism, the category has been embodied in a Federal statute.[4] The Court's finding concerning the right of association occurred in the case *NAACP v. Alabama* in 1958; writing for the majority Justice Harlan said:

> It is beyond debate that freedom to engage in association for the advancement of beliefs and ideas is an inseparable aspect of the "liberty" assured by the Due

> Process Clause of the Fourteenth Amendment, which embraces freedom of speech.[5]

This statement, that it is "beyond debate" that we have a right of association at least in relation to the advancement of beliefs and ideas would be most reassuring if decisions of the Supreme Court were bound by the principle *stare decisis* (let the decision stand), but the Court is not bound by this principle (and probably should not be, since it needs the freedom to correct its own errors or adjust old rulings to new conditions) and as students of the Court well know, it has reversed itself on many important decisions.[6]

Thus the recognition by the Supreme Court of a right of association for a specific category of activity (whether implicit or explicit) is insufficient as a legal ground for the right, both because the right should be established in a more general (as against piecemeal) way, and because a right that is essential to a democratic society should not be dependent upon a Court not reversing itself; what nine justices choose to provide in one term they or their successors may find it desirable to rescind or modify severely in another.

The supreme law of the land, however, is not limited to the Constitution and Bill of Rights. Article VI, section 2 of the U.S. Constitution incorporates all treaties into the supreme law of the land and thus incorporates Articles 55 and 56 of the United Nations' Charter. These articles were the basis for the United Nations' epoch making *Universal Declaration of Human Rights* of 1948, Article 20 of which proclaims a right of association for all persons regardless of nationality or citizenship. The right of association is also contained in Article 22 of the *International Covenant of Civil and Political Rights* of 1966, which became part of international law in 1976, and was ratified by the United States in 1992.[7]

> Article 22 1. Everyone shall have the right to freedom of association with others, including the right to form and join trade unions for the protection of his interests.

Now the fact that there is a strong tradition of freedom of association in the United States, that the Supreme Court has recognized the right as implicit in the Constitution, and the fact that—with Article 22—it is technically already part of the supreme law of the land, may seem sufficient protection of the right. Yet this right has such a unique and vital role in creating and maintaining a democratic society that there is still reason to believe it should be made an explicit part of the Constitution as an amendment. The argument for this vital role has two overall premises, as follows:

1. Among the rights necessary for a democracy are the First Amendment rights of freedom of speech, the press, and assembly.
2. The right of association is presupposed by these First Amendment

rights; hence, it is a necessary condition for a democratic society.

Each of these two premises has supporting argument; the argument for the first premise has been made in a number of versions; I will outline one of them here.[8] It is as follows: first, if there is to be democracy even in a minimal sense of the term, then citizens must be able to participate in self-government in at least two ways: by exercising the right to vote and by exercising the right of petition. Voting may be chiefly a matter of periodically choosing representatives from among competing candidates (and not, for example, voting on State policies), but the right of petition will have to include the right to petition these representatives directly concerning private or public law, the right to give testimony at legislative and administrative hearings, the right to petition the courts, and the right to petition by public demonstration. If either the right to vote or petition is absent, then there is grave doubt as to whether the society is really a democracy. Second, if the rights to vote and to petition are to be exercised effectively, three conditions must be met (they may not be the only conditions that must be met, but they are three very important ones):

A. Citizens must have access to all the information about prospective representatives and current and alternative government policies relevant to the rational assessment of both;
B. They must be able to freely debate or discuss any issues they see fit to consider; and,
C. They must be able to freely exchange information and opinion by as many means of as possible.

Now the best way of securing these conditions is by grounding them in a set of constitutional rights, and the above mentioned rights of the First Amendment cluster are one such set; that is the argument for premise (1) above.

The argument for the second premise, that the right of association is implicit in the First Amendment, is now as follows. The rights of freedom of speech, assembly, and publication are generally exercised for a purpose or purposes. These purposes normally require more than an immediate or spontaneous action to reach fulfillment; indeed, for some purposes (such as the attainment of an ideal) there may be no particular end point in time. But for any purposes whose ends require prolonged effort a right of association is needed for their achievement; it is only the right of association that permits the organization of human effort over any period of time, that allows continuity of purpose from the present into the future. Names and addresses must be secured for notification of subsequent assemblies, for the delivery or mailing of publications, for the solicitation of contributions to support the endeavor, for a concerted effort to petition representatives, and for a host of other allied activities. It is the element of organization here that is critical, if the effort is to be more than an ephemeral outpouring of feelings and ideas. The right of association is exactly the right to freely organize human behavior for the satisfaction of chosen goals—*it is the right to freely create social institutions for selected purposes*. This is at once why the right of association is in need of special emphasis, and the reason why it is implicit in the First Amendment, if the rights enumerated in the First Amendment are to be more than a mere caricature of what we want them to be. And this is also why the presence of a right of association makes it impossible for a society to be totalitarian. For the definition of a totalitarian society is surely that of a society in which the State organizes and/or controls all organized or institutionalized human activity of any significance; or a society in which every significant institution is a part of, or allied with, the State bureaucracy, a society in which no organized activity of any social or political significance is permitted outside the jealously guarded perimeters of State control. The right of association is clearly inconsistent with such a society.

Despite the fact, however, that the right of association is a necessary condition for democracy and a sufficient condition to rule out a society being totalitarian, and despite the uniquely important and vital role of the right in guaranteeing the free creation by a people of their own social institutions, it must also be said that it cannot be an absolute right. Associations may, of course, be formed for criminal purposes, or legal associations may engage in criminal activity (e.g., price-fixing by trade associations), but these merely pose a criminal justice problem. More difficult to deal with are associations that provide benefits to society yet at the same time tend to disrupt, destabilize, or undermine democratic institutions, even though these organizations were not intentionally or ostensibly established for any such purpose and are not operated with this end in view. I will be mentioning or discussing some of these cases in Part II. What I want to note here is that the problem posed by associations of this kind arises from the fact that there is nothing in the Constitution or Bill of Rights that requires the United States of America to be a democracy. Indeed, as historians have made clear, the Constitution was not drafted with the intent of establishing a democracy or democratic society; it was intended to be a representative government controlled by a property holding elite.[9] Hence none of the three branches of government is required to scrutinize its acts, orders, or decisions with the preservation of democracy in mind. Changing this situation would require either a constitutional convention or at least a further amendment to the constitution. Such a "Democracy Amendment" could be phrased negatively:

> No article or amendment of this Constitution shall be interpreted as authorizing a decision, act, policy, rule or law by any branch of government or any

part thereof that limits or is detrimental to the preservation of democracy or a democratic society.

I may seem to be arguing at cross purposes here, in saying that we need a constitutional amendment establishing the right of association in order to guarantee a democratic society, and then maintaining that we need a further amendment to protect us from it. The next part will make clear the reason for this view.

Part II: The Right of Association and Corporations

In a series of decisions around the turn of the century the Supreme Court removed both constitutional and legislated restrictions on certain types of economic associations: corporations, trusts, and cartels. In making these decisions over a period of nearly three decades, the Court either gave no explanation at all for its actions, or in justifying its decisions it ignored their potential impact on American democracy and the American economy. The result of this "liberation" of the corporation, trust, and cartel has been, of course, the enormous concentration of economic power in a few hands that we are familiar with today, a concentration that may be illustrated by the following example. Not long ago it was calculated that the 196 chief executive officers of corporations who belong to the Business Roundtable (a corporate political organization concerned with U.S. domestic and foreign economic policy) represented enterprises having aggregate revenues equal to nearly half of the gross national product of the United States.[10] Since the GNP of the U.S. was more than twice that of the former U.S.S.R. (roughly 120 billion more in 1979) the executive officers collected in this one private organization held a power over resources and their use equivalent in extent to that of the old Supreme Council of the National Economy of the U.S.S.R.[11] And while there were very important differences between these two elites, one important similarity most certainly deserves note: although neither body had absolute power, the decisions of neither were subject to democratic review or modification save in the most extraordinary of circumstances. The one elite organization has now disappeared, eventually to be replaced, we may hope, by a more democratic system; the Business Council remains, in effect, an unofficial part of the government of the United States.

The first of four steps in the process that made the above situation possible in the United States was taken by state legislatures in the 19th century, primarily after the Civil War.[12] State legislatures had originally scrutinized each corporate charter application, setting limits on total capital, shares of stock, activities that could be legally pursued, and insuring adequate protections for the rights of stockholders, considering the control of each of these things a matter of proper public concern and legislative responsibility, since the corporation was a creature of the state.

But especially in the last decades of the 19th century and the early decades of this century, state legislatures began passing increasingly liberal acts that soon made it possible to start a corporation merely by filing some papers and paying a set fee. Justice Brandeis explained this surrender of control over the corporation as follows in a dissenting opinion in 1933:

> The removal by the leading industrial States of the limitations upon the size and powers of business corporations appears to have been due, not to their conviction that maintenance of the restrictions was undesirable in itself, but to the conviction that it was futile to insist upon them; because local restriction would be circumvented by foreign incorporation. Indeedlocal restriction seemed worse than futile. Lesser States, eager for the revenue derived from the traffic in charters, had removed safeguards from their own incorporation laws. Companies were early formed to provide charters for corporations in sites where the cost was lowest and the laws least restrictive. The states joined in advertising their wares. The race was not one of diligence but of laxity...[13]

Assuming Justice Brandeis' explanation correct, it would appear that only a federal incorporation law could have halted the process he describes.[14] Whether such a law would have met with the approval of the Supreme Court in the period around the turn of the century may be doubted. Something of the Court's attitude may be surmised from the second major step taken in the liberation of the corporation, a step taken by the Court itself. In 1886 in the case *Santa Clara County v. Southern Pacific Railroad Co.* the Court make a decision that Justice William O. Douglas described as "one of the most momentous of all our decisions."[15] The case concerned a trivial tax dispute between the county and the railroad, but one legal point involved the interpretation of the Fourteenth Amendment; the relevant clause is italicized below:

> Amendment XIV
>
> No State shall make or enforce any law which shall abridge the privileges or immunities of citizens of the United States and of the State in which they reside; *nor shall any State deprive any person of life, liberty, or property without due process of law;* nor deny to any person within its jurisdiction the equal protection of the law.

Without hearing argument or explanation the Court ruled that the italicized clause did not simply apply to real persons, it also applied to corporations as fictitious persons.[16] And in 1889 the Court reinforced this ruling by interpreting the following clause on equal protection of the law in the same way.[17] Thus in two decisions Justice Douglas characterized as "cryptic and oracular", the Supreme Court inserted corporations into a body of law designed for (real) individuals, and thenceforth the real individuals had to compete on the same turf and terms with a judicially created race of economic giants.[18]

A more cautious and conservative approach by the judiciary would have kept corporations legally fenced in, and allowed time, experience, and public policy to determine what privileges they should have had, and for what purposes. Having liberated the corporation, however, the Court could have at least provided its equal blessing to associations of working people in order to help even up the contest in the political realm. But as will be seen in Part III, that was not done until 1932, and by an act of Congress not the Court.[19]

In the same period, that is, in the last decades of the 19th century, the newly liberated corporations began to form associations at even higher levels, that is, associations of associations. These were the cartels and trusts, created for the purpose of monopolizing or trying to monopolize whole sectors of the economy. A cartel is a formal or in-formal association of corporations typically formed for the purpose of securing greater profits, usually by creating an artificial shortage to drive up prices, by dividing up the market, or by the simpler method of straightforward price-fixing. Since such operations could be prosecuted under the common law as conspiracies in restraint of trade, a safer method of monopolizing known as the "trust" was developed; in exchange for trust certificates a number of corporations (it could be, and sometimes was, hundreds) turned over enough of their stock to one of their number, the trust, to make it the legal owner of them all; in this way they transformed an illegal conspiracy of the many into a mere exercise in the private property rights of the one.

To stop this process of monopolization of industry and transportation Congress passed the Sherman Anti-Trust Act in 1890, but unfortunately with little consequence.[20] For in 1895 the Supreme Court ruled, in the famous "Sugar Trust case", that most of the trusts were beyond the grasp of the Act.[21] The Sugar Trust had gained control of 98% of the sugar refining capacity in the U.S. (65% of it located in New Jersey, and 33% in Pennsylvania). The Justice Department prosecuted the trust, but lost its case in U.S. Circuit Court (now called District Court), in the Circuit Court of Appeals, and in the Supreme Court. The arguments of the various courts were substantially the same; Article I, Section 8 of the Constitution gives Congress the power "To regulate commerce with foreign nations, and among the several States, and with the Indian tribes." The courts interpreted this clause—the "commerce clause" as it is called—to mean that Congress was to have the regulatory power over interstate commerce, but commerce was not the same as manufacturing. In the words of Chief Justice Fuller of the Supreme Court:

> Commerce succeeds to manufacture, and is not a part of it. The power to regulate commerce is the power to prescribe the rule by which commerce shall

be governed, and is a power independent of the power to suppress monopoly...[22]

The relief of the citizens of each state from the burden of monopoly and the evils resulting from the restraint of trade among such citizens was left with the States to deal with...[23]

Thus the Sugar Trust, being a manufacturing trust, was beyond the grasp of Congress, as were all other trusts of a similar kind. The Chief Justice did not explain how the individual states could, acting individually, suppress national and international monopolies if they were prohibited by the Constitution from acting collectively through their national government. Nor did he explain how a manufacturing monopoly like the Sugar Trust could avoid, in the normal course of its business, monopolizing the interstate market for sugar. In a long dissenting opinion, Justice John M. Harlan raised what was perhaps the key question:

Suppose another combination, organized for private gain and to control prices, should obtain possession of all the large flour mills in the United States; another, of all the grain elevators; another of all the oil territory; another of all the cotton mills; and another of all the great establishments for slaughtering animals, and the preparation of meats. What power is competent to protect the people of the United States against such dangers except a national power—one that is capable of exerting its sovereign authority throughout every part of the territory and over all the people of the nation? [24]

But there was no national power to accomplish this protection thanks to the Sugar Trust decision, and nine years later, in 1904, John Moody estimated in his monograph *The Truth About the Trusts* that there were 440 large, active and important trusts, including seven great industrial trusts: the Copper Trust (11 companies), the Sugar Trust (55 companies), the Tobacco Trust (150 companies), the Shipping Trust (6 companies), the Oil Trust (400 companies), the Steel Trust (785 companies), and the Smelting Trust (121 companies). Nearly all of these great industrial trusts had been formed after the passage of the Sherman Anti-Trust Act.[25]

The fourth and last major step in the opening up of the economy to the economic associations of capital was the Supreme Court's establishment of the "Rule of Reason" as it is now called. This is the "rule" that only *unreasonable* monopolies, trusts, and cartels are to be regarded as violating the Sherman Anti-Trust Act. The genesis of this rule is well worth considering, since it is still a part of our anti-trust law and since it was clearly instrumental in helping to launch the Trade Association Movement, or as it might be more accurately termed, the "Reasonable Cartel Movement". This movement developed in fits and starts in the early part of the century but finally colonized the whole territory opened up to it by the Rule of Reason decision, and now covers virtually every industry or sub-industry in extraction, manufacturing, transportation, and services.[26] The rule that helped to engender this cartelization of the economy was laid down by the Supreme Court in the great Oil and Tobacco Trust cases of 1911.[27]

The Oil Trust was a combination of some seventy different companies operating under the name of the Standard Oil Company of New Jersey at the time it was brought to trial. It controlled, according to the Court, 90% of the purchasing, shipping, refining, and selling of petroleum and petroleum products in the U.S.; since it was not a pure manufacturing trust it could not escape the Sherman Act by invoking the Sugar Trust decision. After reviewing the twenty-three volumes of the trial record, the Supreme Court decided to uphold the first part of the lower court's decision, namely that Standard Oil of New Jersey had to be dissolved as a trust. But the Court did not accept the second part of the lower court's ruling, that all the (illegal) agreements among the subsidiary companies should also be dissolved. As this network of agreements constituted a major part of the organizational and operational basis of the trust, in allowing them to continue the Court was clearly stepping into territory wherein it could be accused of willfully departing from the intent of the Sherman Act, and so it needed a rationale. Chief Justice White found one by going back into English law to discover the true meaning of `monopoly' and `restraint of trade'. Citing law under Edward VI, James I, George III, and so forth, he discovered that not all monopolies or restraints were condemned as illegal, only undue and unreasonable ones. He saw no need, apparently, to explain why this English feudal law of centuries past—in which kings granted monopolies to their supporters—should govern the national economic policy of the United States in the 20th century. Justice Harlan, however, once again a solitary dissenter, took him to task:

> All who recall the condition of the country in 1890 will remember that there were everywhere, among people generally, a deep feeling of unrest. The Nation had been rid of slavery—fortunately as all now feel—but the conviction was universal that the country was in real danger from another kind of slavery sought to be fastened on the American people, namely the slavery that would result from aggregations of capital in the hands of a few individuals and corporations, for their own profit and advantage exclusively, the entire business of the country, including the production and sale of the necessaries of life.[28]

Justice Harlan then reminded the Court that in interpreting the Sherman Act in a previous cartel case, *U.S. v. Trans-Missouri Freight Association*, the Court had in "clear and decisive language" declared that the Sherman Act was *not* confined to unreasonable restraints of trade; moreover, the Court had reiterated this position the following year in *U.S. v. Joint Traffic Association*.[29] Evidently deeply disturbed by the direction of the Court Harlan concluded his dissent with some remarks on the Court's "usurpation" of the role of Congress, and a warning:

> The Supreme Law of the land, which is binding alike upon all—upon Presidents, Congresses, the courts and the people—gives to Congress and to Congress alone, authority to regulate interstate commerce, and when Congress forbids any restraint of such commerce, in any form, all must obey its mandate. To overreach the action of Congress merely by judicial construction, that is, by indirection, is a blow at the integrity of our governmental system, and in the end will prove most dangerous to all.[30]

Immediately after the Oil Trust case, in the same term, the Court reviewed the case of the Tobacco Trust, operating under the name of the American Tobacco Co. The Court again upheld the dissolution of the trust, but this time ordered the lower court to reassemble it in such a way that it would not be repugnant to the law! This time Harlan (who died five months after the decision) was more acid in his comments; here he is on the "Rule of Reason":

> I have to say that, in my judgement, the majority, in former cases, were guided by the "rule of reason"; for, it may be assumed that they knew quite as well as others what the rule of reason requires when a court seeks to ascertain the will of Congress as expressed in a statute. It is obvious from the opinions in the former cases, that the majority did not grope about in the darkness, but in discharging the solemn duty put on them they stood out in the full glare of the "light of reason" and felt and said time and again that the court could not, consistently with the Constitution, and would not, usurp the functions of Congress by indulging in judicial legislation.[31]

What was involved here was not merely the usurpation of the power of one branch of government by another, it was also—as Justice Harlan had himself suggested in the Standard Oil case—a defiance of the will of the majority, and in that sense a usurpation of the sovereign power of the people. For behind the Sherman Act and its related legislation was the Populist Movement, a series of interrelated political and social movements going back into the 1870's and encompassing the great majority of the American people: of farmers (rich and poor, owners and tenants), of the urban working class, and of the small business and professional classes. In the words of one of its recent historians, it was "the largest democratic mass movement in American history."[32] And while there were many disagreements in the Populist Movement, the one thing that was virtually universal was the demand for a reasonably democratic economy, one in which everyone had a fair chance, one that was not dominated by big banks, big corporations, trusts, and cartels. That this great and sustained outcry, in penetrating the somber halls and chambers of the Supreme Court, stirred only one heart to dissent among the former corporation and railroad attorneys who sat there is perhaps not remarkable, but that the Court was able to carry forward the general policy embodied in the decisions reviewed here for the next fifty years is perhaps one of the most remarkable episodes of our history.[33] Not until 1937, in the second term of the New Deal, did the Supreme Court reverse its position on the question of monopoly, and by then it was too late to reverse the process of monopolization by trustification, cartelization, merger, and other means that had swept through half a century.

Certainly the defeat of the original purpose of the Sherman Act, and subsequently of the Clayton and Federal Trade Commission Acts, were not solely the work of the Supreme Court; other branches of the government made their own kinds of contribution to the process.[34] But we have carried this story far enough to make clear the reasons for my suggesting a Democracy Amendment for the Constitution. The Court in none of the above decisions considered their possible effects on the political life of the nation. It may be argued that these possible effects were too remote or unpredictable in some cases to permit their rational consideration; while this may be true of the *Santa Clara* decision, it certainly was not the case in any of the rest, particularly with Justice Harlan pointing out the perils.

There is a further and equally important aspect of the Court's treatment of the right of association, namely in relation to the right of working people to form effective unions. In the period in which the corporations were amassing a monopoly power over much of the economy, the development of unions represented an organized opposition and a potentially countervailing power, economically as well as politically. The Court, however, while empowering associations of capitalists or investors, effectively crippled associations of working people.

Part III: The Right of Association and Labor Unions

When the colonies became independent at the end of the American Revolution, most of them passed laws incorporating English Common Law into their legal systems, so that the body of law created by English courts up to the time of the revolution became part of their State law.[35] Under Common Law it is illegal to restrain trade or conspire to restrain trade. Some courts regarded the very existence of an association of workmen for the purpose of improving wages or working conditions as a conspiracy to restrain trade. And when, in the latter part of the 19th century, courts acknowledged the right of workers to form unions, they generally regarded strikes, pickets, and boycotts as criminal acts.[36] Employers went to the courts for injunctions against these activities, and were then able to cause the arrest of any person violating the injunction for contempt of court. Federal law was silent on these issues.

When the Sherman Anti-Trust Act was introduced in Congress in 1889 by Senator John Sherman, there was no intent that it be applicable to unions. And Senator Sherman's original bill made that very clear; its first section reads as follows:

> Sec. 1. That all arrangements, contracts, agreements, trusts, or combinations between persons or corporations made with a view or which tend to prevent full and free competition in the importation, transportation, or sale of articles imported into the United States, or in the production, manufacture, or sale of articles of domestic growth or production, or domestic raw material that competes with any similar article upon which a duty is levied by the United States, or which shall be transported from one State or Territory to another, and all arrangements, contracts, agreements, trusts or combinations between persons or corporations, designed or which tend to advance the cost to the consumer of any such articles are hereby declared to be against public policy and void.[37]

However, by the time the Act eventually came to a vote in July of 1890, it had been amended in such a way that its intent was ambiguous. The first two sections follow:

> Sec. 1. Every contract, combination in the form of trust or otherwise, or conspiracy, in restraint of trade or commerce among the several States, or with foreign nations, is hereby declared to be illegal. Every person who shall make any such contract, or engage in any such combination or conspiracy, shall be deemed guilty of a misdemeanor, and on conviction thereof, shall be punished by a fine not exceeding one year, or by both said punishments, in the discretion of the court.

> Sec. 2. Every person who shall monopolize, or attempt to monopolize, or combine or conspire with any other person or persons, to monopolize any part of the trade or commerce among the several States, or with foreign nations, shall be deemed guilty of a misdemeanor, and, on conviction thereof, shall be punished by fine not exceeding five thousand dollars, or by imprisonment not exceeding one year, or by both said punishments, in the discretion of the court.

For whatever reasons the act was passed in the above form, it will be seen that the new section one, taken by itself, is silent as to the intent of the prohibition, simply outlawing restraint of trade or commerce as such. Three years after the passage of the act two cases in federal circuit courts (now called district courts) dealt with the issue as to whether the Sherman Act was applicable to labor unions. The first case, decided in February, 1893, in Massachusetts, was

United States vs. Patterson. In this case Judge Putman, who heard the case, though not called upon to rule on the issue, provided an *obiter dictum*:

> ...it is important to note the rule [of statutory interpretation] that this whole statute must be taken together. The second section is limited by its terms to monopolies, and evidently has as its basis the engrossing or controlling of the market, or of lines of trade. The first section is undoubtedly in pari materia, and so has as its basis the engrossing or controlling of the market or lines of trade...
>
> We are now at the point where the paths separate. Careless or inapt construction of the statute as bearing on this case, while it may seem to create but a small divergence here, will, if followed out logically, extend into very large fields; because, if the proposition made by the United States is taken with its full force, the inevitable result will be that the federal courts will be compelled to apply this statute to all attempts to restrain commerce among the states, or commerce with foreign nations, by strikes or boycotts and by every method of interference by way of violence and intimidation. It is not to be presumed that Congress intended thus to extend the jurisdiction of the courts of the United States without very clear language. Such language I do not find in the statute.[38]
>
> So taking the two sections of the Act together—as called for under the generally accepted rules of statutory interpretation—it is clear that Section (1) does not extend to labor unions.

In the very next month, however, in a case decided in federal circuit court in Louisiana, *United States vs. Workingmen's Amalgamated Council of New Orleans et al*, a Judge Billings held that the Sherman Act did apply to unions:

> The defendants urge that the right of the complainants depends upon an unsettled question of law. The theory of the defense is that this case does not fall within the purview of the statute; that the statute prohibited monopolies and combinations which, using words in a general sense, were of capitalists, and not of laborers. I think the congressional debates show that the statute had its origin in the evils of massed capital; but, when the congress came to formulating the prohibition which is the yardstick for measuring the complainant's right to the injunction, it expressed it in these words: "Every contract or combination in the form of trust, or otherwise in restraint of trade or commerce among the several states or with foreign nations, is hereby declared illegal." The subject had so broadened in the minds of the legislators that the source of the evil was not regarded as material, and the evil in its entirely is dealt with. They made the interdiction include combinations of labor as well as of capital...[39]

With circuit courts offering contradictory interpretations of section (1) of the Act, a decision was needed as to whether the Sherman Act was to be construed, in effect, as the old common law prohibition of conspiracy in restraint of trade raised to the federal level, in which case it could be used against unions, as Judge Billings held, or whether the Act should be construed much more narrowly as Judge Putnam had argued. The Attorney General of the U.S., Richard Olney, in his annual report to Congress of December, 1893, severely criticized the construction of the statute by Judge Billings, saying it was a perversion of the law from the real purpose of its authors.[40]

However, in the following year a strike in the Pullman factory in Chicago, notorious for its exploitation of workers, developed into an extensive action by the American Railway Union headed by Eugene Debs. Olney changed his mind and supported the use of an injunction under the Sherman Act; as a result, Debs and other union leaders were arrested, jailed, and the strike was broken. On a habeus corpus appeal to the Supreme Court, the convictions were upheld on technical grounds that avoided dealing with the main issue.[41]

More than ten years then passed before the Supreme Court ruled on the applicability of the Sherman Act to Labor, and by this time the use of the act to break strikes had become routine. The issue was settled in the case of the Danbury Hatters, in which a manufacturer of hats in Danburry, Connecticut, filed suit in federal circuit court against the Danbury Hatters union for engineering a nationwide boycott, and asked for triple damages as permitted under the Act. When the union filed a demurrer, on the grounds that the Sherman Act did not apply to labor boycotts, the Circuit Court sustained the demurrer and passed the issue to a Circuit Court of Appeals, which in turn passed it to the Supreme Court. The Supreme Court agreed with Judge Billings, quoting a part of his remarks above, in their opinion.[42]

As a result the case was returned to the trial court and the Danbury Hatters Union was assessed a fine of $250,000 in damages, a staggering sum for a small union in 1908. To avoid the individual members having to give up their homes and other assets, the AFL conducted a national fund raising drive that collected $216,000. But it was clear that if the Hatters decision was to stand, unions in the United States ran a very serious risk in striking, picketing, or boycotting. In addition to the problem of the loss of wages, they could be enjoined against any such activities under section (1) of the Sherman Act and held in contempt of court and arrested if they persisted, and they could be sued in a civil action under Section (7) of the Sherman Act for any losses suffered by the employer, who could collect triple damages. So by 1911, the year of the Standard Oil and Tobacco cases, the situation stood as follows with respect to Capital and Labor. Capital could exercise the right of freedom of association to the extent of monopolizing whole industries, provided the monopoly was "reasonable". Organized labor, representing the only potential counterbalance to the power of Capital, was now effectively prevented from exercising the right in any meaningful way.

Confronted with this situation, organized labor began a drive to reverse the Danbury Hatter's decision through congressional legislation. A similar situation had previously occurred in England. In the Taff Vale case in 1901 the House of Lords had made a railroad union liable for the damages sustained by a company in a rail strike.[43] The unions sought the help of Parliament and succeeded in changing the law with the Trade Disputes Act of 1906. In the United States, a similar legislative campaign culminated with the passage of the Clayton Anti-Trust Act in 1914. The Act included two sections that exempted unions from antitrust law:

> Section 6: That the labor of a human being is not a commodity or article of commerce. Nothing contained in the antitrust laws shall be construed to forbid the existence and operation of labor...organizations, instituted for the purposes of mutual help, and not having capital stock or conducted for profits, or to forbid or restrain individual members of such organizations from lawfully carrying out the legitimate objects thereof; nor shall such organizations, or the members thereof, be held or construed to be illegal combinations or conspiracies in restraint of trade under the antitrust laws.

Taken by itself the first clause of this section would simply be false, since the labor of human beings in a capitalistic economy is in fact an article of commerce, whether paid for by the hour or on some other basis. Taken as part of the statute, however, it exempts labor unions from section (2) of the Sherman Act; unions cannot be sued or indicted for monopolizing labor. Section (1) of the Sherman Act, under which they could be indicted or sued for actions in restraint of trade was taken care of by Section 20:

> Section 20: That no restraining order or injunction shall be granted by any court of the United States, or a judge or the judges thereof, in any case between an employer and employees, or between employers and employees, or between employees, or between persons employed and persons seeking employment, involving, or growing out of, a dispute concerning terms or conditions of employment, unless necessary to prevent irreparable injury to property, or to a property right, of the party making the application, for which injury there is no adequate remedy at law...[44]

With the enactment of sections (6) and (20), Samuel Gompers, head of the AFL, declared the Clayton Act to be a "Magna Carta" for labor in the United States. That is, until the Supreme Court found an opportunity to interpret the two sections in question. The case was *Duplex Printing Co. v. Deering*, heard in 1920. Four companies made printing presses in the United States; three had agreed to the machinists union's demands for an eight hour day, a minimum wage scale, and a union shop. Duplex refused, thus imperiling the agreements with the other three companies. The union attempted a secondary boycott, i.e., employees of the trucking company used by Duplex were persuaded to strike, repair shops persuaded not to repair the presses, and so on. The Supreme Court ruled that an injunction could be issued under the Sherman Act for conspiracy to restrain interstate commerce. The relevant part of the summary reads as follows:

> Section 6 of the Clayton Act, in declaring that...[labor] organizations or their members shall not be construed to be illegal combinations or conspiracies in restraint of trade, assumes that the normal objects of such organizations are legitimate, but contains nothing to exempt them, or their members from accountability when they depart from objects that are normal and legitimate and engage in an actual combination or conspiracy in restraint of trade.

With respect to Section 20 the Court determined that the prohibition on issuing injunctions applied only to a dispute between an employer and employees, and so did not apply where employees were on strike and no longer employed, or where the dispute was between an employer and a union or unions; hence:

> The first paragraph of section 20 of the Clayton Act...is merely declaratory of the law as it stood before.[45]

And the Magna Carta of Labor was reduced to a mere summary of preexisting law. Unlike the Danbury Hatter's case, however, this time there were dissenting voices on the Supreme Court. Justice Brandeis, who had acted as an advisor in the drafting of Section 20 before being appointed to the Court, wrote a ten-page dissent in which he was joined by Justices Clarke and Holmes. In it he pointed out that "This statute was the fruit of unceasing agitation, which extended over more than twenty years and was designed to equalize before the law the position of workingmen and employer as industrial combatants." And that "...Congress, not the judges, was the body which should declare what public policy in regard to industrial struggle demands." And further, on Section 20:

> ...Congress did not restrict the provision to employers and workingmen *in their employ*. By including "employers and employees" and "persons employed and persons seeking employment" it showed that it was not aiming merely at a legal relationship between a specific employer and his employees. Furthermore, the plaintiff's contention proves too much. If the words are to receive a strict technical construction, the statute will have no application to disputes between employers of labor and workingmen, since the very acts to which it applies sever the continuity of the legal relationship.[46]

The *Duplex* case was heard in 1920; it was followed by a period of long and bitter strikes in the coal industry (involving more than half a million workers), railroads (another 500,000 workers), and textile industries, all over efforts by the companies to cut wages. Sherman Act injunctions, readily available and outlawing virtually every strike connected activity, placed the power of the state behind the companies, with results such as these prior to a coal miner's strike in New England:

> Police authority has been vested in the constabulary and the state is taking no chances of being caught unprepared. Scattered through the anthracite belt are squads of the state police who are prepared for any emergency. They are equipped with riot clubs and well trained horses, and pistols and machine guns are at their command. These squads will cooperate with the sheriffs of the different counties, and there has been fair warning that any disturbance of the peace will be strenuously dealt with. There are numbers of deputy sheriffs in readiness for any call.[47]

Or these, in a 1922 railroad strike:

> Anticipating disorder when the railroad shops of the country open to-day for return of such strikers as may wish to save their seniority and pension rights and for new employees, the authorities of five states have mobilized their national guard. The sixth, Illinois, with 300 men already on strike duty in Clinton, is practically in a state of mobilization with militiamen in camps or on waiting order at many points. The five states mobilizing are California, Indiana, Missouri, Mississippi, and Kansas.[48]

Working people thus not only had to deal with the carnage in factories, mines, and railroads—between 30 and 35 thousand accidental deaths a year according to the U.S. Bureau of Labor—but faced organized violence in attempts to exercise the right of association on their own behalf. Felix Frankfurter (later appointed to the Supreme Court by Franklin Roosevelt) and a colleague detailed some of the abuses of the Sherman Act in their book, *The Labor Injunction*, published in 1932.[49] In the same year Congress, the first of the New Deal, finally remedied the *Duplex* decision with the Norris-La Guardia Anti-Injunction Act. The Act begins:

> Be it enacted...that no court of the United States...shall have jurisdiction to issue any restraining order or temporary or permanent injunction in a case involving or growing out of a labor dispute, except in a strict conformity with the provisions of this Act; nor shall any such restraining order or permanent injunction be issued contrary to the public policy declared in this Act.

Section 2 goes on to summarize the inequity regarding the right of association to be remedied by the policy:

> Whereas under prevailing economic conditions, developed with the aid of governmental authority for owners of property to organize in the corporate and other forms of ownership association, the individual unorganized worker

> is commonly helpless to exercise actual liberty of contract and to protect this freedom of labor, and thereby to obtain acceptable terms and conditions of employment, wherefore, though he should be free to decline to associate with his fellows, it is necessary that he have full freedom of association, self-organization, and designation of representatives of his own choosing, to negotiate the terms and conditions of his employment...therefore, the following definitions of, and limitations upon, the jurisdiction and authority of the courts of the United States are hereby enacted.. [50]

The Act was found constitutional in 1938[51], and in 1941 Justice Frankfurter, writing for the Court in *U.S. v. Hutcheson*, declared that "The Norris-LaGuardia Act removed the fetters upon trade union activities...", and noted that the public policy of the United States was now that whether trade union conduct constituted a violation of the Sherman Law could be determined only by reading the Sherman Law together with Section 20 of the Clayton Act and the Norris-LaGuardia Act as a single harmonizing text.[52] There were other decisions of the Supreme Court in line with Hutcheson, as *Thornhill v. Alabama*, in which the Court struck down an anti-picketing statute, bringing peaceful picketing under the protection of the First Amendment.[53] But this long overdue recognition of the rights of working people was complicated by another development that undermined it. That was the passage of the National Labor Relations Act.

Confronted with the problem of bringing the nation out of the depression the Roosevelt government was divided in 1932 as to what should be done. A number of the cabinet, with the backing of leading business organizations, prevailed in supporting a plan similar to the corporate fascism of Italy.[54] Trade Associations, that flourished after the "Rule of Reason" decision, would establish codes of "fair trade" practice; that is, minimize competition, raise prices, limit production, and divide markets. This would theoretically restore profits, production, and re-employ the work force. With the passage of the National Industrial Recovery Act (NIRA) in 1933, General Hugh Johnson, an admirer of Mussolini, was appointed head of the new authority and began the effort to create codes for all the largest industries, integrating all of business into a vast cooperative nationwide structure. Labor was to be integrated into this structure by having every industrial code contain the provision that:

> employees shall have the right to organize and bargain collectively through representatives of their own choosing, and shall be free from the interference, restraint or coercion of employers of labor, or their agents, in the designation of such representatives or in self-organization or in other concerted activities for the purpose of collective bargaining or other mutual aid or protection.

This provision, known as NIRA Section 7(a), was interpreted by corporations as compatible with company unions, a view reinforced by Johnson, who also held that it did not obligate employers to agree to or accept any collective bargaining contracts.[55] While the promise of 7(a)—seen as another Magna Carta for Labor—prompted a great expansion of union membership, the unwillingness of business to engage in real collective bargaining and the absence of any encouragement from the administration led to a wave of strikes. In the following year there were 1,826 strikes involving over a million and a half workers, "strikes and social upheavals of extraordinary importance, drama and violence which ripped the cloak of civilized decorum from society, leaving exposed naked class conflict."[56] In the general strike in San Francisco, union offices were destroyed by police, strikers were beaten and two were killed. Speaking during the strike General Johnson did nothing to ease the situation in calling for "responsible" labor organizations to "run these subversive influences out from its ranks like rats."[57]

All this together with the Supreme Court's ruling the following year that the NIRA was unconstitutional, led to a more carefully constructed act designed to establish collective bargaining as the primary means of settling labor-management disputes, preserving industrial peace and the continuity of production and commerce—the Wagner, or National Labor Relations Act of 1935.[58] The Act guaranteed the right to strike and the right to collectively bargain, establishing a Board that could seek enforcement of its decisions in Federal District Courts. Its effectiveness was mired in the lower courts for two years until the Supreme Court ruled on its constitutionality. The Court found that Congress' power to manage interstate commerce gave it the authority to regulate labor relations in order to avoid the industrial strife that could or would otherwise interfere with that commerce.[59] A major case the following year made clear the danger implicit in so subordinating the rights of labor to the goal of the uninterrupted flow of commerce.

Mackay Radio & Telegraph Co. of San Francisco promised strikebreakers they could retain their jobs after a strike against the company, even though this meant that many strikers would not be rehired. The U.S. Supreme Court in 1938 found no violation of the Wagner Act:

> Although Section 13 provides, "Nothing in this Act shall be construed so as to interfere with or impede or diminish in any way the right to strike," it does not follow that an employer, guilty of no act denounced by the statute, has lost the right to protect and continue his business by supplying places left vacant by strikers. And he is not bound to discharge those hired to fill the places of strikers, upon the election of the later to resume their employment, in order to create places for them. The assurance by respondent to those who accepted employment during the strike that if they so desired their places might be permanent was not an unfair labor practice nor was it such to reinstate only so many of the strikers as there were vacant places to be filled.[60]

Assuming a right of the employer to protect and continue his business (it is unclear whether this was based on the policy of maintaining the free flow of commerce, or on the traditional rights of private property or both) the ruling effectively eliminated a right to strike, making it equivalent to the right to forfeit one's job. A similar ruling the next year voided a reinstatement order of the National Labor Relations Board in connection with a sit-down strike.[61] The right of association was evidently not to be considered a fundamental right in the case of labor unions. As we have seen no similar position was taken by the Court with regard to corporations or associations of corporations.

The notion that the rights of working people should be subordinate to government policies was carried even further in the Taft-Hartley Act of 1947. This Act imposed further restrictions on pickets and boycotts, but in Section 9(h) it went even deeper and imposed government control over the political opinions of labor union officers. Any union that wished to be certified as a bargaining agent was required to have on file with the Board:

> ...an affidavit executed contemporaneously or within the preceding twelve-month period by each officer of such labor organization and the officers of any national or international labor organization of which it is an affiliate or constituent unit that he is not a member of the Communist Party or affiliated with such party, and that he does not believe in, and is not a member of or supports any organization that believes in or teaches, the overthrow of the United States Government by force or by any illegal or unconstitutional methods. The provisions of section 35 A of the Criminal Code shall be applicable in respect to such affidavits.[62]

Needless to say, no such requirement was imposed on the officers or Board of Directors of corporations engaged in collective bargaining, although if national security was the issue, the recent experience of World War II had made very clear the fact that U.S. corporations were quite capable of obstructing or subverting the war effort.[63]

In 1950 the Supreme Court ruled on the constitutionality of section 9(h), in *American Communications Association v. Douds*.[64] The Court decided that since the Communist Party could be expected to engage in political strikes that were disruptive of the national economy the statute fell within the Congressional power to regulate interstate commerce.

We have, then, two very different lines of thought and policy beginning with the New Deal. On the one hand there is the line represented by the Clayton Act Section 20, the Norris-LaGuardia Act, Hutcheson and Thornhill, which accords to working people the right of association, albeit with some restrictions. But there is also the line of thought and policy represented by NIRA Section 7(a), the NLRA, Mackay, and Taft-Hartley, which regards working people's interests and rights as clearly subordinate to the trouble-free (including the politically trouble-free) continuous operation of the industrial system. It is the latter policy that is presently dominant, and with the Taft-Hartley law it came uncomfortably close to the right of association as conceived in Article 51 of the constitution of the former U.S.S.R., i.e., labor organizations turned into agencies of the State.

The history of the right of association in the United States, then, as reviewed in Part II and III above is indeed a shameful one in terms of its favoritism toward organized capital and its hostility toward organized labor. If justice is either fairness or equal treatment under the law, then either both organized capital and organized labor should have been allowed to exercise the right of association, or alternatively, both should have been brought under a coordinated regulatory policy of the State. It is now too late, however, to simply look toward fairness and equal treatment. For we are facing the consequences of a century of this lopsided history, and one of those consequences is an aggregation of political power in the hands of corporations so great that it threatens the existence of the limited democracy that we still possess.

The situation thus demands fundamental reform in our legal system. One element of such a reform is the amendment to the Constitution I have called the Democracy Amendment. It has the virtue of simplicity, and if honored by the Court, over time it would have far reaching effects. It must be accompanied by a further amendment, making freedom of association a universal right instead of—as it has been in Federal law—the privilege of a particular class.

During and after World War II a common characterization of the difference in political philosophy between the Axis or fascist powers and the Allied or democratic powers was put in the following terms. The Allied powers subscribed to the view that the State exists to serve the individual, while the Axis nations held that the individual exists to serve the State. It is ironic that today, half a century after this world struggle, we are faced with a similar conflict of principles and practice. There is the principle of what can properly be called corporate fascism: *The people exist to serve the interests and purposes of corporations*. And there is the democratic principle that *corporations exist to serve the interests and purposes of the people*. The twisted history of the right of association is part of the reason for this unhappy state of affairs.

Human Rights vs. Classical Liberalism

An Essay on Metaphysics and the Theory of Value

IN 1976 TWO TREATIES CAME into force in international law that embody the highest ideals that have ever been expressed in law, let alone in international law. They are the Covenant on Civil and Political Rights and the Covenant on Economic, Social, and Cultural Rights.[1] The nations that have ratified these treaties—and that now includes the majority of nations on the earth—have in so doing surrendered a large measure of their sovereign powers over the populations of their countries, have committed themselves to making periodic reports to the United Nations on their progress in implementing the human rights established by the Covenants, and have committed themselves to periodic public examinations by that body on their progress.[2] They have thus made themselves parties to the greatest collective project ever undertaken by our species. The success of this project over the next century will depend in part on the removal of many obstacles; some of these obstacles are entrenched political and economic interests, and some of them are ideas, attitudes and habits of thought that are equally well entrenched. In the United States the most important obstacle of the latter kind appears to be the ideology of Classical Liberalism.

By the ideology of Classical Liberalism I mean the constellation of ideas and theories developed from the late 17th through the 19th centuries, and associated with John Locke, Jeremy Bentham, James Mill, Adam Smith and many others.[3] As an ideology Classical Liberalism has been the most powerful influence on the Western world since Christianity. Part of the explanation for this influence is undoubtedly the role it played in promoting the development of industrial capitalism; but part of the explanation is also the fact that it was an ideology built upon the premises—already widely accepted—of modern philosophy. Since these premises include a metaphysics, or conception of the nature of reality, it is perhaps better to speak of Classical Liberalism as a full-fledged *Weltanschauung* rather than simply an ideology.

Part I will sketch those aspects of the Classical Liberal world-view that are inherently hostile to the implementation of important rights now held through the International Covenant on Social, Economic, and Cultural Rights and other international human rights conventions. The conflict is rooted in the Classical Liberal theory of value and associated moral principles. Part II will present an alternative to Classical Liberalism in the form of a systemic theory of value that is more compatible with human rights law. That this alternative is also more in accord with the realities of the present system of production in the United States occupies the third part of the paper. Part IV considers some of the implications of the preceding parts for the institution of private property. The last part returns to the subject of the International Bill of Human Rights as the blueprint for the Common Good in the 21st century.

Part I: The Classical Liberal Weltanschauung

Modern philosophy rests on a philosophical premise that established itself in the period of the Renaissance, the premise that *only individual things exist or are real.*[4] Although the premise was stated as and appears to have been understood as an empirical and verifiable claim, it is in fact an *a priori* principle whose main function has been as a guide in the construction of theories, explanations, and justifications in science, ethics, and law. The real "individual things" for many of the new scientists of the 17th century, for example, were the atoms (hard particles) out of which everything else was held to be composed. In theories concerning human society, including Classical Liberalism, the real "individual things" are individual persons, and society was seen as a mere aggregation of persons, having no reality beyond them. Thus any explanation of the characteristics and history of a society had to be found in the nature of its inhabitants or in the particular characteristics of particular individuals. This "reduction" of society to the individuals who compose it, however, is not the only aspect of modern philosophy relevant to Classical Liberal ideology. The premise that only individual things exist has two corollaries regarding value, referred to above as the Classical Liberal theory of value. If only individual things exist, then:

1) Only individual things can possess value.
2) Only individuals are capable of creating value.

Both corollaries probably seemed very reasonable in the period in which the industrial revolution was gathering steam, where those individual things capable of being bought and sold—raw materials, manufactured commodities, tracts of land, productive machinery, precious metals—were the sorts of things that had value, at least to those involved in market agriculture, commerce, manufacturing, and invention. And the notion that individuals were the sole or primary source of value was evidenced in the merchant adventurer, the inventor and the entrepreneur; the class that was creating wealth and transforming the world.

At the same time, however, these new premises had profound implications. For example, if only individual things exist, then there can be no such thing as an ecological system in the sense of something greater than the mere sum of its individual constituents; and to one whose thought was habituated to these premises, it would seem irrational to look for or consider such a system. Again, if individuals alone can produce or create value, then *Nature* as such cannot be creative of value. Indeed, in early modern philosophy Nature was not regarded as creative of value for another reason as well: it was considered to be wholly mechanical. "Mind is active, Matter passive" was a formula taken for granted by proponents of early modern philosophy.[5]

In this intellectual framework value would have to be created by individuals expending labor on dead matter, that is, altering in some respect some part or aspect of a passive and mechanistic physical world. So the value of something produced would reasonably be equatable with the amount of labor required to produce it. And as labor was assumed to be painful, it was evidently regarded as moral common sense to require that the producer should enjoy the full value of what he or she produced. We have, then, two further principles:

3) The real value of a thing is the amount of labor required to produce it.
4) The individual should have the full value of the product of his labor.

Principle (3) is the Labor Theory of Value, and (4) is one of the foundations of private property, provided that having "full value" is understood to include freedom of disposition.[6] Both principles play an important role in the theory of the Free Market, which lies at the heart of Classical Liberalism. Before stating the main thesis of that theory, one more principle needs to be added, that of Utility:

5) What is right is whatever promotes the greatest happiness of the greatest number.

This is a principle of many faces. It assumes that every person has a moral claim to be counted, and in this respect it was a powerful battering ram historically against Feudalism and Monarchism.[7] It asserts the primacy of worldly happiness, and so also confronted the moral hegemony of the Church. Unfortunately, it also assumes something that is commonsensically false, namely, that there is no such thing as a *common good* or *public good* apart from the sum total of individual goods. And the history of moral theory in the era of Classical Liberalism is virtually silent on any competing principle regarding the right as what promotes the public good. Lastly, the Utility principle has been used and is still used to justify the sacrifice of the few in the name of scientific and/or industrial progress for the many. In this role it legitimizes the primary goal of the Free Market: maximizing the production of those things that would promote the greatest happiness of the greatest number; viz., food, clothing, shelter and other manufacturable necessities of life.

The Free Market itself is envisioned as a price-competitive economy with multiple individual producers of every commodity, in which everyone enjoys freedom of investment, freedom of exchange, and freedom of contract. I will refer to these freedoms as "economic liberties," in order to keep them separate from the economic rights which are accorded by the International Convenant, such as the right to a decent standard of living, the right to employment, and others.[8] The central hypothesis concerning the Free Market is as follows (after Adam Smith):

6) If there is a free market, then:
   A) There will be the most efficient use of resources for the production of the necessities of life,
   B) There will be a maximum increase over time in productivity, and
   C) There will be a reasonably fair distribution of what is produced.[9]

What is meant by 'productivity' here is output per man-hour. In the 18th and 19th centuries it may have seemed obvious that goals (A) and (B) should have priority over any and all other concerns; at the end of the 20th century—confronted as we are with a host of environmental and ecological problems—it is no longer so obvious. In any case, a system that would maximize wealth in the form of exchangeable commodities and at the same time provide everyone with the full value of his or her labor must have appeared to the 18th century as a system inspired by angels. Indeed, trying to show that these results were truly sound has preoccupied more than a few 19th and 20th century economists.[10] The following passage, for example, is from John Bates Clark's *The Distribution of Wealth*:

> It is the purpose of this work to show that the distribution of the income of society is controlled by a natural law, and that this law, if it worked without friction, would give to every agent of production the amount of wealth which that agent creates.[11]

The basic idea, first stated by Adam Smith, is that a free market will always tend to equalize the supply and demand for any commodity, and if the supply equals the demand, then the market price of the commodity will equal its real value, i.e., the labor time required to produce it. Clark put it this way:

> Normal prices are no-profit prices. They afford wages for all the labor that is involved in producing the goods, including the labor of superintending the mills, managing the finances, keeping the accounts, collecting the debts and doing all the work of directing the policy of the business. They afford, also, interest on all the capital that is used in the business, whether it is owned by the *entrepreneur* or borrowed from some one else. Beyond this there is no return...[12]

There is, of course, a problem in justifying the profits of capital within this schema, since capital expends no labor, and the problem comes out here in the evident contradiction between prices being "no-profit prices" on the one hand, and yet including the profit (interest) on capital on the other. Adam Smith dealt with the issue by saying the profit of capital would have to be a deduction from workers' wages.[13] But the deduction would be justified on his view, since over time rising productivity would cause the real value of commodities to decline, and thus the buying power of wages would increase. Whether this makes sense (if labor is itself a commodity) is another question, but it shows that Adam Smith took seriously the principle that "the whole produce of the laborer" should belong to the laborer.[14]

The Liberal Opposition to Economic Rights

Now there are at least two main areas of conflict between Classical Liberalism and economic rights. One concerns the labor principle, principle (4), and the other concerns the principle of Utility and the primary goals of the Free Market. In what follows I will confine my remarks to a simple statement of the problem, without considering various qualifications of the principles that have been urged that might tend to mitigate but not eliminate the basic conflict.[15]

Assume then for the purpose of illustration the *a priori* principles of Classical Liberalism: (1), that there are only individuals, and (2), that only individuals are producers of value. The conflict arises when one class of persons is productive of value and another class, for whatever reasons, is not. The term 'productive' here is highly tendentious, usually understood to mean engaged in the production of marketable commodities or services; so 'unproductive' means not so engaged.[16] If government intervenes in this situation to tax the former on behalf of the latter, on principle (4) there would be a serious breach of ethics. Government is taking by force of law what rightfully belongs to productive citizens, who are deprived of the full value of their labor.

Moreover, a further sin is committed as well by a government appropriating a share of an individual's labor for purposes of providing for the "non-productive" class. The wealth that would otherwise be invested in creating new enterprises, improving existing ones, or upgrading productive skills will be reduced, so the economic growth rate of the economy will be slowed, interfering with the main purposes of the Free Market. And this is wrong on the Utility principle, since the government is using its power to benefit a few today at the greater expense of the many tomorrow. The same objection would be made to the possibility of the government owning and operating sufficient profit making enterprises to provide for the so-called unproductive class. So it would appear that within the worldview of Classical Liberalism it is morally problematic as to how a State could go about implementing the right to a minimum standard of living, medical care, and education; these would require continual "expropriations" of private property or "wastage" of capital on those who did nothing to earn it.

Part II: An Alternative View: The Primacy of Systemic Value

A very different position on economic rights is made possible by the view that it is not individuals that are the primary source of value, *but the social system as such*. Before explicating the statement that the social system is the primary source of value, there are two preliminary comments, one on the existence or reality of social systems, the other on the meaning of the term.

That there are social systems is a matter of common sense; within the Liberal perspective, however, a social system is regarded as being reducible to the individuals that make it up, so any and all social phenomena must be explained in terms of the nature or characteristics of those individuals. The counter claim that social systems are not so reducible, and exist in their own right, does not entail postulating the existence of a mysterious and transcendent metaphysical entity (that would be to construe the category of system as if it belonged to the category of individual thing); nor does it require acceptance of the view that social systems exist independently of the individuals that make them up. It does require acknowledging that social systems may exist independently of any particular set of inhabitants, in the same way a corporation exists independently of any particular set of directors, officers, and employees.

Second, the term *social system* is being used here to include the legal, political, cultural, and economic systems of modern society, as distinguishable parts of one and the same overall system. All are thus subsystems interconnected to the point that none could or would be what it is without existing in the relational matrix of the whole social system, and all have both mental and material aspects. If this view is correct, and I believe it is, then any theory that treats one of these subsystems as if it were isolable from the rest would appear to have very limited usefulness in explanation or prediction. There could be, for example, no set of variables such that knowing their values and the relevant laws, one could predict future states of the economic subsystem, the way we can predict the future states of the solar system. Not only because the economic subsystem is part of a larger more complex system and not easily defined, but also because we are dealing with systems that are both material and mental, and the material and mental aspects of societies appear to interact in unpredictable ways. The same thing would be true of the social system as a whole, since it exists within the greater ecological system of the planet.[17]

Now the claim that the social system is the primary source of value does not entail that the labor performed by individuals is unnecessary or that it is illusory or has no value. What it does mean can, I think, be summed up in three points:

1. For virtually every kind of employment, it would not *exist* at all, or would exist only marginally, outside a particular social system and generally for a limited historical period. For example, the manufacture of square-head nails (ending in the 1870s), or the manufacture of glass radiotubes (ending after the invention of the transistor in 1948), or family farming (dying out in this century).
2. Further, it means that most kinds of products or services would have little or no *value* save within that particular social system.
3. Finally, it is the continuous operation of the entire social system that makes possible the individual contribution to the creation of value; stated in another way, it is a necessary condition for one's being engaged in a productive employment or service that the entire system be functioning on a more or less continuous basis. The reason for this is simply the fact that modern society is temporally, physically, economically, and administratively integrated into one system. If this social system "slows down" or "stops," individual production of goods or services slows down or stops. The integration of the social system, particularly the economic system, will be considered at length below, but there is first another principal regarding value and the social system that needs to be considered.

It will be recalled that the Classical Liberal perspective developed on the basis of the ideas that only individuals can produce value, and that only individual things can possess value. In like manner if social systems exist, *they may possess value in themselves as well as being a source of value*. In the case of a social system there would of course be no question that for its inhabitants it has value at least insofar as it is a life sustaining system (although it may have other characteristics that are life threatening as well). In either case, recognition of the existence of systems as such would make possible their protection in law and their modification by law.[18] Thus an ecosystem could be protected in its own right, rather than as a by product of the protection of individual members of an endangered species.

That a social system may have great value in itself as well as being the primary source of value does not entail that the individuals who constitute it at any particular time must be subordinate to it in the sense indicated below; attribution of value to the one does not threaten the value of the other. This is a point that is often misunderstood and so requires some comment. Recall that under international law now in force, every individual has civil, political, economic, social, and cultural rights. This means that a principal criterion for the evaluation of any social system is now the degree to which the society has observed and implemented the International Bill of Human Rights.[19] Recognition of the reality, value, or causal role of social systems is thus in no way equivalent to a political philosophy that subordinates the individual to the needs or purposes of the State.

However, the protection in law of social systems, ecological systems, and even the human immune system, will require restrictions on economic liberties, that is, on the rights of private property. So will, of course, the implementation of the economic, social and cultural rights of the Second Covenant; for example, under the Covenant individuals have the right to security, employment, and a decent standard of living.[20] Corporations therefore cannot be permitted to discharge them merely for the purpose of increasing quarterly earnings and/or temporarily raising the value of their stocks. An assessment of just what is involved in the conflict between private property rights and human rights, requires a close look at what has become of private property in the late 20th century. But first it is necessary to consider some of the reasons for the view that the economy of the United States has the nature of an integrated system.

Part III: The Nature of the Productive System

In 1904 Thorstein Veblen described the beginnings of an integrated industrial system in the United States in *The Theory of Business Enterprise*:

> As was noted above, each industrial unit, represented by a given industrial "plant," stands in close relations of interdependence with other industrial processes going forward elsewhere, near or far away, from which it receives supplies—material, apparatus, and the like—and to which it turns over its output of products and waste, or on which it depends for auxiliary work, such as transportation...
>
> By virtue of this concatenation of processes the modern industrial system at

> large bears the character of a comprehensive balanced mechanical process. In order to insure an efficient working of this industrial process at large, the various constituent sub-processes must work in due coordination throughout the whole. Any degree of maladjustment in the interstitial co-ordinations of this industrial process at large in some degree hinders it working...The higher the degree of development reached by a given industrial community, the more comprehensive and urgent becomes this requirement of interstitial adjustment.[21]

This integrated industrial system, heavily dependent on science and engineering, was distinguished by Veblen from what he called the business system, dedicated to profits rather than production. And *The Theory of Business Enterprise* described a number of ways in which the latter profited by and from the disruption of the former. The solution of those who embraced the Technocracy Movement was to stabilize the industrial system by removing it from the hands of businessmen and putting it into the hands of the engineers and scientists. What actually happened, to much the same end, was the stabilization of the system through vertical and horizontal monopolization of industries by means of patent hoarding, trusts, holding companies, acquisitions and mergers; a major role was played by investment bankers, beginning with the railroads:

> What were the economic consequences of the rise of investment banker control over the railroads? There were four inter-related economic consequences which were most significant. First, the investment banks encouraged consolidation of the railroads into giant systems, both before the 1890's and during the period of reorganization. Second, the investment bankers succeeded in reducing competitive behavior among the railroads. As Carosso puts it, "Their purposes...were to bring order and stability to an industry sorely in need of it, promote cooperation and harmony among competitors, and restore the investors confidence in railroad securities." [22]

The third and fourth consequences mentioned above were the establishment of a monopolistic rate structure and an unprecedented concentration of economic power over the railroads in the hands of a small number of investment bankers.[23] This process of the concentration of economic power—by a variety of means—has of course continued throughout the century, but at the same time a number of other tendencies toward further integration and interdependency have also been significant. Trade Associations and/or Cartels, Corporate Joint Ventures, Interlocking Directorates, Government-Industry Advisory Bodies, and Corporate Domestic and Foreign Policy Organizations have all played a role. To appreciate the extent to which these developments have organized the economy into a unified system, a few examples will be useful.

Beginning in the 1910's, industrial trade associations have played a central role—especially in World Wars I and II—in the standardization of production methods and materials, product lines, accounting methods, credit procedures, and so on. And having standardized an industry or sub-industry, many associations took the next step and operated or tried to operate as cartels, restricting production, dividing up markets, or simply fixing prices. A very successful and sophisticated example is the domestic oil cartel, here described in a U.S. Senate Small Business Committee report:

> There is a mechanism controlling the production of crude oil to market demand (or below) that operates as smoothly and effectively as the finest watch...
>
> The oil-control policies in effect in the United States consist of a series of State and Federal statutes, recommendations of committees, made up of integrated oil-company economists and recommendations as to market demand made by the Bureau of Mines of the Department of the Interior. No single item is itself controlling; taken together they form a perfect pattern of monopolistic control over oil production, the distribution among refiners and distributors, and ultimately the price paid by the public.[24]

Starting in 1935, at the request of the American Petroleum Council (trade association of the oil industry), the Bureau of Mines, acting on information provided by the oil companies, issued monthly forecasts of the total quantity of crude oil required for the ensuing month. The quantity forecast by the Bureau was then divided up among the oil producing states and among the producing companies in each state, on the authority of the Interstate Oil Compact Commission (IOCC), the Texas Railroad Commission, and the oil conservation laws that were passed in the oil-producing states. The IOCC was created by an interstate agreement ratified by Congress in 1935; in addition, in the same year, Congress passed the "Connally Hot Oil Act," which prohibited interstate transport of oil in excess of the monthly allocations.[25] And in 1955 came the capstone, an act giving the President of the United States the authority to limit the importation of foreign oil, which President Eisenhower did in 1959, assigning the cartel 88% of the market.[26] Thus in effect an industry wide price-fixing cartel was supported, as the above report put it, by three legs of a tripod: the state laws, the federal laws, and the major oil companies interest in doing away with any real competition. And the industry is careful to maintain its position; for example, in the early 70's Gulf Oil's Government Operations Division, to keep track of 61 different federal agencies having something to do with the energy business, employed four vice presidents and forty five personnel with an annual budget of over two million dollars a year.[27]

Not all domestic trade associations are as powerful as the oil industry, of course, and only some of them have been successful in the institutionalization of market control; however, once an industry has been standardized throughout it is far easier to make informal and spontaneous agreements on limiting production or prices. And virtually every industry or subindustry in the United States is so standardized and has its own trade association; over a hundred of the thousands of national industrial trade associations had budgets of five million dollars or more a year in 1990.[28]

The melding together of the private and public spheres into one system that is illustrated by the domestic oil cartel has been a major tendency particularly following the Second World War. One area in which the two join together is the Government Advisory Body, where representatives of the corporations in an particular industry or industries meet with officials of government agencies or departments. There were, for example, 820 such advisory bodies in December of 1979, with 18,742 members.[29] Considering personnel from the private sphere serving in government in every kind of capacity, a 1955 survey found over one hundred thousand "WOC's" in government agencies, departments, commissions and the like. WOC's are persons serving "without compensation"; that is, their salaries are paid by the industry from which they are borrowed.[30]

The cooperative relations between corporations that have become an integral part of the system is illustrated by Corporate Joint Ventures. Commenting on the results of a study of jointly owned subsidiaries in the iron and steel industry, the author observed:

> More significant, perhaps, is the new light thrown on the structure of the industry. The more than seventy joint subsidiaries is a substantially larger number than heretofore was thought to exist—and there are probably others that this study was not able to discover. The interest groupings into which they fall indicate that we can no longer think of the steel industry as comprising some dozen large and ten smaller integrated producers...*The joint subsidiaries are quasi-mergers...*[31]

A similar study of the twenty largest oil companies for the period of the early and mid-1970's found 2755 joint ventures among them.[32] The Webb-Pomerene Act, 1918, has been regarded by corporations as exempting such ventures from anti-trust law, although it specifically exempts only associations "entered into for the sole purpose of engaging in export trade,... [and] provided such association, agreement, or act is not in restraint of trade within the United States...."[33] In any case, the U.S. government has either looked the other way or actively promoted joint ventures. For example, to stay with the oil companies:

> In the mid-20s the U.S. government fought strenuously to help Exxon and Mobil gain admission to the Iraq Petroleum Company, which successfully united British Petroleum (BP), Royal Dutch/Shell, Exxon, and Mobil in a joint venture that led to the 1928 Red Line Achnacarry agreement—both the joint venture and the cartel agreement were, on their face, violations of U.S. antitrust laws.[34]

A further level of integration of the economy is represented by interlocking boards of directors, where one corporation shares a member or members of its board of directors with others. Morgan Guaranty and Trust, for example, had members of its board of directors on 233 other company boards in 1968; Chemical Bank had 278, Chase Manhattan Bank, 193, and so on. While it is illegal under the Clayton Act for a director to sit on the boards of two "competing" companies, it is not illegal for directors of Morgan Guaranty, for example, to sit on the boards of three oil companies, three chemical companies, four drug companies, and so on, since they are not competing with these companies.[35]

Finally, a program of the Committee for Economic Development will illustrate the work of corporate policy and planning organizations. The Committee for Economic Development (CED) is an organization originally formed in 1942 to work out plans for shifting from a wartime economy to a peacetime economy.[36] It is made up of the Board Chairmen, Presidents, and Vice Presidents of 200 of the largest financial and non-financial corporations in the country. From the beginning, the organization engaged in a very active research and economic policy program under the direction of Theodore Yntema, Chair of the Finance Committee of Ford Motor Company. In 1962 the fifty member Research and Policy Committee issued a statement on national policy entitled "An Adaptive Program for Agriculture." The Committee determined that a "massive adjustment" needed to be made in the human resources committed to agricultural production. In the words of the report:

> What we have in mind in our program is a reduction of the farm labor force on the order of one third in a period of not more than five years.[37]

According to the 1959 Census of Agriculture there were 3,703,000 farms in the United States; a reduction of this number by one third would mean over a million two hundred thousand farms shut down in the recommended five year period. The reasons given for this policy were to make farming profitable without government controls and to establish a free market for farm products. What was to become of the million two hundred thousand farm families and their employees was left to the reader's imagination. In the imagination of the CED they would all somehow shift to employments that were in some way more profitable to them and to the nation.

Clearly the place for deciding on a national farm policy in a democratic society is its elected legislative body, and the Congress of the United States has never adopted a policy of eliminating small farms in favor of large corporate farms. In fact, the Agricultural Act of 1961 adopted a policy of acting "to encourage, promote and strengthen" the small farm.[38] However, far more federal law and policy is created by unelected federal department and agency bureaucracies than by the U.S. Congress (the ratio is 18 to 1).[39] In this case, the relevant bureaucracy, the Department of Agriculture, has long favored the agribusiness corporation over the small farmer, through the policies and regulations of its Agricultural Stabilization and Conservation Service, its Extension Service, and its Agricultural Research Service.[40] And according to Department of Agriculture statistics, between 1960 and 1970 some six million persons did indeed leave American farms.[41] It should be noted that whatever the Department did or did not do to encourage this exodus, the corporations that developed the CED farm policy could implement it on their own by various means. For example, a 1963 Giannini Foundation Research Report showed that farms of 80 acres or less received no discounts on fertilizers, insecticides, crop dusting or aerial spraying, compared to discounts of 10, 14 and 25 percent for the largest farms (more than 3200 acres). And a Federal Reserve survey of 1966 showed that small farms consistently paid higher rates for bank loans than large farms. While these figures are not evidence of a cooperative corporate effort to implement CED policy, they do make clear some of the kinds of things that can be done to effect such a policy, with or without government complicity.

Aside from the warning to those who might think of taking up farming, there are several points to be made here. One is that a line of separation between private and public governance of agriculture would be difficult to draw and would often be quite arbitrary, as we have seen in the case of the oil industry. Second, agriculture in the United States is clearly a subsystem managed by a mix of powerful private organizations and public agencies; and third, the subsystem is managed in such a way as to promote the end of the "Free Market" system, increased efficiency in output per man-hour. It is an end that allows for the profitable growth of corporations, but in the case of American farms at the cost of great suffering on the part of millions of our farm families, many of whom struggled for years to hold on to their land, having no knowledge of the above policy of the CED or Department of Agriculture or reason to believe there even was such policy.

Part IV: The Theory of Systemic Value and Private Property

Part III has presented evidence that the economy of the United States is a highly organized system and a system that is jointly administered in the main by two institutions, neither one of which is dealt with in Classical Liberal political or economic philosophy and neither one of which is addressed by the Constitution. The first is the corporation, which the U.S. Supreme Court brought to life in 1886 by the simple expedient of declaring that corporations were to be regarded as "persons" under the Fourteenth Amendment, and therefore would enjoy some of the same constitutional rights as those possessed by real persons.[42] The second is the Federal agency that embodies all three powers of government in one institution: legislative, judicial, and executive. These agencies presently comprise the fourteen executive departments (as Agriculture, Defense, Commerce, or Energy) and the sixty-two independent institutions (as the Federal Reserve System, Central Intelligence Agency, or Nuclear Regulatory Commission); almost all of these are the work of the past century. As noted above, 95% of Federal law is enacted by these agencies, and while they are required by the Administrative Procedures Act of 1946 to conduct public hearings on proposed laws, these hearings are typically attended largely or solely by representatives of corporations. That one agency should embody all three powers appears to violate the principle of the separation of powers, and indeed the Supreme Court ruled, in 1892, that Congress cannot delegate legislative power, as this "...is a principle universally recognized as vital to the integrity and maintenance of the system of government ordained by the Constitution." [43] In this century, however, the Court has stepped around this earlier ruling by distinguishing Congressionally legislated laws from the "administrative rules" of agencies, and most recently the Court has made the Federal agencies even more independent of Congress by eliminating the Congressional veto power over agency legislation.[44] What has evolved over this century, then, is a political/economic system administered in the main by these two institutions, corporations and government agencies, in symbiotic relationship. It is a situation that lies outside the Constitution and outside Classical Liberal political theory in the sense that neither the corporations nor the triple-powered agencies were envisaged by either and do not appear to be justifiable by either. Let us now have a look at the institution of private property, one of the great foundations of Classical Liberal thought, to see how it has been effected by and fits into this system.

The concept of private property embedded in the Classical Liberal tradition—call this the classical conception of private property—has two aspects that are of particular interest here. Private property has been understood, first of all, as the *individual* ownership of things, tangible or intangible. Second, the meaning of ownership has been understood in terms of a set of rights held by the owner in relation to the things. These rights would include, following the analysis of private property by Honore', the right to possess, use, manage, and receive income from the property, as well as the right to transfer, waive, abandon or destroy it.[45]

The institution itself has been justified on the basis of the moral principles of Classical Liberalism considered above. We have considered one of the moral principles justifying private property in principle (4): if the individual should have the full value of his or her labor, then the individual should have the rights that secure full value to the product of that labor. Closely connected with this justification is a further one also based on the individual, and that is the idea that private property is essential to the free development of the individual's personality and powers; the quotation following is from Thomas Hill Green, founder of the British Idealist movement in the 1860's:

> One condition of the existence of property, then, is appropriation, and that implies the conception of himself on the part of the appropriator as a permanent subject for whose use, as instruments of satisfaction and expression, he takes and fashions certain external things, certain things external to his bodily members. These things, so taken and fashioned, cease to be external as they were before. They become a sort of extension of the man's organs, the constant apparatus through which he gives reality to his ideas and wishes.[46]

The property envisaged here as an extension of the individual's person or personality was probably thought of as tangible property, as real property and chattels; it would be difficult to see how a securities portfolio or other similar intangibles could be conceived of as an extension of one's bodily organs or person or how any credence could be given to such a conception.[47] The justification of most property of the intangible kind rests, therefore, on a second traditional argument based on the principle of Utility.

The argument here is essentially the argument for the Free Market economy as promoting the greatest happiness; if the goals of the Free Market are accepted as having moral priority over all other concerns and policies, then the institution of private property is justified since it is a necessary condition for the existence of the Free Market. It is the legal foundation for the Free Market's economic liberties—freedom of investment, contract, and exchange. But if there is to be private property, is there no limit on how much property an individual may accumulate? The standard answer is that any such limit would interfere with the availability of capital for purposes of investment, and so would have the effect of retarding technological advancement and/or economic growth; and these ends, once again, have the highest moral priority.

This argument, however, lost its force for any practical purpose with the coming of the corporation, an exercise in the freedom of association that allows an unlimited number of individuals to pool unlimited capital. And today, even the sale of stock by corporations is no longer a principal means of raising capital, since almost all investment in productive and service industries comes from funds raised internally.[48] Indeed, the problem in the late 20th century is not that of raising more capital for investment in new technology, but the rate of technologically driven social change that we can tolerate without social and ecological destabilization and chaos.

Two Kinds of Property

In considering the nature and status of private property as it exists today, it will be useful to distinguish between *income producing property*, and *income reducing property*. This is a very rough distinction, but still a very useful one. Income reducing property is, for the most part, tangible and personal property; for example, a person's dwelling, automobile, clothing, a pet, and so on. It is property that requires the expenditure of income over time in order to keep it in useable condition, to operate it, to keep it clean or in good health, and so forth. Income producing property, on the other hand, is in greater part property of the intangible kind that provides regular income, as patents, stocks, bonds, and other securities. The distinction is not absolute; depending on its use, for example, a vehicle might belong to either category or both, and a professional license could be regarded as both.

More and more, over the past century or so, income producing property has lost the attributes of private property as listed above; an owner of corporate stock has a very limited property right in the corporation: the right to receive dividends, to propose motions at annual meetings of stockholders, and in some cases to vote for directors (depending on the kind of stock held); but no control over the operations and policy of the corporation or even over the portion of profits to be made available as dividends; indeed, the stockholder is even the last to be paid, after creditors and employees.[49]

Of the more than eight trillion dollars worth of stock held in 1995, the ownership of nearly half is even further removed from the classical conception of private property than the above. Some two trillion is held by private and public pension funds; here the individual investor is not the legal owner of any stock, but has only a beneficial interest—a limited property right—with little or nothing to say regarding the investments of the fund or its officers. Another trillion is held in mutual funds, in which again the shareholder has no legal ownership of the stocks purchased with his or her money. Outside of pension and mutual funds, five or six hundred billion is owned by financial and non-financial corporations, legally and beneficially, and a great part of the remainder is held by non-profit private foundations, non-profit institutions such as charitable or educational corporations, and various kinds of trusts in which the trustee (often a bank or trust institution) is the legal owner. Thus nearly half of the publicly traded stock in the United States is legally owned by corporations rather than individuals. This is again a state of affairs that lies entirely outside the Classical Liberal political or economic theory, made possible by the Supreme Court decision mentioned above that, with a wave of the judicial wand, made corporations into "persons."

Private property in the classical sense has thus virtually disappeared *as far as the category of income producing property is concerned*. In the classical sense private property involved a real owner, something owned, and a set of rights held by the owner over what is owned. As we have seen, much of the property in this category is not legally owned by individuals at all, and for what is so owned, the traditional rights do not obtain or obtain only in a severely limited sense. Thus the Classical Liberal arguments to justify property as a product of individual labor or as an extension of self or expression of personality are not applicable; corporations are really not individuals, and corporate stocks or mutual fund shares are really not private property in the classical sense.[50] The arguments would still apply, of course, in the case of personal property, the largely tangible property that is held by real individuals. Let us consider now how these two categories of property—income producing and income reducing—are distributed in the population as a whole.

Somewhat more than half of the publicly traded stock is still held by individual owners, or by "households" in the terminology of the Federal government. If households are ranked according to ownership of stock, the top .5% of the population held 58.57% of this stock in 1995. The top 5% held 94.49% of the stock; the top 10% held 99.11%. Eighty percent of U.S. households had none.[51] Ten percent of households, then, held 99% of the stock that is not owned by corporations, to which must be added a healthy percentage of bonds and other securities. In the case of stocks alone, this amounts to a bit over four trillion, one hundred and fourteen billion dollars at 1995 market value.[52] In the case of the top .5% of households, this would amount to roughly $2,409,569,800,000.00, or 2.409 trillion dollars. Much of this wealth is *dynastic*, i.e., it is held and managed in such a way so as to increase from one generation to another. Here is one example of the magnitude of such holdings:

> Of some 1,600 living Du Ponts, only 250 constitute the inner circle. Of these, only about 50 make up the all-powerful inner core of the family. Together, these 50 Du Ponts control or share control over $211 billion worth of assets, greater than the annual Gross National Product of most nations. They own huge or controlling interests in over 100 multimillion-dollar corporations and banks, including some of the world's largest...[53]

The existence of dynastic fortunes requires that the transfer of property from decedent to heirs be permitted in law, and that the bulk of the property transferred escapes estate or inheritance tax. The Classical Liberal tradition was divided on the issue of passing such wealth from one generation to another.[54] Some took the view that there is a natural right to bequeath property; others, as Thomas Jefferson, took a diametrically opposite position:

> The earth belongs in usufruct to the living; the dead have neither powers nor rights over it. The portion occupied by any individual ceases to be his when he himself ceases to be and reverts to society.[55]

That there is no natural right to bequeath property is now the prevailing view in the law, as expressed here rather tersely by a California Court:

> It is entirely immaterial whether the statutes relative to inheritance comport with the court's or counsel's idea of justice, morality or natural right. The matter is in the plenary control of the state Legislature and depends entirely upon the provisions of the statutes.[56]

The issue, then, is the extent to which society should permit accumulated wealth to be passed on to heirs. I have argued that our economy is an integrated system and that this system is the primary source of value. From this standpoint, individuals who possess stocks and bonds possess *entitlements to future systemic value*. That is, they have a legal or beneficial interest in value to be produced in and by the economic system; the exact return depending on the particular investments, but primarily on the performance of the system as a whole. Now the economic system responsible for generating that value and the social system that sustains it required hundreds of years of thought, labor, and struggle by millions of persons to attain its present level of sophistication, complexity, and productive power; its continued operation requires the regular labor of millions of individuals carrying out a myriad of specialized tasks. Holders of stock, however, will receive regular shares of the value produced by this system in the form of dividends without the need to do or contribute anything. In this respect *entitlements to future systemic value* are morally objectionable; the case of dynastic wealth is particularly egregious.

An individual born into dynastic wealth inherits a portfolio of entitlements to part of the product of the labor of countless other human beings into the indefinite future; and not only has the individual done nothing to earn this status, it is a violation of the basic democratic principle against special privileges by birth. It would also appear to be a violation of the 14th Amendment to the Constitution, which requires that no one be denied equal protection of the law; those who are born into the position of having part of their future labor automatically appropriated by others are clearly not enjoying equal protection under the law.

Lastly, dynastic wealth is wealth that goes far beyond what any individual or family could ever use for any ordinary purpose of life, even allowing as ordinary purposes the possession of houses and apartments in a number of cities in this country, chateaus in France, castles in Spain, any number of vehicles, airplanes, yachts, fine art collections, and the income to keep up all these properties and the staffs they require. It is wealth that is not consumable. It has, therefore, only one purpose, a purpose that should never be among the ordinary purposes of property: it is a source of political power over other people and of *political power over the operation and direction of the social system itself*. We have considered one example of this above, where the controlling interests and boards of the largest corporations initiated or acquiesced in driving millions of fellow Americans off their farms to replace them with more "efficient" agribusiness corporations.[57] Those who inherit dynastic wealth are thus not only economically privileged to live off the labor of others, they are politically privileged with an inherited and illegitimate power over the lives of their fellow citizens.

After the American Revolution virtually all of the states abolished laws providing for primogeniture and entail, either by statute or constitutional provision. These were laws that made dynastic wealth possible in the form of land holdings, land being the principal form of wealth in the early states. It was believed by many that there was no place in a democratic society for an aristocracy perpetuated by inheritance.[58] The form of wealth has shifted in the last one hundred years, land having given way to securities, but the belief is just as valid.

Part V: The Common Good

Parts III and IV have attempted to describe the peculiar stage that we have reached in the evolution of the political economy of the United States. We have developed an economic system of extraordinary technical complexity; its fundamental units of production, the corporations or corporate conglomerates, are themselves organized in a complex mosaic of trade associations and national and international policy making bodies, and these organizations have in turn developed symbiotic relationships with quasi-sovereign governmental agencies. At the same time legal title to this system of production has been shifting slowly over this century from individuals to financial and non-financial corporations, further removing the control of the economy from a moral and political community of persons that alone makes civilized society possible. None of this accords with the Classical Liberal political and economic theory that continues to be put forward as its moral and theoretical foundation.

If the foregoing analysis is correct the worldview that has guided the developed nations since the Enlightenment—the Classical Liberal *Weltanschauung*—has helped to promote changes so profound as to undermine its own applicability and utility. We are therefore in a situation requiring a change in some basic premises and values. I have argued that it is the social system as such that is the primary source of value. A social system cannot conceivably be private property, if for no other reason than that it consists in part of all of the persons who have been socialized as its members. If any concept of ownership is to be applied here, it would have to be that of a *collective ownership* of the social system and its product. Collective ownership would have at least the following implications:

1) Private property in the income producing category would be a public trust to be managed for the common good.
2) Every member of the social system would have a rightful claim to the social product, meaning in practical terms a decent standard of living, including medical care, security in old age and disability, education, and meaningful participation in the social, cultural and political life of the society.

This brings us back to the International Bill of Human Rights with which we began. For the kinds of rights that all of us *should* have as collective owners, we *already do have* in this international treaty law.[59] It is an outgrowth of a seed planted in the Charter of the United Nations, in the form of two articles:

> Article 55
>
> With a view to the creation of conditions and stability and well-being, which are necessary for peaceful and friendly relations among nations based on respect for the principle of equal rights and self-determination of peoples, the United Nations shall promote:
>
> a) higher standards of living, full employment, and conditions of economic and social progress and development;
> b) solutions of international economic, social, health, and related problems; and international cultural and educational cooperation;
> c) universal respect for, and observance of, human rights and fundamental freedoms for all without distinction as to race, sex, language, or religion.
>
> Article 56
>
> All Members pledge themselves to take joint and separate action in co-operation with the Organization for the achievement of the purposes set forth in Article 55.

These articles became the basis for what I characterized above as the greatest collective project ever undertaken by our species. The third clause of Article 55 led to the adoption of the *Universal Declaration of Human Rights* in 1948. The United Nations Human Rights Commission, chaired by Eleanor Roosevelt until

1953, began work immediately on turning the Universal Declaration into international law in the form of two Covenants; that work continued for eighteen years.[60] In the interim, sixty-six new nations had joined the United Nations, a non-aligned nations movement had been organized (1961), and the General Assembly declared the decade of the 60's a decade of international economic co-operation in accordance with the first and second clauses of Article 55.[61] Human Rights law, in other words, was being developed along with planning for the international economic and political co-operation that would be necessary for its implementation. These two aspects of the program of the United Nations, the creation of the law and the effort to modify the global economy to implement that law continued through the 1960's and 70's. Together they constitute a global blueprint for the Common Good of all peoples, and they have been supported by virtually all of the one hundred and ninety some nations that are currently members of the organization. Only a minority of rich and powerful nations, the "Group of Seven" (G-7), the U.S., Britain, Germany, France, Japan, Italy, and Canada, have consistently stood in opposition.[62]

International Human Rights Law

The international law concerning Human Rights may be divided into four categories, the first two of which are together referred to as the *International Bill of Human Rights*:

I. The Universal Declaration of Human Rights (1948);
II. The Covenant on Civil and Political Rights (1976), and the Covenant on Economic, Social, and Cultural Rights (1976);
III. A series of nearly 40 independent supplementary conventions.
IV. A series of related declarations, principles, rules, standards, and guidelines having an advisory status.[63]

In the main the above categories go from the very general statement of human rights in the Declaration, to the more detailed statements of the Covenants, and then to the still more specific law of the various conventions. For example, the Declaration states in Article Seven: "All are equal before the law and are entitled without any discrimination to equal protection of the law." The Covenants are more specific; each of them pledges States Parties to the Covenants not to discriminate on the basis of "race, colour, sex, language, religion, political or other opinion, national or social origin, property, birth, or other status." Still more specific are, for example, the Convention Against All Forms of Racial Discrimination (1969), or the Convention Concerning Discrimination in Respect of Employment and Occupation (1958).[64] Lastly, it is expected that at the level of particular cases, the judiciary of each country will have the task of interpreting international human rights law into the specific context of its own languages, culture, and tradition. Together the body of human rights law represented by all four categories now occupies over 900 pages in the 1993 compilation published by the United Nations.[65] That the governments of nations with different languages, cultures, political systems, religions, traditions, political and economic interests could all agree on so comprehensive a body of human rights law is surely the greatest co-operative achievement of a century that has otherwise been the most barbaric and destructive in human history.

The Implementation of Human Rights Law

With the exception of war crimes and the crime of genocide, the United Nations makes no attempt to enforce international human rights law, if enforcement means the use of police power. First of all the organization is a voluntary association of politically sovereign nations, the governments of which are presumed to have joined this collective project in good faith. Thus in the main the role of the United Nations is properly that of being supportive of their efforts at implementation. And implementation means the creation of the political, economic and social conditions that make possible the exercise or enjoyment of the rights that people now possess by law. This may require anything from internal changes in social practices or changes in law or administrative policy, to changes in the economic relations between nations. Two principal means of implementation have been developed by the organization. One is a reporting process that is built into the various treaties, and the other is the project for what is referred to as the New International Economic Order (NIEO).

An example will illustrate the reporting process. Ratification of the Covenant on Economic, Social, and Cultural Rights requires a government to submit a report within two years on the measures it has adopted to give effect to the Covenant rights and on the progress made in their enjoyment, and reports are expected to be submitted every five years thereafter.[66] Reports are reviewed by an 18 member Committee on Economic, Social, and Cultural Rights, made up of experts in the field of human rights nominated by States Party to the treaty, elected by the United Nations Economic and Social Council and serving in their personal capacity rather than as official representatives of any government. Reports are reviewed by the Committee in open public sessions, with the assistance of the various United Nations Agencies whose work is intimately related to the implementation of specific treaty rights, as the International Labor Organization, the Food and Agriculture Organization, the World Health Organization, and UNESCO.[67]

As important as the reporting process is in keeping governments in mind of and answerable to their treaty obligations, an enormous problem is posed by the limited resources that developing nations can devote to the implementation of human rights. World economic planning was therefore seen, very early on, as a necessary part of the implementation process. The first step in this direction was the formation of the United Nations Conference on Trade and Development (UNCTAD) in 1964. The Final Act of this conference, fifty-five pages in length, begins as follows:

> The States participating in the Conference are determined to achieve the high purposes embodied in the United Nations Charter "to promote social progress and better standards of life in larger freedom"; to seek a better and more effective system of international economic cooperation, whereby the division of the world into areas of poverty and plenty may be banished and prosperity achieved by all; and to find ways by which the human and material resources of the world may be harnessed for the abolition of poverty everywhere.[68]

This same conference saw the formation of the Group of 77, a caucus of developing nations representing the non-aligned movement; their joint declaration on international co-operation concluded:

> Such co-operation must serve as a decisive instrument for ending the division of the world into areas of affluence and intolerable poverty. This task is the outstanding challenge of our times. The injustice and neglect of centuries need to be redressed...[69]

A series of actions by the General Assembly to promote the aims of the Charter and the first UNCTAD conference led to the adoption in 1974 of a *Programme of Action on the Establishment of a New International Economic Order* (NIEO).[70] Some of the goals of this ten part program were bringing an end to all forms of foreign occupation, racial discrimination, apartheid, colonial and neo-colonial domination and exploitation; establishing permanent sovereignty of the developing nations over their own natural resources; creating measures to eliminate the instability of the international monetary system (to prevent, for example, the currency fluctuations that can be devastating to developing nations); and regulation and control of the conduct of transnational corporations (proscribing, for example, "their collaboration with racist regimes and colonial administrations" and regulating "the repatriation of the profits accruing from their operations, taking into account the legitimate interests of all parties concerned.")[71] Adoption of the NIEO was followed in the same year by the General Assembly's approval of a *Charter of the Economic Rights and Duties of States*, making clear the responsibilities of States in their internal affairs as well as in their relations with other States, and establishing a quinquennial review by the Assembly of the progress made in its implementation.[72] The Director of the United Nations Institute for Training and Research (UNITAR) commented on the magnitude of the NIEO undertaking in one of the 17 volumes on the project produced by that organization:

> ...humanity's complex problems in the area of economics, the environment, disarmament, food production, the transfer of technology and other areas as well, have become so large, interrelated and urgent that they require the enormous efforts of thousands of international researchers and scholars at hundreds of international research institutions simply to survey the extent of the problem. Moreover, the recommendations of these experts on the various world problems must then be assessed at the many dozens of international forums, both within and without the United Nations, now dedicated to developing solutions to humanity's ever-growing dilemmas.[73]

Recognition of the interrelatedness of the world's social, economic and political problems means understanding that they cannot be resolved in isolation from one another. The same interrelatedness exists for the implementation of human rights; no right or category of rights can be fully implemented or enjoyed in the absence of the rest. In 1993 the World Conference on Human Rights stated this clearly in the *Vienna Declaration and Programme of Action*:

> All human rights are universal, indivisible, and interdependent and interrelated. The same document adds that democracy and human rights are mutually dependent on one another: "...democracy, development, and respect for human rights and fundamental freedoms are interdependent and mutually reinforcing."[74]

Written into international treaty law, then, is an astonishing, and in its implications, a revolutionary manifesto. It represents one of the two directions in which Classical Liberalism has evolved in this century, one progressive and one retrogressive. The progressive direction -the *Human Rights Movement*- has built upon the civil and political rights of Classical Liberalism, adding economic, social and cultural rights and a commitment to democracy. The retrogressive direction, now being referred to as *Neo-Liberalism* or *Neo-Conservatism*, celebrates the extension of civil and political rights to corporations, typically rejecting any kind of economic, social or cultural rights for real persons. In the late 1960's, George W. Ball, investment banker and Undersecretary of State during the Kennedy and Johnson administrations, sketched the position in a talk before the International Chamber of Commerce in London that now seems prophetic:

> We recognize that we live in a world whose resources are finite and whose demands are exploding. To avoid a Darwinian debacle on a global scale we will

> have to use our resources with maximum efficiency and a minimum of waste...
>
> This can be achieved only when all the factors necessary for the production and use of goods—capital, labor, raw materials, plant facilities and distribution—are freely mobilized and deployed according to the most efficient pattern. And this in turn will be possible only when national boundaries no longer play a critical role in defining economic horizons.

However, "corporate persons" as the Undersecretary calls them, are impeded in carrying out these tasks, as developing countries are fearful their economies will fall under foreign domination and so impose obstacles to the entry of foreign firms; moreover:

> A greater menace may come from the actions of governments addicted to a regime of planning, who see in the global corporation a foreign instrumentality that may frustrate their economic designs. The basis for their concern is easy to understand, especially in countries where a world company, if allowed in, would become the largest employer of national labor and consumer of national materials.

A solution favored by Undersecretary Ball was the establishment by treaty of an international companies law, administered by a supra-national body:

> An international companies law could place limitations, for example, on the restrictions nation-states might be permitted to impose on companies established under its sanction. The operative standard defining those limitations might be the quantity of freedom needed to preserve the central principle of assuming the most economical and efficient use of world resources.[75]

In the 1960s this program seemed rather less than likely. However, beginning in the 1970's the developed countries, reacting to the United Nations' proposal for a New International Economic Order and spearheaded by the G-7, began to work on many fronts to undermine the NIEO and the global implementation of human rights law. This campaign involved the World Bank, the International Monetary Fund (IMF), the General Agreement on Tariffs and Trade (GATT), the World Trade Organization (successor to GATT), the power of the U.N. Security Council, and even the overthrow of democratically elected governments.[76] It has reached the point of proposing George Ball's international companies law in the form of an international treaty that would give corporations virtually unimpeded access to any nation's economy that wants to participate in the world market.[77] At the same time, the transnational corporations are in the process of carrying out a palace revolution in the United Nations, negotiating a framework with U.N. leadership for their regular involvement in U.N.

decision making, including the disbursement of development funds to developing nations.[78]

This concerted attack by transnational corporations and the governments of developed nations on an international project for the Common Good of humanity, however, is hopefully the last phase in a period characterized by the philosophical hegemony of the Classical Liberal Worldview. For even though its contemporary Neo-Liberal proponents are attempting to arm-twist the rest of the world into accepting its articles of faith, they are now faced with a much more powerful moral alternative that has been enacted into international law and is backed by the majority of the nations on earth. The struggle between these two philosophies will very likely be a protracted one, and will surely be as turbulent and confused as the long struggle that ended the middle ages and produced the modern world.

Some Legal and Moral Consequences of Philosophic Individualism

THE UNITED STATES GOVERNMENT ratified the International Covenant on Civil and Political Rights on June 8th, 1992; it is unclear if and when the government will ratify its companion document, the International Covenant on Social, Economic, and Cultural Rights (ICSECR).[1] One source of opposition to the latter is powerful legal and moral traditions that go back to the 18th century. They are logically derivable from a metaphysical or foundational premise occasionally referred to as Nominalism; however, to avoid the ambiguities connected with that term I will refer to it as the premise of Philosophic Individualism.[2] The first part of this paper considers some of the main implications of this premise and the connection between these implications and the legal and moral traditions in question. The category of rights specifically at issue here is the category often referred to as "positive" as against "negative" rights, *i.e.*, post-New Deal entitlement rights as against traditional constitutional rights; examples of positive rights from the ICSECR would be the right to an adequate standard of living (Article 11), the right to the highest standard of physical and mental health (Article 12), or the right to education (Article 13).[3]

If the metaphysics of Philosophic Individualism is logically incompatible with the ICSECR for the reasons developed in Part I, an alternative foundational premise that appears to be gaining ground in this century is much more favorable to it. In part II of the paper I consider this alternative premise, Philosophic Holism, and some of its relevant implications. I will end with a comment on the nature of metaphysical or foundational propositions as such; they are clearly a category that is *sui generis* but hardly vacuous or nonsensical as philosophers maintained in the late 19th and early 20th centuries.[4] Indeed, having a wide range of implications, they serve an organizing function in the intellectual life of a society.

Part I

The premise of Philosophic Individualism can be stated in several different ways which I will take to be synonymous:

I) *Only individual things exist,* or alternatively, *Only individual things are ultimately real.*

The best way to explore the meaning of (I) is to consider a series of its corollaries. They are derived by coupling the premise with a commonsensical notion and then deducing the appropriate conclusion. The causal corollary will serve as a useful example:

II) *Only individual things can be causes or causal agents.*

This corollary is derived from (I) by adding the premise that *only real things can be causes;* what is meant here is that if something has never existed, does not now exist, and will never exist in the future, in any form and in any sense whatever of the term 'exist', then commonsensically it can never act as a cause. And when this commonsensical notion is added to (I) the result is the corollary (II) that leads in many directions. For example, in the sciences (II) would require that to explain any natural phenomenon we must discover the individual things that are the ultimate causes of the phenomenon in question.[5] The idea was extraordinarily productive; in biology, for example, it led to the theory of the cell as the basic unit of life in the first half of the 19th century, to the germ theory of disease in the second half, and to the theory of the gene as the basic unit of heredity in the 20th. Our interest here, however, is not the various consequences of philosophical individualism in the sciences, but those for social life and legal theory.

In the realm of social life the premise requires human society to be a mere aggregation of individuals; society or community as such was regarded as a fiction.[6] So it followed that with respect to human society only individual persons are capable of being causal agents. And if rights are powers (such as the right to make a will), or at least presuppose powers, then only those things that are active agents can have rights, and it must follow that:

III) *Only individual persons can have moral or legal rights.*

Notice that while (III) restricts the sorts of entities that can be holders of rights, excluding, for example, institutions, groups, forests, rivers, other species, and so on, by itself it permits no conclusion as to which categories of individuals would have rights, what rights they would have, and under what conditions. The same is true of a related deduction from (II), namely:

IV) *Only individuals can have moral or legal obligations.*

What we have here—in these abstract corollaries—is a set of limitations within which various theories regarding rights, obligations, and responsibilities can be developed—so long as they conform to the fundamental premise of philosophic individualism. A more general way of stating (III) and (IV) would be: only individuals can have status as moral or legal agents or entities.

One of the limitations of (IV) is immediately relevant to the matter of entitlements. While individuals can be obligated to or be responsible for other individuals (IV) does not recognize institutions as such, whether private or public, as capable of being obligated or responsible either to individuals or to other institutions. This is not to say that the individual officers or officials of institutions cannot have obligations or responsibilities in their limited capacities as officers or officials, but that is not the same as the institution itself having an obligation.

Within the framework of Philosophic Individualism, then, there is no metaphysical elbow room for governments, corporations, or other institutions, and so in law there was no provision for them; the constitution of the United States deals with the powers and relations of the various branches of government, and the rights of individuals, the latter primarily in the Bill of Rights. But there are no provisions concerning groups or organizations. This problem was solved in the case of corporations by the Supreme Court ruling in *Santa Clara County v. Southern Pacific Railroad Company*, 1886, that in the eyes of the law corporations will be considered "persons" and so fall under the Fourteenth Amendment (and thus have legal status to sue and be sued).[7] In the case of the government this option was ruled out, since it would require including the government as a "person" under the very provisions that were intended to protect persons *from* the government.

On the other hand having a government that is not a moral or legal person in the law creates serious practical problems. A government that is not a moral or legal person is one that cannot be morally or legally obligated. And if government cannot be obligated, then one cannot have a right to any benefit one receives from it, whether the benefit is a pension, job, welfare, disability payment, or government contract. So any such transfer of value to an individual by government would have the status of a mere gratuity, a matter of charity. Thus if Congress passed an act to provide benefits to veterans, Congress could modify or repeal it at will, and veterans would have no recourse; due process of law would not be available, because there is no legally recognized individual entity to sue. It is this framework of thought that probably explains, or helps to explain, a series of cases in which Federal District Courts and the U.S. Supreme Court ruled continually against individuals who sought redress for terminated benefits, pensions, jobs, and contracts. In these cases the courts routinely declared that the benefits in question had the status of mere "gifts" without providing any explanation or justification for the claim except precedent. For example, in *Lynch v. United States*, Justice Brandeis said:

> Pensions, compensation allowances and privileges are gratuities. They involve no agreement of parties; and the grant of them creates no vested right. The benefits conferred by gratuities may be redistributed or withdrawn at any time in the discretion of Congress. *United States v. Teller*, 107 U.S. 160; *Frisbie v. United States* 157 U.S. 160,166; *United States v. Cook* 257 U.S. 523,527.[8]

In none of the cases cited here does the Court provide any explanation or justification for the view that benefits must be regarded as gifts; the earliest case cited, *United States v. Teller*, 1882, refers us to *Walton v. Cotton*, 1856; *Walton* again assumes the gratuity position:

> The pension is undoubtedly a bounty of the government, and in the hands of an administrator of a deceased pensioner it would not be liable to the claims of creditors, had the acts of Congress omitted such a provision. But the legislative intent is shown to be in accordance, in this respect, with the law.[9]

Walton cites no precedent, and says no more on the issue than the above (regarding which it should be noted that it was not and is not necessary to categorize pensions as gratuities in order to block creditors of a deceased pensioner).

The gratuity doctrine has been somewhat tempered since *Goldberg v. Kelly*, 1969, in which the Court ruled that New York State could not terminate welfare benefits without a prior notice and hearing. Justice Black, in dissent, held on to the older point of view:

> The Court...relies upon the Fourteenth Amendment and in effect says that failure of the government to pay a promised charitable installment to an individual deprives that individual of *his own property*, in violation of the Due Process Clause of the Fourteenth Amendment. It somewhat strains credulity to say that the government's promise of charity to an individual is property belonging to that individual when the government denies that the individual is honestly entitled to receive such a payment...[10]

If a welfare payment is charity then there is clearly no property right to it, but that was the very point at issue and Justice Black provided no explanation for his position.

Now the argument here has not been that in these pre-Goldberg cases the courts consciously relied on the premise of Philosophic Individualism in deducing or endorsing the view that government benefits must be construed as gifts. There is no way of knowing what the private reasoning of the Court may have been; we only know that in none of the cases did the Court see any need to make it part of the public record. And this suggests that the Court probably considered the matter too obvious to require argument or discussion. What I am arguing here is that the court decisions were consistent with the premise of Philosophic Individualism, that this premise was a characteristic feature of our intellectual life throughout the period covered by these decisions, and that to someone reasoning within that framework, it would "strain credulity," as Justice Black put it, that the rights and obligations that held between individuals could be extended to government or society or such. Hence it is not unlikely that the intellectual framework of Philosophic Individualism is part of the explanation of this string of decisions.

It is only in this century and largely after the New Deal period that the courts began to take a somewhat different view on government benefits; one of the principle events helping to bring about this change of view was probably the passage of the Social Security Act in 1935 (ruled constitutional by the Supreme Court in two cases in 1936 and 1937 respectively).[11]

As will be seen when we turn to the corollary on value, there is a second line of reasoning that leads from the premise of Philosophic Individualism to the view that government payments must be mere gifts, although this time it is a matter of ethics: that any transfer of value from government to an individual citizen *ought* to be an act of charity. Before going on to the corollary on value, however, there is a further line of decisions by the Court that it never explained and that appear to be connected with the problem considered above. This is a series of cases upholding the doctrine of sovereign immunity, a series that begins with *Cohens v.Virginia* in 1821. In that case Justice Marshall announced the doctrine (without argument) that it was impossible for a citizen to sue the government:

> The universally received opinion is, that no suit can be commenced or prosecuted against the United States; that the judiciary act does not authorize such suits.[12]

It should be noted that neither the Judiciary Act nor any of its amendments prior to this case declared that a suit could not be commenced or prosecuted against the United States; the Act is silent on the issue.[13] Nonetheless this view was taken without question to be "universally established" and "universally assented to" until 1882. In that year Associate Justice Samuel Miller reviewed the possible reasons for it in the case *United States v. Lee*. Looking into "the laws and practices of our English ancestors...," he could find no satisfactory reason for the doctrine but still did not explicitly reject it. The tradition in English law that the King cannot be sued in his own court was inapplicable, since we had no king. The modification of this view that it would be inconsistent with the very idea of supreme executive power did not apply, since we had no person with supreme executive power. Justice Miller concluded:

> It seems most probable that it has been adopted in our courts as a part of the general doctrine of publicists, that the supreme power in every State, wherever it may reside, shall not be compelled, by process of courts of its own creation, to defend itself from assaults in those courts.[14]

But the real question was why shouldn't the government be required to defend itself in its own courts, and that remained unanswered. Within the intellectual framework that allows only individuals as real entities, however, there are few alternatives. There is no one individual with supreme power, and as noted above, officials of various branches or departments—while responsible for their own torts as private individuals—can't reasonably be held responsible as individual officials for tortious conduct of the government as such. In fact, since the government is not a moral or legal agent, it would appear to be incapable of tortious conduct. Perhaps this explains the rather shocking statement of the Court in *Gibbons v. United States*:

> No government has ever held itself liable to individuals for the misfeasance, laches, or unauthorized exercise of power by its officers or agents.[15]

Like the doctrine of government benefits as gifts, the doctrine of sovereign immunity persisted until the passage of legislation by Congress, in this case the Federal Tort Claims Act in 1946, an act that gave citizens at least a limited right to sue the government.

The Corollaries on Value

There are two further corollaries that are important in filling out the picture of Philosophical Individualism. These extend the meaning of (I) into the domain of value, i.e., they are formulae that apply to value in any shape or form in which it presents itself (aesthetic, material, spiritual, economic, or whatever). The first one is:

V) *Only individual things can be sources of value.*

With regard to human society, from the 17th century on the source of value was taken to be human labor. Locke says, in his *Second Treatise*:

> "...nay, if we will rightly estimate things as they come to our use, and cast up the several Expenses about them, what in them is purely owing to *Nature*, and what to *labour*, we shall find, that in most of them 99/100 are wholly to be put on the account of *labour*."[16]

And of course, when an individual produces something of value, he is entitled to the product:

> "Whatever then he removes out of the State that Nature hath provided, and left it in, he hath mixed his *Labour* with, and joyned to it something that is his own, and thereby makes it his *Property*."[17]

Now what is relevant to our concerns here is what becomes of the product of an individual's labor, for as James Mill put it over a hundred years later, "if you give more to one man than the produce of his labor, you can do so only by taking it away from the produce of some other man's labor."[18] So it follows that:

> "The greatest possible happiness of society is, therefore, attained by insuring to every man the greatest possible quantity of the produce of his labor."[19]

From this perspective then, the problem for entitlements is—in a nutshell—the problem that one person's entitlement must be some other person's loss. It is not that there are no conditions under which part of the value produced by an individual can be taken. One such condition is spelled out by Adam Smith:

> "As soon as stock has accumulated in the hands of particular persons, some of them will naturally employ it in setting to work industrious people, whom they will supply with materials and subsistence, in order to make a profit by the sale of their work, or what their labour adds to the value of the materials."[20]

And the laborer will not then receive the value of his or her labor:

> "In this state of things, the whole produce of labour does not always belong to the labourer. He must in most cases share it with the owner of the stock which employs him."[21]

But this deduction of a portion of the value created is justified because the accumulation and investment of capital "occasions, in a well-governed society, that universal opulence which extends itself to the lowest ranks of the people."[22]

Certain other deductions from the value produced by an individual may also be justifiable, as a deduction by government to provide security of person and protection of private property; here again there is, theoretically at least, a tacit agreement. However, there seems to be no possible justification for taking away part of the property produced by one person's labor in order to support other individuals who are unemployed or unemployable; within the framework of Philosophical Individualism, this is tantamount to compulsory labor or slave labor, so entitlements seem *prima facie* to be unethical. The support of the unemployed and unemployable can properly only be through charity.

There are, then, two lines of objection to "entitlement" rights both of which rest on the premise of Philosophic Individualism. It is unethical to force some individuals to assume obligations to others involuntarily, and there is no institution that can assume these obligations since institutions are not recognized as having any reality above and beyond their own individual denizens. And both of these objections rest on the premise that at rock bottom there are only individual persons and their individual labor. There are no other "entities" that can be productive of value or saddled with real obligations.

I turn now to the second and last corollary of (I) regarding the theory of value:

VI) *Only individual things can have value.*

In more practical terms this corollary could well be restated for much of the last several hundred years as "Only things that can be turned into private property or things that can be commoditized have value." And the measure of their value is, again, the amount of labor required to produce them:

> Labour, therefore, is the real measure of the exchangeable value of all commodities.[23]

The relevance of the preceding to our subject, however, is indirect; it is what is excluded here that is important. And what is excluded from the realm of value in this framework is all of those things that are not individual things, that cannot be commoditized, that cannot be transformed into private property, and so have no exchangeable value. Two of these are of particular importance; one is the ecological system, or systems, that sustain life. The ICESCR touches on this in Article 12-2-b, calling for "The improvement of all aspects of environmental and industrial hygiene." Under this clause the argument can be made that we are entitled, among other things, to non-disease producing air, water, and food supply, all of which can be provided only by a healthful environment and a healthy ecosystem.

But these things are not individual things, and are excluded from the realm of value in the conceptual framework of Philosophic Individualism. An ecological system dissolves on this view into the individual things that are its component parts. And while each individual part could be of value, the whole can have no value in itself since it has no ontological status as reality.

A second thing that is excluded from value in this framework that is important is *human society*; this has both a formal and informal aspect. The formal aspect is the legally organized social system that sustains us (with all its various interlocking subsystems: legal, economic, financial, political, and so on); the informal aspect is civil society or community. By the latter I mean the very complex fabric of relationships that include custom, habit, mores, morals, and human caring or concern for others, relationships that must normally obtain and be taken for granted between people in order that an ordinary and desirable social life can continue.

Thus in relation to the formal aspect of society, we had no law to prevent the "take over" of the American economic system by trusts, monopolies, and cartels. The Supreme Court was under no legal obligation to do so, and in fact aided and abetted the same.[24] Or to take a more recent example, we had no law to protect whole sectors of the American economy from being purchased by foreign companies.[25]

In regard to the informal aspect of society, we have no law preventing corporations from producing commodities that undermine the very existence of human community (e.g., motion pictures, videos, and magazines that depict women as sexual objects, commodities, willing or deserving victims of rape or violence, and so on). And no law against establishing franchise outlets of big corporations in small neighborhoods that undermine and eliminate the small family enterprises that are vital to the existence of the neighborhood as a community. One may argue that there should be no such laws, or that they are impossible (a debatable matter), but the point I want to underline here is the absence of law protective of systems as such.

Clearly all these subjects deserve far more discussion than I have given them here, but if the particulars remain to be sorted out, the general implications of (VI) seem evident enough. Generally speaking, in the realm of value the conceptual framework that is represented by (VI) cannot consistently accord value to things vital to our survival such as human community or the ecological system of the earth. I turn then to an alternative metaphysics that has very different implications.

Part II

In its strong form the premise of Philosophic Holism can be stated as follows: *only complexes or systems exist or are ultimately real.*[26] Two things need to be noted regarding this premise. First, I take the basic idea to be that wholes—in various ways—are more than the sum of their parts, so that the term 'complex' will include systems, organizations, institutions, and the like. In this form the premise is incompatible with Philosophic Individualism in its strong form, proposition (I) above. A weaker form of Holism asserts that there *are* complexes or systems, but does not maintain they are the *only* things that exist or are ultimately real, as a weaker form of Philosophic Individualism would assert the reality of individual things but would not insist that they are the only ultimate reality. The weaker forms of the two positions are compatible, and may together constitute a more desirable metaphysics than either (I) or (VII). In what follows I will explore the implications of the weaker form of Holism:

> VII) *Complexes, institutions, or systems exist as such; they are part of the ultimately real.*

And a corollary regarding value:

> VII) *Institutions or systems can be sources of value.*

In the case of human society (VIII) means that the social system as such can be productive of value. Since there are different forms of value, if we allow real individuals as well as systems it is possible that individuals are productive of some forms of value and the social system of others. In the case of economic value the great tendency of the past several hundred years clearly has been from the individual as the primary productive unit of society to the corporation as the primary unit, and lastly to a whole interlocking productive system with the government at the head.[27] The latter point may be said to been reached in the United States during and following the Second World War, particularly with the passage of the Employment Act of 1946.[28]

That individuals are not ordinarily independent sources of economic value in modern society seems reasonable enough; given the staggering complexity of contemporary societies, and the seemingly never ending division of labor, the manufactures or services that individuals cooperatively or collectively produce could not in 99% of the cases be produced at all outside the existing system, and would not ordinarily have a use (let alone value) outside that same social system.

If the primary source of economic value is the social system, however, then entitlement rights do not pose an ethical dilemma; there is no compulsory surrender of economic value produced by an individual since the individual does not as such produce economic value. That is not to say the labor of the individual is without value, since were it not for the labor of individuals nothing at all could be produced by the social system. It is to say, however, that the labor performed by the individual is typically dependent on a pre-existing technological substratum and that the product of that labor is useless outside a particular technological matrix, and this is as true of most "knowledge" products as it is of others.

If it is the social system that is the primary source of economic value, then what follows with regard to its distribution? The premise (VIII) is neutral here.

Whether the social system is one that accords value to individuals as such depends on the character of the social system. There are social systems in which the individual member is evidently valued as such, most of them technologically and socially much simpler than ours, as the indigenous tribal peoples of the rain forests. And there are all too many examples of social systems in which individuals are not valued as such and exist only as means to some end. What can be said is that (VIII) is consistent with a universal and equitable distribution of the value produced by a social system. What principles should govern this distribution and how it could be accomplished are subjects that deserve extensive and independent attention.

If value were to be distributed equitably throughout society, however, it may be objected that even if all forms of value are products of the social system, not all individuals within the society participate in some way in the productive process. Thus even if there are not, on this view, productive individuals who are being taxed to support the unproductive, there is still the ethical principle that individuals should get what they deserve. Part of the answer to this objection is that according to *The International Bill of Human Rights*, there are certain things that people deserve simply as human beings; among them is the right to an opportunity for work that is freely chosen or accepted, for a remuneration that provides a decent standard of living for self and family (ICSECR, Articles 6, 7). A further part of the answer to this brings us to another corollary:

IX) *Institutions or systems can be causes, or causal agents.*

If complexes or systems are causes, it is clear that their causal agency differs in kind from that of individual things. The employment level, for example, is a variable property of the economic system, and although it is possible to predict increases or decreases in unemployed persons given specific changes in the economy, it is impossible to predict which individuals in particular will be employed or unemployed. The causation is "random"; the term is double quoted because reasons could doubtless be given as to why some particular person fell into either class. But to give these reasons would be to move to a different level of cause and effect, the level of individual rather than systemic causation. Many years ago it was shown that the rate of incidence of certain crimes, as robbery and burglary, increase with the unemployment rate and decrease with its decrease.[29] More recently it has also been shown that the rate of admissions to mental hospitals, of suicides, homicides, and cardiovascular mortality rates also rise with the unemployment rate, and decline with its decline.[30] The point I am leading up to here is that since World War II—as noted above—the State has taken a direct hand in managing the economic system. On occasion this management has taken the form of fiscal and/or monetary policies that have the effect of increasing unemployment (whether, for example, to combat or discourage inflation or for some other purpose).[31] In such cases, and they are not infrequent, it seems justifiable to require that the State provide for the persons it causes to be unemployed, for those who are admitted to mental hospitals, and for those forced into bankruptcy or loss of home.

In like manner, where government policies on carcinogenic food additives, pesticide residues in foods, radionuclide emissions from power plants, industrial plants, aboveground and underground bomb testing and the like are known to cause a specifiable number of cancers in the population (very roughly in the range of eight to ten times more than would result from natural background radiation), it seems only moral common sense that the State should bear the burden of the health costs.[32]

But what is moral common sense in the framework of (VII) is not moral common sense in the framework of (I). In the latter case cause and effect is a relation that holds between individual things; thus to show liability it is necessary to trace the causal chain step by step from final effect to original cause, and that is almost certainly a practical impossibility in the case of either example considered, unemployment or cancer. What has to be recognized is the reality of systemic causation, and therefore the reality of systemic liability and systemic obligation; hence the next corollary:

X) *Institutions or systems can be legally or morally obligated.*

This principle seems to be a developing one in American law; schools and school districts have been sued for not educating their students, corporations as such have been indicted for criminal activities, and under the Federal Tort Claims Act the responsibility of the Federal government as such for tortious acts is debated in the courts. Yet there are still many court cases, such as those involving cigarette smoking and cancer, in which it is assumed that there is liability only if there is evidence tending to show a direct non-statistical causal chain. If the conceptual framework of Philosophic Individualism stands in the way of realizing systemic liability and obligation, it also stands in the way of recognizing the intrinsic value of institutions and systems, and that brings us to the last corollary:

XI) *Institutions or systems can have value as such.*

It is probably not exaggerating to say that examples of systems that are accorded value as such are presented to us in the daily newspapers on a regular basis; the ongoing struggles over the preservation of whole ecosystems as valuable in themselves and as valuable as parts of greater systems (as the importance of the vast virgin forests of Siberia in the earth's biosystem), the need to protect human communities as such, and so on. It is only a step to the declaration that complexes or systems have rights, meaning that they can be parties in legal actions, and lawsuits can be initiated in their names. Unfortunately we have not yet reached this point, so that important ecosystemic resources still have to be defended on the basis of preserving an endangered species, rather than the preservation of the ecosystem itself. If the examples of ecosystems and human community are a reliable guide, then it would appear that what the older metaphysics of Philosophic Individualism missed were the necessary conditions that made the existence and survival of individual things possible. This probably should not be surprising, since there was no reason to notice these underlying conditions until their absence or deterioration brought them to our attention, and/or we had developed the technologies that allowed us to discover them.

The Nature of Metaphysical Premises

I want to conclude with a note on the nature of metaphysical premises in general and human rights in particular. In the late 19th and early 20th century, as proponents of science and the scientific method were finally defeating the proponents of theology and establishing a secular culture, metaphysics was rejected on the grounds that it was obviously not scientific, that it was impossible to verify claims such as "Only spiritual things exist," and the like. Since much of the history of philosophy is in fact the history of metaphysics, it is not surprising that much academic philosophy sought shelter in a new role as "handmaid" to science, concentrating on logic and philosophy of science and abjuring metaphysics.

Metaphysics, however, has roots far deeper than anyone thought. It is clearly not about the nature of the world in general, as had been assumed by its critics; it is not, in that sense, *about* anything. Rather, it provides, as a foundational premise with its series of corollaries, a deeply lying conceptual substratum that organizes the intellectual life of society. As such it restricts the kinds of explanations that can be given for both natural and social phenomena and events, it limits the sphere of what can be considered of value or worth, and it shapes —to borrow Locke's phrase—"the nature and extent of human knowledge."

As we have seen, with respect to rights, the metaphysics of Philosophic Individualism places severe limits on both the kinds of rights that are possible, and the kinds of things that can be possessors of rights. Since all these limitations constitute a bar to both thought and action, why is such a foundational framework tolerated? Why is there such a foundational framework at all? I believe there are two answers to this question; the first and most important is that if there were no such common intellectual framework there would be complete intellectual anarchy, followed by social disorganization. This is the danger posed by a shallow "Deconstructionism" in contemporary philosophy. The second is that such a conceptual framework constitutes the ground of our rationality, and so of our confidence in bringing reason to bear on action; without such a ground reason has no stable premises and cannot function.

So the problem is not the elimination of metaphysics, but that of adjusting metaphysics to the situation in which we find ourselves. The premise of Philosophic Individualism has been the foundational premise of the modern Western world, the premise on which its institutions and fields of knowledge have been painstakingly constructed since the late Middle Ages. For all those who now support the vision, the spirit, and the law that constitute the International Bill of Rights, I have argued here that the premise of Philosophic Individualism has outlived its usefulness. The intellectual life of modern society must be reconstructed on a different basis, as we continue the process of modifying old institutions and creating the new.

The Metaphysical Basis of Racism in Western Civilization

WE DO NOT USUALLY THINK of metaphysics and racism as having significant connections. Yet there are important connections, and understanding them helps make clear why racism has been so firmly rooted in modern Western civilization. In examining the relations between the ideas or concepts in what follows, I do not for a moment wish to suggest that material or economic motives and reasons are not equally important.

One of the deepest premises of this civilization from the late Middle Ages up to the present century has been a premise that can only be described as metaphysical, i.e., it is a philosophical view that appears, *prima facie*, to be about the world but is neither empirically testable nor verifiable. In the fourteenth century it is the premise that *ens* and *unum* are identical, that if anything has being it must be one, i.e., one individual thing. In the seventeenth century it was the premise that only substances exist, where substances are, again, individual things. In the latter half of the twentieth century as a consequence of the disrepute into which metaphysics had fallen, the proposition that only individual things exist has survived largely as a methodological principle.[1] Whatever form it has assumed in whatever century from the 14th to the 20th, however, for purposes of this exploration I will refer to it as the premise of *philosophic individualism*. The premise of philosophic individualism, then, is the premise that only individual things have ultimate reality; all other things are composed of and analyzable into, individual things.

The first part of this paper explores the relation between the premise of philosophic individualism and the ideology of racism. I will begin with definitions, since it is important to be clear about what one is dealing with, and because the standard dictionary definitions of racism are themselves in conformity with the premise of philosophic individualism. I will then go on to consider the connection between racism (in the standard definition) and that premise. What I have to say about the connection between racism and philosophic individualism in general is also applicable to sexism and classism, but I will make no specific references to these.

In the second part of the paper I turn to the last decades of the 19th century, for these are decades in which "scientific" race theories became an integral part of Western culture, and they are also decades of high theorizing.[2] There are several theories and movements from this period I want to consider, and they have the same parentage in philosophic individualism as racism, sexism, and classism; the relations between the former and the latter offspring are complex and disturbing.

Part I

Definitions

The term racism is standardly defined as follows:[3]

> A) Racism is (1) a belief that race is the primary determinant of human traits and capacities and that racial differences produce an inherent superiority of a particular race, and (2) behavior in accordance with such a belief, racial prejudice or discrimination.

Contrast this definition with one from a different perspective:

> B) Racism is (1) a characteristic of a social system in which the organization of social life is such that one racial group is systematically benefited at the expense of others, and (2) the ideology of racial superiority that is associated with such a social system.

What we have in (A) is an example of how a metaphysical premise is reflected in the standard definition of a term; viz., if only individuals exist, then whatever racism is, it must be some kind of characteristic or characteristics of individuals. And the two characteristics given in (A) are a belief and a pattern of behavior. The same kind of individualistic definition is typically given for our other two terms as well, 'sexism' and 'classism'; there is a belief that one sex or social class is superior to another, and there is the discriminatory behavior consistent with that belief.

The structural definition in (B), on the other hand, ignores individual beliefs and individual behavior and focuses on the social system. Racism is defined as a structural property of the system; that is, it may be built into the social system in any number of ways, in the legal system, the *de facto* segregation of housing, differential wage scales, and so forth. From this perspective an individual may reject racism in sense (A) and yet still be an unwilling or even unknowing participant in a social system that is inherently racist. The second part of the definition in (B) addresses the set of ideas and values that help maintain this structural property of the social system.

From the standpoint of philosophic individualism, this structural definition would be acceptable only on a provisional basis, since social systems are not individual things (unless we want to entertain the idea of society as some kind of ghostly superindividual) and so cannot really have properties. Whatever characteristics the social system may appear to have must on analysis turn out to be characteristics or behavior patterns of the individuals that compose it.

The first expression of the premise of philosophic individualism, then, concerns the manner in which the phenomenon in question is defined. And if the individualistic definition of racism is the controlling one, then that definition will be the one that is employed in the law as well as in government policy. In that case racism as a structural property of the social system will be very difficult to eliminate; I will return to this point in the section on adjudication below, but first I want to consider a similar distinction between types of explanations. If only individual things exist, then only individual things can be causes, or causal agents. All explanations would thus have to be based on facts about individual things.

Explanations

It will be useful to refer to the phenomenon that is to be explained as the *explicandum*, and the cause or reason that is given for it as the *explicans*. Then an individualistic definition can be defined as follows:

> An explanation is *individualistic* if the explicans is found in the nature of, a property or properties of, or some change in, an individual thing or things.

And a structural explanation may be defined in like manner:

> An explanation is *structural* (or systemic) if the explicans is found in the nature or structural properties of a social system, or a change in such properties.

If philosophic individualism is the controlling premise in a culture, then individualistic explanations will be the standard. Explanations of this type will be what people hear, what they read, what they are given at home and in schools, and what they will therefore make use of themselves, since explanations that depart from the social standard (for example, one of the structural type) would not be apt to be taken seriously. In these circumstances one could say that the proposition that only individual things exist has the status of an *a priori* truth in that society, a cultural *a priori*.

That an explanation is of a particular type, of course, does not mean that it is either good or bad, true or false. One may have a good individualistic explanation or a poor structural one. Nor are the types mutually exclusive as such. The problem is that where one type is *a priori*, i.e., where it is socially presupposed, it excludes any other. If only individual things exist then there can be no other type of explanation acceptable but the individualistic, although for any given explicandum there may be any number of different explanations of that same type.

What is the connection, then, between the individualistic type of explanation and racism? The connection is that when an attempt is made to explain real or imagined differences between individuals of different races, or differences between cultures or civilizations, the *explicans* is automatically found in innate differences between the individuals in question. And where these differences are ranked on a scale of superior to inferior or the equivalent, the conclusion follows that individuals must be superior or inferior to one another by nature.

> The different progress of various nations in general civilization, and in the culture of the arts and sciences, the different characteristics and degrees of excellence in their literary productions, their varied forms of government, and many other considerations, convince us beyond the possibility of a doubt, that the races of mankind are no less characterized by diversity of mental endowments, then by...differences of...body structure...[4]

This is a passage from a lecture given in London in the early 19th century. The author has explained the differences between civilizations by appealing to a difference in the mental endowments of the individuals that compose them. He is also convinced of his conclusion "beyond the possibility of a doubt," meaning, presumably, that he sees no alternative explanation that is anywhere nearly as plausible. Different races must have different mental endowments.

> In the forms of their highest governments, those of the Aztecs, Mayas, and Peruvians, we see repeated on a large scale the simple and insufficient models of rude hunting tribes of the plains. This is also true of the black race of Africa. The powerful monarchies which at times have been erected in that continent over the dead bodies of myriads of victims have lasted but a generation or two... Indeed the law of "thus far shalt thou go and no farther" tells the story of most of the failures of races and peoples. They fell through mental inability to succeed. They had reached the natural limit of their activities.[5]

This is from a work published in 1890 by a professor of linguistics and archaeology at the University of Pennsylvania. It is somewhat confused, but if the *explicandum* is why the cultures and/or monarchies in question perished, the *explicans* given is the limited mental endowments of their inhabitants. Notice that the connection between the purported cause and the effect is left unclear, and that in addition no other possible explanation is considered (true also of the first example). The first of these deficiencies could be a matter, simply, of the author's enthusiasm for his conclusion. The second may be a property of the explanatory mode. Let me explain.

In the first example, where the fact to be explained is why one civilization is more advanced than others, one could say, for example, that some civilizations are younger than others, and this is why they are not as far advanced, or that some civilizations exist in a much more hostile physical environment than others. These are not, of course, individualistic explanations, and within that framework they would simply be further *explicanda*, further facts to be explained. For example, if one civilization is younger than another, that could be because the people of that civilization took a much longer time to become organized in such a way as to advance themselves, which would be taken to show that they were less favored in mental and/or physical endowments. If a civilization in a hostile physical environment is less advanced, that may be because the inhabitants are less able to overcome adversities, again a result of lesser mental endowments.

The point I want to make, then, is that when a mode of explanation has the status of being a culturally *a priori* mode, what happens is not that explanations of various types are compared and those of one type consistently chosen or favored over others. What seems to happen is that there is a prior sorting of the facts into those that need explaining and those that do not, or those that are capable of explanation and those that are not (because a fact of the latter sort would function as an explicans). In this sense any culturally presupposed mode of explanation is a bar to rationality, though it must be added that *without* a culturally presupposed mode of explanation it would doubtless be impossible to avoid intellectual anarchy.

Adjudications

The problem posed by the individualistic perspective is not limited to definition and explanation; if there are only individual things then only individuals can have existence in the law, and this means that only individuals can have rights (which is not to say that all individuals would in fact have rights). But this means that groups, peoples, species, social systems, ecological systems, and so forth, cannot have rights. Hence the legal system, being constructed on the basis of individual rights, makes it very difficult to address the structural problems of the social system and the environment. All such issues devolve into the rights of some individuals versus the rights of some others, both sides having the equal protection of the law. To really deal with racism, sexism, or classism as structural properties of the social system it would be necessary to introduce *group* rights in addition to *individual* rights. Two legal cases will illustrate the problem, one from the nineteenth century and one from the more recent past. Before considering those cases, however, two comments are necessary. (1) If there are only individual rights, then any legislation to outlaw racial discrimination must be written in such a way as to apply to each and every individual regardless of race or color. For example, the Nineteenth Amendment to the Constitution:

> Section 1. The right of citizens of the United States to vote shall not be denied or abridged by the United States or by any State on account of sex.

This does not say that the right of women to vote shall not be abridged, for that would be introducing a group right, i.e., a right (in this case a constitutional protection) that is not universal but is limited to a specific class of persons. (2) Legislation that confers a group right may be based on a biological difference such as sex, or it may be based on what is primarily a social or political category, like race or nationality.[6] In the first of the cases to be considered below, the law was written to apply universally but was interpreted by the Court as conferring a group right and therefore rejected. In the second case the law in question was written as a group right and was therefore rejected.

At the end of the Civil War Congress passed a series of constitutional amendments and statutes that were intended to abolish slavery and establish full civil status for all ex-slaves:

1. The Thirteenth Amendment, January, 1865. (Outlawing Slavery)
2. The Civil Rights Act of April 9, 1866.
3. The Fourteenth Amendment, June, 1866. (Equal Protection in the Law)
4. The Fifteenth Amendment, February, 1869. (The Right to Vote)
5. An Act to Enforce the Fifteenth Amendment...; May 27, 1870.
6. An Act to enforce the Fourteenth Amendment...; April 20, 1871. (The Klu Klux Klan Act)
7. The Civil Rights Act of March 1, 1875.

Read together, these enactments constituted a powerful assault on the racial apartheid of the South, but there was little opportunity for them to take effect. Beginning in 1883 with the *Slaughter House Cases*, the Supreme Court struck down key parts of the statutes and hedged in the amendments until there was virtually nothing left of the Congressional program. *Slaughter House* informed the nation that the Fourteenth Amendment did not extend the Bill of Rights to citizens in relation to their State governments, although many had understood that to be the intention of the amendment.[7] And where the Fifteenth Amendment says:

> SECTION 1. The right of citizens of the United States to vote shall not be denied or abridged by the United States or by any State on account of race, color, or previous condition of servitude.

The Supreme Court interpreted the amendment as narrowly as possible—not as prohibiting any interference with the exercise of the right to vote—but as merely forbidding the states, counties, or cities from passing laws that explicitly excluded racial groups from the franchise. In the words of the Court:

> The Fifteenth Amendment does not confer the right of suffrage upon anyone.[8]

So the right of Black citizens to vote was left open to be abridged by whatever laws a state or county government could devise so long as they did not mention race or color; for example, laws requiring payment of a registration or voting fee, or a requirement that voters be able to recite the constitution from memory.

Speaking of the Court's treatment of the amendments, Justice Harlan, whose position as a lone dissenter on the Court was very similar to that of Justice Thurgood Marshall on the Rehnquist Court, made the following comment:

> I cannot resist the conclusion that the substance and spirit of the recent amendments of the Constitution have been sacrificed by a subtle and ingenious verbal criticism.[9]

Behind the verbal subtleties, of course, there were real issues, and one of those was the above mentioned problem of individual versus group rights, a problem that surfaced in the *Civil Rights Cases* of 1883, from which the above quote is taken. In this case the Court declared key sections of the Civil Rights Act of 1875 unconstitutional. Section 1 of this Act made it illegal for any "inns, public conveyances on land or water, theaters, and other places of public amusement" to discriminate against people on the basis of race, color, or previous condition of servitude. Further sections made it a criminal offense punishable by imprisonment for 30 days to a year for so discriminating, and allowed the victim to file suit in Federal court.

The Court ruled that Congress had no power to enact this legislation either under the Fourteenth or the Thirteenth Amendments. With respect to the Fourteenth Amendment the Court took the position that the amendment applied only to governments, not to private business. With respect to the Thirteenth, the Court allowed that the amendment did empower Congress "to pass all laws necessary and proper for abolishing all badges and incidents of slavery in the United States." But the issue turned on whether the denial of accommodation or admission to an inn, conveyance, or theater on the basis of race or color constituted the imposition of "a badge of slavery." And the Court was unwilling to rule that it was, apparently believing that to do so would be to create, in effect, a legally privileged position for a particular group:

> When a man has emerged from slavery, and by the aid of beneficent legislation has shaken off the inseparable concomitants of that state, there must be some stage in the progress of his elevation when he takes the rank of a mere citizen, and ceases to be the special favorite of the laws, and when his rights as a citizen, or a man, are to be protected in the ordinary modes by which other men's rights are protected.[10]

The "favored" position conferred by the Civil Rights Act of 1875 was, evidently, that of having the local U.S. District Attorney, Marshall or other Federal officer required by Federal law to institute proceedings against any inn, conveyance, or theater that refused admission or accommodation on the basis of race, color, or previous condition of servitude, and the fact that a person so discriminated against had the right to file a civil suit in Federal court for the same violation; neither qualified as "ordinary modes" by which rights are protected in the states.

One could argue here that the Civil Rights Act was written in universal terms, and did not in its language specify Black people as the category to whom alone the law applied. Practically speaking, however, the law was intended to provide remedies for a specific group, its membership determined by "race," and the Court did not approve. (One may also wonder if the Court really understood the position of ex-slaves in the South, but that is another matter.)

In the case *Regents of the University of California v. Bakke*, on the other hand, a rule that was written as a group right was rejected by the Court on the same basis, that the Fourteenth Amendment protects all individuals equally, in this case from discrimination.[11]

Allan Bakke, a white medical school applicant, twice rejected by the school, filed suit against the University of California arguing that its admissions program violated his rights to equal protection of the law under the Fourteenth Amendment, and also under section 601 of Title VI (Nondiscrimination in Federally Assisted Programs) of the Civil Rights Act of 1964. Neither the California Supreme Court nor the U.S. Supreme Court dealt with Title VI; however, the problem posed by its section 601 is the same as that posed by the Fourteenth:

> Sec. 601. No person in the United States shall, on the ground of race, color, or national origin, be excluded from participation in, be denied the benefits of, or be subjected to discrimination under any program or activity receiving Federal financial assistance.[12]

The section is written as a universal right, whereas the admission program created a group right: sixteen of the one hundred seats available in the entering class had to be reserved for minorities. The California Supreme Court held that this program was a violation of the Fourteenth Amendment's equal protection clause, which required that:

> ...no applicant may be rejected because of his race, in favor of another who is less qualified, as measured by standards applied without regard to race.[13]

On appeal by the regents the U.S. Supreme Court agreed with the California court:

> The fatal flaw in petitioner's preferential program is its disregard of individual rights as guaranteed by the Fourteenth Amendment. Such rights are not absolute. But when a State's distribution of benefits or imposition of burdens hinges on the color of a person's skin or ancestry, that individual is entitled to a demonstration that the challenged classification is necessary to promote a substantial state interest. Petitioner has failed to carry this burden.[14]

There is, then, no group right of the minority to be proportionately admitted to medical schools. And no group right in general means there is no right of any racial or ethnic minority to have, proportionately, as many doctors, nurses, teachers, airline pilots, or what have you as the white population. But if there is no such right, then there is not necessarily a violation of the Fourteenth Amendment's equal protection clause if there are none at all.

The difference between an individual and a group right may be further illustrated in relation to the right to run for office. Every woman who qualifies has the right to run for the office of United States Senator; women as a class, however, have no right of representation in that body. If women had a group right to representation it could be secured, for example, by the requirement that at least one of the Senators from every State be female. It seems clear that the establishment of group rights could profoundly restructure the social system; it also appears to be the only effective means of accomplishing the objective of full integration. And this is the direction in which we ought to go if we are serious about social equality. There is, however, a difficult legacy to overcome, the legacy not only of philosophic individualism but also its offspring.

Part II

Further Implications of Philosophic Individualism

We have considered some of the implications of the premise of philosophic individualism in relation to definition, explanation, and one important aspect of legal rights. I want to end by considering some further offspring of the premise in the late 19th century that have had a profound impact on the 20th century. These have to do with the explanation of crime, poverty, madness, and disease.

In 1873 a serious economic depression occurred in England which continued, on and off, into the 1890's; it spread rapidly into all of the industrialized countries including the United States, which had developed much of the Midwest on the basis of the exportation of meat and grain.[15] Whatever poverty, disease, crime, and insanity existed before the "Great Depression" as it was called, was considerably exacerbated by it. No doubt partly in response to this situation, as well as to urbanization and industrialization in general, there was a burst of theorizing regarding the root causes of these social problems. And just as the international depression had made clear the economic interdependence of the industrialized nations, so these decades of "high theory" suggest the coming to maturity of an international intelligensia. What is striking about this international theorizing is the way in which the individualistic mode of explanation acted as a common lens, to focus the cause of these problems on the very individuals who were poor, sick, insane, or in prisons.

The New Criminology

In April 1891, Robert Fletcher, M.D., the retiring President of the Anthropological Society of Washington delivered an address called "The New School in Criminal Anthropology," an address subsequently published in *The American Anthropologist* in July of that year. In that address he extolled the work of this new school, or School of Lombroso, about which nothing had yet been published in the United States. The School had begun with the publication of Lombroso's *L'uomo delinquente*, in 1876, and had already secured a fair number of followers in his native Italy, as well as France, Austria, Germany, Argentina, England, Spain, and Portugal. Its basic theses were two: (1) that much of society's crime was due to the presence of individuals who were criminal by nature and (2) that such individuals could frequently be recognized by their physical features alone. For example, the murderer:

> He has a cold concentrated look; sometimes the eye appears injected with blood; the nose is often aquiline or hooked, always large; the ears are long; the jaws are powerful; the cheek-bones widely separated; the hair is crisp and abundant; the canine teeth well developed, and the lips thin; often a nervous tic or contraction, upon one side of the face only, uncovers the canine teeth, producing the effect of a threatening look or a sardonic laugh. [16]

Purportedly based on empirical studies, the power of these rather frightening Lombrosian characterizations was reinforced in the doctor's lecture by the tale of the infamous Jukes family; in 75 years the descendants of this single criminal pair amounted to 1,200 persons, all of whom, or very nearly all, became devoted to a life of crime. Moreover, Fletcher pointed out, there is a difference of opinion in the new school as to whether the criminal is a regression to prehistoric man or to an even earlier bestial ancestor of prehistoric man. And having created this nightmare image of semihuman prehistoric beasts stalking their prey in the streets of modern cities and reproducing themselves more rapidly than the human population, Fletcher went on to recommend the death penalty as a social defense measure.

While the Lombrosian theory that criminal individuals could be recognized by visible physical features died out soon enough, the notion that criminality is hereditary did not. The "socialist" school of criminology, as Fletcher called it, held that crime was generated by the individual's physical and moral surroundings. But from the individualist perspective, of course, the surroundings were the product of the degenerate individuals that inhabited them, and the Eugenics movement reinforced that view.

The Eugenics Movement

The Eugenics movement is generally taken as beginning in 1869, the year of the publication of Francis Galton's *Hereditary Genius: An Inquiry into its laws and consequences*. This work, surveying the genealogies of the British upper class, appeared to provide evidence that intelligence as well as sociability (i.e., capacity for social life) were hereditary characteristics. It opens with a call to action:

> I propose to show in this book that a man's natural abilities are derived by inheritance, under exactly the same limitations as are the form and physical features of the whole organic world. Consequently, as it is easy, notwithstanding those limitations, to obtain by careful selection a permanent breed of dogs or horses gifted with peculiar powers of running, or of doing anything else, so it would be quite practicable to produce a highly-gifted race of men by judicious marriages during several consecutive generations. I shall show that social agencies of an ordinary character, whose influences are little suspected are at this moment working towards the degradation of human nature, and that others are working toward its improvement.[17]

Of course the improvement of the human race by the same methods used in breeding horses is something of a problem in civilized society, nonetheless the Eugenics movements had taken root in thirty different countries by 1930.[18] Early enthusiasts hoped to use such means as financial inducements to early marriages between superior persons, State support for desirable families, rewards for larger families of good stock and the like. Unfortunately since the "good stock" was generally discovered among the upper classes, these methods appeared to be gilding the lily. And as evidence was compiled through many "scientific" studies that many undesirable traits were heritable, it was the darker side of the movement that came to be implemented. These undesirable traits or tendencies were mental retardation, insanity, criminality, epilepsy, alcoholism, drug addiction, tuberculosis, blindness, physical deformities, pauperism, and orphanism.[19] Where such "traits" or "tendencies" were found the cause was taken to be some defect in the individual; where they were found to run in families (orphans begetting orphans) the conclusion had to be that the defect was inheritable. The methods used to curtail reproduction could include restrictive marriage laws, abortion, financial or other inducements to voluntary sterilization, but most frequently, involuntary sterilization.

In the United States by 1930 at least thirty states and Puerto Rico enacted legislation permitting forcible sterilization of various categories of persons, as the mentally retarded, persons with epilepsy, confirmed criminals, rapists, and others.[20] It must be said that not all Eugenicists favored this practice; those that did not hoped that it would be terminated by the United States Supreme Court. However, in an opinion written by Justice Holmes in *Buck v. Bell*, 1927, the Supreme Court ruled for enforced sterilization:

> We have seen more than once that the public welfare may call upon the best citizens for their lives. It would be strange if it could not call upon those who already sap the strength of the State for these lesser sacrifices, often not felt to be such by those concerned, in order to prevent our being swamped with incompetence...[21]

By 1963 63,678 persons were known to have been forcibly sterilized in the States that had legalized the procedure.[22] Many of these occurred in state mental hospitals and penal institutions, and involved a disproportionate number of Blacks.[23] In addition, it is unclear how many persons were unknowingly or "accidentally" sterilized, or how many were sterilized by enforced consent, i.e., the practice of agreeing to perform abortion only if the patient agrees to simultaneous sterilization.[24]

What I am arguing here is not that the individualistic mode of explanation is the cause of forcible sterilization laws; there were many factors involved. It does, however, appear to be a necessary condition for these laws; it creates a presumption in favor of explaining the characteristics and behavior of persons as due to their own innate constitution, and without this presumption, the idea that these characteristics are heritable and the social acceptance of the sterilization programs as "rational" policy would not be sustainable.

Social Darwinism

Among the various reasons that led to these programs not the least among them was the influence of Darwin's *Origin of Species: The Preservation of Favored Races in the Struggle for Life*, 1859. Viewed through the lens of philosophic individualism, Darwin's theory of the natural selection of species became "Social Darwinism," the natural selection of favored individuals. But this natural process did not necessarily entail selective sterilization. To some people it meant that the poor and diseased should be allowed to perish quietly in their slums, as decreed by Nature.[25] To others, modern biological science and the medical arts should be enlisted in an effort to guide and refine the natural process of the gradual elimination of the weaker, degenerate, or atavistic stocks. The latter position was greatly reinforced by the larger idea of a world struggle between the races. Theodore Roosevelt, shortly before his two terms as President of the United States, wrote:

> We cannot avoid the responsibilities that confront us in Hawaii, Cuba, Porto Rico, and the Philippines. All we can decide is whether we shall meet them in a way that will redound to the national credit, or whether we shall make of our dealings with these new problems a dark and shameful page in our history...
>
> The timid man, the lazy man, the man who distrusts his country, the over-civilized man, who has lost the great fighting, masterful virtues, the ignorant man, and the man of dull mind, whose soul is incapable of feeling the mighty lift that thrills "stern men with empires in their brains" - all these, of course, shrink from seeing the nation undertake its new duties...
>
> I preach to you, then, my countrymen, that our country calls not for the life of ease but for the life of strenuous endeavor. The twentieth century looms before us big with the fate of many nations. If we stand idly by, if we seek merely swollen ease and ignoble peace, if we shrink from the hard contests where men must win at hazard of their lives and at the risk of all they hold dear, then the bolder and stronger peoples will pass us by, and will win for themselves the domination of the world.[26]

This is not the place to consider what the stern men with empires in their brains did in Hawaii, Puerto Rico, and the Philippines. But it is the place to note that imperialism was one of the methods suggested by John Stuart Mill for dealing with economic depression, and there seems little question that the vast imperial expansion of the West in the decades at the turn of the century was stimulated in no small measure by the economic crises of the period.[27] That these great land grabbing operations did not provide, with some exceptions, immediate revenue to the empire builders is testimony to the motivating power of the ideas we have been considering here, viz., racism, eugenic theory, and social darwinism. Into this volatile mixture one could also stir other ingredients from the same period, as the theory of elites of Gaetano Mosca, Vilfredo Pareto and others; these theorists attempted to show that human societies, whatever type they may be, are always and invariably run by small elites, though not necessarily by the kind of hereditary upper class Galton studied in England.[28] It is the matter of science and religion, however, that I want to consider in conclusion.

Science and Religion

Near the end of the 20th century, I believe it is difficult to appreciate the intellectual climate at the end of the 19th century when the struggle of science against the cultural domination of religion was in its last stages. Cornell University, founded in 1876, was the first secular university in the United States. It was attacked from virtually every side, and in defending it in public lectures, Andrew Dickson White developed the material for his great two volume work, *A History of the Warfare of Science with Theology*, 1896. The following passage is from the introduction:

> My book is ready for the printer, and as I begin this preface my eye lights upon the crowd of Russian peasants at work on the Neva under my windows. With pick and shovel they are letting the rays of the April sun into the great ice barrier which binds together the modern quays and the old granite fortress where lie the bones of the Romanoff Czars.
>
> This barrier is already weakened...The waters from thousands of swollen streamlets above are pressing behind it; wreckage and refuse are piling up against it; everyone knows it must yield...The barrier, exposed more and more to the warmth of spring by the scores of channels they are making, will break...and the river will flow on beneficent and beautiful.
>
> My work in this book is like that of the Russian *mujik* on the Neva. I simply try to aid in letting the light of historical truth into that decaying mass of outworn thought which attaches the modern world to the medieval conceptions of Christianity, and which still lingers among us—a most serious barrier to religion and morals, and a menace to the whole normal evolution of society.
>
> My hope is to aid—even if it be but a little—in the gradual and healthful dissolving away of this mass of unreason, that the stream of "religion pure and undefiled" may flow on broad and clear, a blessing to humanity.[29]

I have quoted White at some length here because the passage conveys something of the *fin de siecle* sense of being on the verge of an entirely new era when the sciences will have finally swept away the ignorance and superstition of the past and progress can move rapidly ahead without hindrance; but I have also quoted it because it poses an unanswered question: what would pure religion be when the whole "decayed mass of outworn thought" is finally dissolved away by the tireless "*mujiks*" of scholarship and science?

Francis Galton had worked out one answer to this question, an answer prompted in part by his assessment of the situation in general:

> It has now become a serious necessity to better the breed of the human race. The average citizen is too base for the every day work of modern civilization. Civilized man has become possessed of vaster powers than in old times for good or ill, but has made no corresponding advance in wits and goodness to enable him to direct his conduct rightly.[30]

Bothered by this apparent inability of people to cope with modern civilization and make use of its powers in a rational and ethical manner, Galton conceived of a marriage of science and religion:

> A passionate aspiration to improve the heritable powers of man to their utmost, seems to have all the requirements needed for the furtherance of human evolution, and to suffice as the basis of a national religion, in the sense of that word as defined by J.S. Mill, for, though it be without any ultra-rational sanctions, it would serve to 'direct the emotions and desires of a nation towards an ideal object, recognized as rightly paramount over all selfish objects of desire.'[31]

There is no doubt that the Eugenics movement became a secular religion for many, and there is also no doubt that many persons who were active in it or supported it in different countries, including Germany, had idealistic motives.[32] There is also no doubt that many believed it to be scientifically sound; indeed, the editor of a set of recent studies of the movement in France, Brazil, Russia, and Germany attacks the "myth...that eugenics was essentially a pseudo-science"

What we have here, then, is a very potent combination of religion, science, and idealism; yet at the same time it helped to create the views and attitudes that led to the worst genocidal crimes that humanity has ever encountered. The earliest of these appears to be the attempt by Germany to eliminate the Herero and Nama tribes in South West Africa in the period from 1904 to 1907. A missionary reported on settler attitudes:

> The real cause of the bitterness among the Hereros toward the Germans is without question the fact that the average German looks down upon the natives as being about on the same level as the higher primates (baboon being their favorite term for the natives) and treats them like animals. The settler holds that the native has a right to exist only insofar as he is useful to the white

> man. It follows that the whites value their horses and even their oxen more than they value the natives.[33]

This attitude toward Blacks as closer to apes than humans was supported by the published views of European and American ethnologists, anthropologists, psychologists and medical personnel.[34] It was shared in Southwest Africa by colonial administrators, and at home by a large proportion of the Reichstag and higher government officials including the Kaiser; it made possible the campaign to eliminate the Herero people, reducing their number from 80,000 to some 15,000 by the time Germany surrendered the colony in 1915.[35]

One can say that it was not, after all, the fault of science that such things happened. Not all scientists agreed with the racist views of their colleagues. Furthermore it was not (as most would now agree) good science; so science itself is not to blame. There is reason, however, to disagree. For the science that we developed in the West after the Renaissance, whether physical or social science, was based on the very same premise that underlies racism, sexism, classism, and the eugenics movement. The premise that led to the scientific and technological superiority of the West is also the premise that led to its barbarism. It is the premise that a proper explanation must be an individualistic one; without this fundamental step it is difficult to see how all the rest could have occurred. The great barrier to moral progress that is now beginning to melt is not the one that Andrew Dickson White envisaged, it is the barrier of philosophic individualism.[36]

The Decline of the West

An Essay on Western Civilization and Its Values

Around the end of the First World War two unusual and prophetic works were published in Germany concerning the nature and the destiny of Western civilization: Oswald Spengler's *Der Untergang des Abendlandes* (The Decline of the West), and Albert Schweitzer's *Kulturphilosophie* (The Philosophy of Civilization).[1] Both authors regarded Western civilization as being obviously in decline; on Spengler's view the decline was an inevitable stage in the organic evolution of any culture. The title of Volume I of Schweitzer's work, however, suggested a less pessimistic view—*Verfall und Wiederaufbau der Kultur* (The Decay and Restoration of Civilization).

The questions raised by these works—whether Western civilization is indeed in decline, what exactly is meant by decay or decline and what it portends, and whether the decline is irreversible—have lost none of their interest; indeed, after a further world war and Holocaust, and after nearly a half century of socially disruptive and politically destabilizing Cold War, they seem more pertinent than ever.

Part I of this essay is concerned with the principal theses of Spengler's *Decline of the West* and the assumptions on which they are based. Part II considers the contrasting view of Western decline and its causes in the first volume of Albert Schweitzer's *Kulturphilosophie*.[2] As will be seen, both works are limited by their individualistic perspective; part III presents an alternative view from a systemic perspective.

Part I: Oswald Spengler

It is difficult to find—in *The Decline of the West*—a straight-forward statement of its main theses. Spengler distinguished eight different cultures in human history and a number of stages in the evolution of every culture, on the basis, presumably, of his method of analogy; thus much of the *Decline* deals with comparisons of one culture with another in regard to music, art, philosophy, science, architecture, mathematics, politics and various other subjects.[3] The basis of the comparisons or analogies is not always clear, however, nor is their value or significance for his main theses. In any case empirical or historical evidence plays a minor role, as the theses turn out to be independent of the classifications and comparisons of cultures; they have, as will be seen, a decidedly *a priori* character.

The following passage is an example of Spengler's style, and is also a passage in which his two principal theses come out fairly clearly. The passage occurs in a section in which he is objecting to historians' attempts to write a history of mankind-in-general when on his view there is no such thing; there is only the history of particular cultures:

> "Mankind," however, has no aim, no idea, no plan, any more than the family of butterflies or orchids. "Mankind" is a zoological expression, or an empty word. But conjure away the phantom, break the magic circle, and at once there emerges an astonishing wealth of *actual* forms—the Living with all its immense fullness, depth and movement—hitherto veiled by a catchword, a dryasdust scheme, and a set of personal "ideals." I see, in place of that empty figment of *one* linear history which can only be kept up by shutting one's eyes to the overwhelming multitude of the facts, the drama of *a number* of mighty Cultures, each springing with primitive strength from the soil of a mother-region to which it remains firmly bound throughout its whole life-cycle; each stamping its material, its mankind, in *its own* image; each having *its own* idea, *its own* passions, *its own* life, will, and feeling, *its own* death. Here indeed are colours, lights, movements, that no intellectual eye has yet discovered. Here the Cultures and the stone-pines, the blossoms, twigs and leaves—but there is no ageing "Mankind." Each Culture has its own new possibilities of self-expression which arise, ripen, decay, and never return. There is not *one* sculpture, *one* painting, *one* mathematics, *one* physics, but many, each in its deepest essence different from the others, each limited in duration and self-contained, just as each species of plant has its peculiar blossom or fruit, its special type of growth and decline. These cultures, sublimated life-essences, grow with the same superb aimlessness as the flowers of the field.[4]

The two main theses of the *Decline* are expressed here as clearly as anywhere and I have tried to state them concisely in the two propositions below, adding his subordinate thesis regarding Western civilization since that will be a main concern.

I) Every culture has its own unique nature, the which nature determines its destiny (unless it is obstructed by some external forces).

II) Every culture necessarily passes through a youth, maturity, and old age or decline (or, alternatively, a Springtime, Summer, Fall, and Winter).

III) Western civilization is a such unique culture and is presently in the Winter of its life-span.

Now a peculiarity of these theses (and certainly of the above quotation) is the treatment of cultures as if they were independently existing entities capable of having their own natures. This notion is clearly not derived from any empirical or comparative study of history and culture, but the basis for it does not become clear in *Der Untergang* until we get to Volume II, Chapter V, and a section entitled "Peoples, Races, Tongues." Here it becomes clear that the above theses are derivative of certain others:

IV) There are distinct races of human beings arising in and out of different geographical areas.

V) Every such race has a unique nature, responsible for its own unique culture and destiny.

Proposition (IV) here is otherwise expressed as a concurrence of blood and soil:

> A race has roots. Race and landscape belong together. Where a plant takes root, there it dies also. There is certainly a sense in which we can, without absurdity, work backwards from a race to its "home," but it is much more important to realize that the race adheres permanently to this home with some of its most essential characters of body and soul. If in that home the race cannot be found, this means that the race has ceased to exist. A race does not migrate.[5]

The reference to plants is not a mere analogy; Spengler distinguishes being or "being-there" (*Dasein*), from waking-being, or waking-consciousness (*Wachsein*). The former is the more primitive being (characteristic of plants) that carries or participates in the cosmic rhythms of life and is correlated in animals and humans with blood; the latter is connected with sensation, understanding, and language.[6] A race is described as a "current of Being," and language as " ... the efficient form of *one* great waking-consciousness that connects many individual beings."[7] Although Spengler sometimes appears to hypostatize race and culture, I find no clear evidence that—behind the rhetoric—he really regards race or culture as substantive entities in themselves. Culture is an expression of race, and race is produced by the "mysterious power of the soil," some individuals being better exemplars of the "race-being" than others, the latter having no necessary connection with any specific physical characteristics.[8]

The fifth thesis is a form of racial Neo-Kantianism: by Neo-Kantianism I mean the view that our fundamental conceptual framework is innate in the mind, so that we automatically bring to experience concepts we may (mistakenly) believe we have derived from that experience. The racial version of Neo-Kantianism assumes that there are distinct races and that every race has its own peculiar conceptual framework, its own peculiar form of cognition and feeling, and therefore necessarily creates its own form of art, music, architecture, science and so forth. Thus each race produces a culture that cannot be meaningfully shared with others; for this reason something can be borrowed by one culture from another only if it can be transformed into something else or put to a use specific to the borrowing culture. Further, when the creative potentialities intrinsic to the race are fully developed and expressed in every area of life, a culture necessarily passes into the stage of sterility and decline. This stage is marked by the growth of great world-cities like ancient Rome, modern Berlin or New York:

> In place of a type-true people, born of and grown on the soil, there is a new sort of nomad, cohering unstably in fluid masses, the parasitical city-dweller, traditionless, utterly matter-of-fact, religionless, clever, deeply contemptuous of the countryman.[9]

In the megalopolis of this final stage capitalism develops, traditional relationships are replaced by those based primarily on money, and with its inner creative potential exhausted, the energy of the civilization turns into a simple "will to power," and is directed outward in the form of imperialism.[10] Spengler is not always clear as to exactly what period he is thinking of, or what he means by various terms (e.g., 'capitalism'), but the leading characteristics of decline were clearly being exemplified by the West at the turn of the century—the megalopolis, the advent of the reign of finance capital, the race for colonies by the imperialistic Western powers.

Since he found similar signs of decline in ancient Rome, and regarded Greco-Roman culture as being the product of a Mediterranean race while European civilization is the product of a Northern race, Spengler rejected the view that Western history is properly divisible into three periods: ancient, medieval, and modern. On his view 'Western civilization' refers to the period from roughly the tenth century to the present. He was thus one of the few European intellectuals in his period that rejected the Enlightenment view (or myth) that Western civilization began in ancient Greece and Rome, and is therefore one of the oldest civilizations on earth.

There seems little doubt that Spengler's application of racial Neo-Kantianism on the grandiose scale of the history of human civilization, and the great popularity of the *Decline of the West* in the Germany of the 1920's, did much to help create a favorable climate for the rise of the National Socialist movement as well as supply some of its ideological positions.[11] For example, the premise of racial Neo-Kantianism provides a basis for the otherwise bizarre view of the Nazi party that there is a "German physics" essentially different from Jewish or any other physics. The idea that the final stage and destiny of Western civilization is necessarily found in imperialism and in fact should be expressed in a Third Reich, provided support for the militarist and imperialist program of the Army and the Party. His essay "Prussianism and Socialism" undertook the task of "liberating German socialism from Marx" by identifying it with Prussianism. And Prussianism was the structuring of society along lines of command and obedience in a rigid social hierarchy.[12] Spengler was never a Nazi Party member, however, and was accused by the Party of "betraying" the cause because he believed that the old German aristocracy ought to be leading the program of imperialist expansion rather than the Nazi Party.[13]

Stripped of its racialism, however, *The Decline of the West* still leaves us with some questions worth pursuing, questions to which I will return in part III.14 It raises the question as to whether there is some sense in which the evolution of a civilization is built into it and is thus in some sense inevitable. It raises the question whether the evolution of the West is devoid of, or must be devoid of, any relation to an ultimate moral purpose or purposes, so that we are indeed simply evolving like a "family of butterflies or orchids." And in the characterization of the stage of decline as one in which normal or traditional human relations break down and leave only naked pecuniary relations, an issue is raised that Schweitzer made central to the first volume of his *Philosophy of Civilization*: why have we created material conditions of life that threaten the existence of our own civilization?

Part II: Albert Schweitzer

In the preface to his *Philosophy of Civilization*, Schweitzer maintained that "the real essential nature of civilization ... is ultimately ethical."[15] From this perspective the First World War was a clear testimony that Western civilization had ceased to progress as a civilization and had entered into a state of barbarism. Further testimony could be found, on his view, in the barbaric treatment by Europe of its colonial peoples.

The question Schweitzer set out to answer in the first volume of what became a trilogy on the philosophy of civilization was when and why Western civilization had gone off course. Before considering his answer to that question, however, I want to look at his account of decline. It is presented in terms of the individual person confronted with the conditions of modern life.

First of all the phenomenon of urbanization—Spengler's megalopolis—creates a situation in which normal human relations deteriorate:

> The normal conduct of one person to another is impeded. Owing to the haste in our mode of life, the increasing traffic, the necessity for living and working with many others in a constricted space, we are brought together continually and in diverse ways as one stranger to another. Circumstances do not permit us to behave as one human being to another, and the restrictions imposed on our natural activities as human beings are so everyday and general that we are habituated to them and we no longer perceive our impersonal behavior as unnatural.[16]

In the light of what has occurred in this century since the publication of this work, I believe it is worth underlining this point—that normal human relations are undermined by the conditions of modern life. Schweitzer continues:

> Wherever there is lost the consciousness that every man is an object of concern for us just because he is a man, civilization and morals are shaken, and the advance to fully developed inhumanity is only a question of time.
>
> As a matter of fact, the most utterly inhuman thoughts have been current among us for two generations past in all the ugly clearness of language and with the authority of logical principles. There has been created a social mentality which discourages humanity in individuals. The courtesy produced by natural feeling disappears, and in its place comes a behavior which shows entire indifference, even though it is decked out more or less throughly in a code of manners. The standoffishness and want of sympathy which are shown so clearly in every way to strangers are no longer felt as being really rudeness, but pass for the behavior of the man of the world. Our society has also ceased to allow to all men, as such, a human value and a human dignity; many sections of the human race have become merely raw material and property in human form. We have talked for decades with an ever increasing light-mindedness about war and conquest, as if these were merely operations on a chess-board; how was this possible save as the result of a tone of mind which no longer pictured to itself the fate of individuals, but thought of them only as figures or objects belonging to the material world?[17]

There is a good deal more to Schweitzer's account of the decline in the ethical consciousness and behavior of the individual and the conditions of modern life that produce it; for example, the over-organization of work with the concomitant loss of independence and creativity of the individual, the overspecialization of work with the loss of any understanding of its wider social and moral implications, the overworking and overstressing of the individual so that no one has the time or inclination to reflect on the deeper questions of life or those of right and wrong.[18] And much of what Schweitzer attributes to society in the early years of this century appears to describe the present with even greater accuracy.

Why then, according to Schweitzer, are these civil and human values allowed to be undermined by the conditions of modern life? His answer was that it is primarily due to the failure of philosophy and theology, particularly since the mid-19th century.[19] In the period of the Enlightenment philosophy offered a fairly integrated worldview that affirmed the value of civilization and its material and spiritual progress, as well as providing a basis for ethics and the civil and human values. However, in the last half of the 19th century philosophy and theology were unable to maintain this leadership role, and abdicated to the natural sciences. The sciences, of course, were in no way capable of providing a *Weltanschauung* that could provide an intellectually respectable ground for civilization in the ethical sense, nor was that any part of their purposes. Without a unifying and guiding worldview, however, a gradual fragmentation of civilized life occurred, with the consequent erosion of civilized behavior and civil society.[20]

This is an interesting view and one that clearly has some merit; it is true that individual philosophers in the Enlightenment period tried to develop an integrated worldview, and it is true that this aim was abandoned by most post-Enlightenment philosophers, who have turned to a variety of narrower and more technical problems.[21] It is true that in the second half of the 19th century the cultural hegemony of philosophy and theology was considerably weakened and later displaced by the triumph of the scientific outlook and the scientific method on the one hand, and by the impact of biblical criticism on the other.[22] And it is also true that philosophers made a series of attempts to develop a generally acceptable theory of ethics and failed to do so; indeed, by the 1930's many philosophers had arrived at the position that ethical statements were devoid of cognitive content.[23]

Were Schweitzer's analysis correct, the solution to the problem would clearly be the creation of a *Weltanschauung* that would provide a unified vision of life in accord with the ideals that emerged from the Enlightenment.[24] This Schweitzer himself attempted to provide in the last volume of his *Philosophy of Civilization*, and there is no doubt that this work has happily influenced many individuals. The analysis, however, is idealistic in the sense that it attempts to explain the decay of the West solely in terms of the intellectual and spiritual realm, as if this realm were quite independent of the material conditions and social circumstances of people's lives.

But this is not the only problem—nor is it the main problem—with Schweitzer's analysis. Both his and Spengler's analyses are examples of explanations that may be called *individualistic*, i.e. they are explanations of the sort that find the cause or reason for something in the nature, the characteristics or changes in an individual entity or entities. It may be contrasted with a *systemic* type of explanation, one that finds the cause or reason for something in the nature, properties, or changes in a system; for example, an ecological system or social system.

Spengler's explanation for the rise and fall of civilizations is individualistic as it finds the cause of the rise and inevitable fall of a civilization in the immutable nature of the individuals that constitute it. Why the individuals in a particular civilization have the particular nature they do remains unexplained, although it appears to have some mystical connection with the supposed geographic "homeland" of the race.

Schweitzer's account is also individualistic, finding the reason for the decline of modern society in the inadequate or wrongful ideas, attitudes, and values of its inhabitants, a situation that its intellectuals have failed to correct by providing a coherent and life-affirming worldview. Why people have the "wrong ideas" they do in the first place and why intellectuals failed to create a guiding *Weltanschauung* for European civilization remain unexplained.

In thinking about Western civilization, then, both Spengler and Schweitzer appear to have conceived of a society as little more than an aggregation of individual persons. Such a view is dangerously misleading because it leaves out of account the most important part of the problem we are facing, namely the nature of the social system that has evolved in the West over the past several hundred years.

Part III: A Systemic Perspective

Human societies are not mere aggregations of individuals, they are complex social systems that have evidently evolved from more primitive primate social systems. So the questions posed at the end of Part I need to be raised in regard to the nature of the basic social system that is common to Western developed nations and not in regard to the characteristics of individual persons. These questions were whether the evolution of Western civilization is in some sense built into its nature and is inevitable; whether there is moral purpose, in some sense, in that evolution, and lastly, why material conditions of life have been created that threaten to reverse the process of civilization. What follows is a brief and preliminary sketch that attempts to consider these questions from a systemic perspective.

A social system may be defined as the sum total of its institutions together with the network of formal and informal relationships obtaining between them. The term institution here includes everything from an established social practice or custom to a conglomerate corporation or federal agency. This institutional mass can be conceptualized in a number of different ways. A social system as complex as the one we have inherited, for example, can be usefully analyzed for some purposes as a complex of interrelated subsystems (such as the legal system, political system, economic system, educational system, and so on), each of which is itself a complex of related institutions.[25] And each of these latter institutions or kinds of institution has a purpose or set of purposes, in most cases established in or by the law and enforceable by law. Hence the question as to whether the social system itself has a purpose can be explicated to mean the question whether there are institutions that are dominant and dominating to the extent that their institutionalized purposes determine the general direction in which the system is evolving.

I believe the answer to this question is clear: over the past century there are three closely connected institutions—or complexes of institutions—that have emerged as dominant in Western societies: *industrial capitalism, industrial science, and industrial technology*. Like the holy trinity in Christianity, they can be seen as one institution or as three interdependent institutions depending on one's purposes; together they dominate the social systems of the West. By *industrial capitalism* I mean a social system institutionally organized around the primary purpose of accumulating capital through wage labor and industrial production, and justified on the grounds of social and material progress.[26] By *industrial technology* I mean the technologies that primarily serve the purpose of industrial production, directly and indirectly, from the methods of harnessing of basic energy sources to computerized monitoring of production lines or typing pools. It is technology that is geared to efficiency in one specific sense of that term: generating the maximum product with minimum labor. Not all technologies are of this kind; indeed, there is a wide range of those that are not, from organic farming to the technologies used by Australian aborigines to survive in the desert. Finally, by *industrial science* I mean science that has as its primary function the acquisition of what may be called transformational knowledge, i.e., knowledge that is useful in transforming some aspect or part of the natural environment or entity into something else, whether this is the simple extraction of ores and their transformation into usable metals, the organic chemist's transformation of crude oil into thousands of usable chemicals, or the bioengineer's transformation of living animals into pharmaceutical factories.[27] Science of this kind clearly serves the industrial process; but not *all* science does so, e.g., biological studies devoted to preserving a species or saving an ecosystem, or the astrophysicists' attempts to determine the size of the universe. The individual scientist, of course, may have as a principal motive the search after truth, either for its own sake or for the benefit of humanity. Yet the use of that truth depends on the nature of the social system in which it is discovered, as some of the scientists who developed the atomic bomb realized to their dismay.

These three institutions, then, having as their primary purposes the accumulation of capital, the acquisition of transformative knowledge, and efficiency in the use of labor time, are the dynamic core of contemporary Western social systems. None of these institutions could exist without the others, and none could progress without progress in the others. We have no specific word for this institutional complex, despite it being a social engine of enormous power that has shaped and reshaped much of society many times since the late 19th century.[28] *Moreover, the ideas, attitudes, values, practices and purposes associated with this complex have come to be—over the past century—the dominant and dominating culture of the civilization.*

It is therefore possible to say, literally, that the civilization has a purpose or purposes, and that the civilization has a set of values; they are the purposes and values of these systemically dominant institutions. I will refer to their collective values and purposes as *industrial* values and purposes, as distinct from the *human and civil* values mentioned earlier. Speaking broadly, industrial values are what guide the behavior of individuals in their assigned roles in the systemically dominant institutions, behavior that is often very different from that in an extra-systemic or civil context. Thus a corporate officer who would not think of doing anything personally to injure a family in his own neighborhood, will sign an order at the corporate office for the layoff of thousands of employees as part of a day's business, regardless of the potentially devastating effects on the employees and their families. Part of the reason for this apparent moral schizophrenia seems to be the dreadful plasticity of our species, a plasticity that allows decent young men to be turned into torturers and concentration camp inmates to take on the values of their oppressors.[29] But part of the reason is the fact that the question of responsibility is deeply clouded when institutions are involved, so that it is easy to rationalize signing such an order. Here, for example, the institution laying off its employees is a legal institution operating within the law and in accord with its chartered purposes and the norms of the business system. The action depriving the employees of income is an act of the corporation, and an action the officer is probably powerless to prevent. Moreover, one cannot be held responsible for what one cannot prevent. Thinking in this way the individual is morally compromised, and brings about a consequence that would be unthinkable in a personal capacity.

Generally speaking people have greater freedom to relate to one another as fellow human beings and as morally responsible persons in extra-institutional contexts and within the context of civil institutions. These institutions—the family, church, unions, clubs and friendship circles, non-profit citizen associations, and publicly supported schools and hospitals—constitute an institutional infrastructure that has been the source and mainstay of a moral community, as well as an important wellspring of moral progress. Schweitzer believed that human and civil values were in decline by the turn of the century or earlier, and attributed this to a moral failure on the part of the European intelligensia. Whether there was in fact such a decline in individual morality or a moral failure of the intelligensia is difficult question, but it seems helpful in considering the question of decline to keep the *dominant industrial values* separate from the *human and civil values.* By *human* values I will mean those having to do with the relations between individual persons, as civility, decency, respect and concern for others and for their rights; by *civil values* I will mean both cultural values, as respect for the cultural and ethical achievements of human civilization, and civic values, the values concerned with or involved in service to the community, city, neighborhood, government, and the human species in general. The distinction between *industrial values* and *human and civil values* provides a standard against which we can speak more objectively regarding the decline of the West. The moral state of the civilization can be seen as a function of the relative strengths of the two value systems, and changes in this relationship will be reflected in changes in the relative status and influence of the associated institutions. [30]

The values associated with the industrial system were formed for the most part in the 18th century, but they did not begin to become culturally dominant until the late 19th and early 20th century.[31] Churches, for example, still dominated colleges and universities at the end of the 19th century, and church membership was a prerequisite to doing business in most towns and cities.[32] At the same time, however, the decades around the turn of the century are the period in which the corporate form of enterprise came into its own, supported by a series of Supreme Court decisions.[33] And it is the period when industrial values began to lay claim to a hegemonic role as evidenced by the spread of Social Darwinism and the related eugenics movements, the growing status of science (including psychology and psychiatry) and the corresponding decline in the status of theology and religion, the creation of secular universities, the exploitation of modern technology and science in the First World War, and so on.

In Germany and Austria, still the intellectual center of the West in the early decades of the century, the intelligensia reacted to these developments in a variety of ways. We have considered Spengler and Schweitzer; in a vein similar to the latter's *Decay and Restoration of Civilization* of 1928, Edmund Husserl's *The Crisis of the European Sciences* (1934-7) expressed a profound concern regarding the positivism (i.e., scientism) of modern science and its inability to deal with the deeper issues of humanity. His philosophical work was intended to provide a new philo-sophical foundation for both science and culture. It was overshadowed in Germany, however, by the philosophy of his former student, Martin Heidegger, who turned to the Nazi party for a solution to the "crisis" of Western civilization.

The impact of industrial values on the social system were delineated by Herman Broch in his trilogy, *The Sleepwalkers* (*Die Schlafwandler*, 1928). The following passage is from one of Broch's essays on the disintegration of values, incorporated in the text of the novel:

> The logic of the soldier demands that he shall throw a hand grenade between the legs of the enemy:
>
> the logic of the army demands in general that all military resources shall be exploited with the utmost rigour and severity, resulting, if necessary, in the extermination of peoples, the demolition of cathedrals, the bombardment of hospitals and operating-theaters:
>
> the logic of the business man demands that all commercial resources shall be exploited with the utmost rigour and efficiency to bring about the destruction of all competition and the sole domination of his own business ...
>
> the logic of the painter demands that the principles of painting shall be followed to their conclusions with the utmost rigour and thoroughness, at the peril of producing pictures which are completely esoteric, and comprehensible only by those who produce them ...
>
> in this fashion, in this absolute devotion to logical rigour, the Western world has won its achievements,—and with the same thoroughness, the absolute thoroughness that abrogates itself, must it eventually advance *ad absurdum*: war is war, *l'art pour l'art*, in politics there is no room for compunction, business is business,—all these signify the same thing, all these appertain to the same aggressive and radical spirit, informed by that uncanny, I might almost say that metaphysical, lack of consideration for consequences, that ruthless logic directed on the object and on the object alone, which looks neither to the right nor the left; and this, all this, is the style of thinking that characterizes our age.[34]

This passage characterizes a society in which industrial values are dominant and their "spirit" has begun to permeate all other areas of social life. It is a style of thinking, as Broch calls it, that was carried to Nietzschean heights by Spengler in his *Der Mensch und Die Technik*, 1931, (Man and Technics, 1932) in which Westerners are counseled not to falter in the will to power, even if doomed to perish in a forthcoming and inevitable struggle with "the inferior races."[35] And the form this final will to power might take was suggested by Ernst Jnger's *Der Arbeiter* (The Worker), 1932. Here modern technology is celebrated in the society of the future, seen as a totalitarian machine that is mobilized from top to bottom for the purpose of war and conquest; "freedom" is found in total submersion of the self in the social process. *Der Arbeiter* thus supplied another ingredient in the intellectual soup that nourished the Nazi Party.

With respect to this first phase in the cultural hegemony of industrialism, then, the European intelligensia appears to have been deeply divided, and in some cases confused, as to the significance of what was happening and what would constitute an appropriate response. The second World War and the period of intellectual and political repression that followed provided scant opportunity or encouragement for further speculation.

A Civilization in Decline

Apart from the unparalleled destructiveness of the second World War itself, it is in the period following the war that we can see—with hindsight—the first clear evidence of a self-destructive tendency in industrial civilization. The evidence is in the poisoning of the physical environment by radionuclides—such as strontium 90 and others—as a result of the atmospheric testing of atomic bombs, on the one hand, and the increasing use of neurotoxic and carcinogenic pesticides on the other. Rachel Carson, who made vividly clear the danger of pesticides in *Silent Spring*, recalled the effect of the bomb on her own thinking:

> Man's attitude toward nature is today critically important, simply because of his new found power to destroy it ... I clearly remember that in the days before Hiroshima I used to wonder whether nature ... actually needed protection from man. Surely the sea was inviolate and forever beyond man's power to change it. Surely the vast cycles by which water is drawn up into the clouds to return again to the earth could never be touched. And just as surely the vast tides of life—the migrating birds—would continue to ebb and flow over the continents, marking the passage of the seasons.
>
> But I was wrong. Even these things, that seem to belong to the eternal verities, are not only threatened but have already felt the destroying hand of man.[36]

Both Andrei Sakarov and Linus Pauling predicted, in 1958, that the testing done up to that time would result in a million cancer deaths worldwide. By 1962, the year Rachael Carson wrote the above, atmospheric tests of atomic weapons had produced a radioactive fallout equivalent of 40,000 Hiroshima size bombs.[37]

It required hundreds of millions of years for the primordial radioactivity of the earth to decrease to a level that made the evolution of life possible, so the promotion of technologies that in their effects contribute to reversing that process strikes one as a form of insanity. We are inclined to speak of collective or social insanity, but these terms are unnecessarily vague. What is involved is institutional derangement, i.e., a derangement rooted in the nature and purposes of particular social institutions. For example, in the 1950's, in addition to the military production of atomic weapons, the U.S. Atomic Energy Commission undertook a program of promoting "peaceful" uses of the atom that included nuclear power plants, nuclear medicine, and nuclear dynamite. In the latter category were such projects as the use of atomic bombs in oil and gas recovery, mining copper, and creating new harbors or canals.[38] These projects were pursued despite the gathering evidence of the medical effects of ionizing radiation. A project for blasting a new Panama canal with nuclear bombs, for example, was not abandoned until 1970. John Gofman, head of the bio-medical division at Lawrence Livermore National Laboratory, reported a conversation that illustrates the conflict of values mentioned previously. After Gofman and a co-worker had made some predictions on cancer and leukemia deaths to be expected from nuclear testing and the nuclear power program, the Atomic Energy Commission asked the head of the lab, Michael May, to pay him a visit:

> 'Jack,' he said, 'I defend your right, in fact your duty, to calculate that a certain amount of radiation will cause 32,000 extra deaths per year from cancer.' But to my disappointment, he then asked, 'What makes you think that 32,000 would be too many?' 'Mike,' I said, 'the reason is very simple. If I find myself thinking that 32,000 cancer deaths per year is not too many, I'll dust off my medical diploma, take it back to the Dean of the Medical School where I graduated, hand the diploma to the dean and say, 'I don't deserve this.'[39]

This is an example of the purposes and values of an institution overriding normal human values; it is a shocking example, but unfortunately it is only too often duplicated. The reason, I believe, is that we have a very strong need to identify with institutions, and to make an institution's values, attitudes, and culture a part of our own raison d'etre. In some cases, people identify so deeply with an institutional role that the self is completely eclipsed by the institutional role.[40] The reason this human proclivity is important is again the issue of institutional balance. In a civilization that is driven by industrial capitalism, industrial science, and industrial technology, there must be a healthy infrastructure of strong institutions that ground and perpetuate the human and civil values. Since the second World War, however, a number of developments have conspired to undermine the effectiveness of this infrastructure, and greatly strengthen the power and authority of the industrial institutions.

There has been one wave after another of corporate mergers and acquisitions, resulting in a staggering concentration of economic and political power. And unlike the general situation in Europe, in the United States this corporate power is not tempered by having representatives of labor or the public interest on boards of directors. The Antitrust Division of the Justice Department has done very little to try to prevent or retard this concentration of power over the 50 years since the second world war. One of the reasons why the Division has been ineffectual lies in a series of decisions of the Supreme Court that eliminated any consideration of the political meaning and consequences of economic power, as well as a narrowing of the economic issues that can be considered.[41]

One dimension of the political significance of concentration has to do with the media; we are now faced with an almost total control of the means of communication by a very few giant corporations.[42] This is an especially serious problem because, outside of schools, the media—books, magazines, newspapers, television programs, radio programs, and films—are the primary determinants of the general level of consciousness, knowledge, and understanding in society. If we consider the vital role that media must play in a democratic society, the ownership and control of the media by a few giant amoral corporations may prove tantamount to a pre-frontal lobotomy on the body politic.[43]

The political meaning of the concentration of economic power in general, however, can best be understood by reflecting on the fact that capital is at bottom the power to organize human labor. Thus in a society in which economic power is largely in private rather than public hands, both the nature and future of the country are to a great extent in those same hands. They have the power to determine how the mental and physical labor of the working majority is to be directed, in what ways, and to what ends. And the power of citizens to determine through their elected representatives what is to be done to resolve the problems they are facing as a society is of course restricted by the legal rights of the holders of capital. Where capital is widely distributed among individuals in the population, this may not be a problem of great moment. However, when capital is held by corporations instead of individuals there is a significant change; corporations are not and by their charters and the law cannot be, members of the moral community of humankind. They are essentially bureaucratic machines set up for capital accumulation. Further, when capital is as concentrated as it is at present—many individual corporations being economically more powerful than most governments—the democratic control of the future of human civilization will be virtually impossible without a radical realignment of the social system.

This erosion of the democratic governance of society, through civil institutions as well as government, reached a new level in the last decades of the 20th century, when the civil institutions of society began to be invaded by the industrial value system through *privatization, corporatization,* and *commercialization. Privatization* is the management of public institutions—institutions serving public purposes and financed by the public—by private companies for their own profit; it has affected schools, hospitals, prisons, and government services on a large scale. *Corporatization* is the imposition on an institution of the corporate model of private hierarchical management, as it has been in the above categories of institutions as well as in non-profit public interest organizations, museums, and universities. *Commercialization*, in the case of public institutions, refers to the situation in which public institutions receive financial support from corporations in return for using the public institution as a vehicle for sales and advertising; for example, the introduction of coca cola machines into grade schools, or the provision of free television sets in return for students watching TV ads during their periods of instruction.[44]

All of these invasions of public space have the effect of legitimizing industrial values and/or delegitimizing human and civil values, as the latter are challenged, implicitly or explicitly, as of lesser importance or no greater importance than the former. This is particularly worrisome because it is our public institutions that are the social infrastructure that maintains and transmits human and civil values from one generation to another. And it is unclear whether the institution of the family can alone maintain the human and civil values when surrounded by other public institutions so degraded by privatization, commercialization, and corporatization.[45]

Western liberal industrial civilization, then, has a number of self-destructive tendencies: the progressive physical contamination of the environment (with the proliferation of environmental diseases), the uncontrolled growth and power of the modern corporation (with the loss of public control of government), and finally, the undermining of the moral infrastructure of society considered above.

The Spengler Questions

At the end of Part I on Oswald Spengler, three questions were posed regarding the nature and evolution of Western civilization. The first was whether the direction in which the civilization has evolved is a consequence of its nature, that is, whether the evolution was in some sense inevitable. The answer to this question seems to be that the direction is indeed a consequence of its nature, understanding that to be the complex of institutions that make up the industrial triad of science, technology, and capitalism. However, at any given time the direction in which this triadic system evolves depends largely on what lines of scientific and technological research appear most promising from the standpoint of possible future profits.[46] Needless to say, these lines of research may or may not result in social, political, or economic changes that are compatible with human and civil values.

In the United States there have been repeated attempts within the federal government to establish some degree of democratic control over the scientific and technological research that is publicly funded, albeit with no real success. During World War II a Senator from W. Virginia, Harley Kilgore, introduced legislation in Congress to put publicly funded scientific research under democratic guidance. He was concerned that the direction of publicly funded research was mostly in the hands of large corporations and elite universities, as were any patents that developed out of the research. Both the corporations and universities opposed the idea, and Kilgore's proposals were defeated.47 Recognition of the need for some degree of public/democratic control, however, would not go away. Neither would the opposition to any form of control by corporations, universities, and the scientific community. The history of this struggle since the Second World War has been traced in considerable detail by David Dickson; it is a history of unfortunate compromises and it wends its way through the National Science Foundation's Ethical Values in Science and Technology program (1971), the policies of the Office of Technology Assessment (1972), the Recombinant DNA Advisory Committee (1976), the Office of Science and Technology Policy (1976), Senator Edward Kennedy's "Science for the People" program (1977), and so forth.[48] Beginning in the Carter administration (late 1970's) the idea of relying on an economic analysis took hold, and "cost/benefit" analyses became the paradigm. However there is really no way for government advisory panels to estimate the costs and benefits to society of policy decisions involving science and technology.[49] The principal reason is that what is to count as "cost" and what as "benefit," and how they are to be measured and how weighed against each other very often involves a conflict between industrial and human values, whether it is explicit in the analysis or remains implicit. For example, how many of the 103 nuclear power plants in the U.S. should be recommissioned for another 20 years, if—according to the Nuclear Regulatory Commission—each will cause 12 cases of cancer within that time period?[50] Ethically, such questions from hell can only be answered through a public and democratic policy making process; certainly not by an advisory panel composed of experts. There is no such thing as expertise in deciding how many persons are to be sacrificed, because no persons should be sacrificed.

Absent any meaningful public democratic control of scientific and technological research, then, the social system evolves in a non-rational manner, like Spengler's butterflies. And if there is an overall direction discernible in this process, it lies not in an eventual control over nature—which is clearly impossible—but in constantly deepening and expanding the transformative powers of industrial technology. Is there any ultimate limit to this process? Any foreseeable end? This was my second Spengler question, and there are at least two things that seem relevant to an answer. The first is the principle of Diminishing Returns (or decreasing marginal utility); this refers to the fact that for any activity that necessarily becomes increasingly complex, the cost of pursuing it will also increase until a point is reached where the returns or benefits are no longer worth the input of time, energy, or money. Joseph A. Tainter has reviewed the literature on this principle in *The Collapse of Complex Societies*, and found that it seems to provide a very plausible explanation for the collapse or decline of previous civilizations.[51] The literature on diminishing returns is extensive, as are the areas in which the phenomenon is operative, as science, technology, agriculture, medicine, education, the extractive industries, and economic productivity. In the sciences, it is often the case that the most general knowledge is established early in the discipline, so what remains is the more specialized work—work that can become prohibitively expensive—a recent example being the Supercollider proposed for research in particle physics and abandoned by the U.S. Congress.[52]

One measure of diminishing returns in scientific and technological research is the number of patents generated. In a survey of 50 countries it was found that inventions per scientist and per engineer have declined in nearly all cases between the late 1960's and late 1970's.53 This is perhaps especially striking because 80-09% of all the scientists that have ever lived were alive in the early 1960's.[54] Medical research has exemplified this same pattern—the conquest in industrial countries of the great epidemic diseases (typhoid, cholera, tuberculosis, and smallpox)

brought about a marked increase in life expectancy. The defeat of polio was a good deal more expensive, while the costs of research on AIDS is astronomically higher in comparison, and the effort so far is merely to hold off a decline in life expectancy rather than extend it. In the case of society in general the evolution toward complexity occurs in different areas at various rates; however, as Tainter points out:

> A society increasing in complexity does so as a system. That is to say, as some of its parts are forced in a direction of growth, others must adjust accordingly. For example, if complexity increases to regulate regional subsistence production, investments will be made in hierarchy, in bureaucracy, and in agricultural facilities (such as irrigation networks). The expanding hierarchy requires still further agricultural output for its own needs, as well as increased investment in energy and minerals extraction. An expanding military is needed to protect the assets thus created, requiring in turn its own increased sphere of agricultural and other resources. As more and more resources are drained from the support population to maintain this system, an increased share must be allocated to legitimization or coercion.[55]

The increasing share allocated to legitimization and coercion, of course, creates further burdens on the support population, until the system ratchets itself into collapse:

> The process of collapse ... is a matter of rapid, substantial decline in an established level of complexity. A society that has collapsed is suddenly smaller, less differentiated and heterogeneous, and characterized by fewer specialized parts; it displays less social differentiation; and it is able to exercise less control over the behavior of its members.
>
> It is able at the same time to command smaller surpluses, to offer fewer benefits and inducements to membership; and it is less capable of providing subsistence and defensive security for a regional population. It may decompose to

> some of the constituent building blocks (e.g., states, ethnic groups, villages) out of which it was created.[56]

In the case of Western industrial societies there seem to be two further tendencies at work—peculiar to itself—although it is possible they fit into the category of diminishing returns. One is the generation of polluting wastes, which seem to increase incrementally in kind and magnitude along with scrap and garbage as industrial civilization evolves. The other is the consequent undermining of human health as a result of the contamination of air, water, food, and environment by these wastes and by other pollutants—radiological, chemical, and electromagnetic.

This brings us to the second principle relevant to the question of a limit in the evolution of industrial civilization. This might be called a Principle of Incremental Endangerment: the deeper and more extensive is the transformative power of industrial science and technology, the greater is the peril to individuals and civilization in general. There are a number of reasons for this. One reason is the potential for greater harm from the deliberate misuse of the more powerful technologies, by individuals, institutions, or States. Another reason is ignorance; it has been repeatedly demonstrated over the last century that our knowledge of the dangers inherent in new technologies is gained primarily by heart rending experience, as in the tragedies surrounding the use of radium, x-rays, and nuclear technology.[57] X-rays, for example, were discovered in 1895 by Roentgen, and came to be used for the "treatment" of a whole catalogue of diseases; not until 1956 were they were shown by Dr. Alice Stewart to be responsible for childhood leukemia even at very low doses, and only in 1999 have they been shown to be a cause of Ischemic Heart Disease by Dr. John Gofman.[58]

A third reason, also related to the above, is the dominant role of industrial values, such as *wissenschaft ueber alles*. Here are two examples. When the atomic bomb was being created at Los Alamos, New Mexico, both Edward Teller and J. Robert Oppenheimer were seriously concerned that the device could set off a chain reaction in the ocean or the atmosphere. That would, of course, have been the end of life on this planet. Fortunately for the world, nothing happened. The fear of an ultimate catastrophe also haunted the creation of the accelerator called Bevelac:

> In the early 1970's Tsung Dao Lee and Gian-Carlo Wick discussed the possibility that a new phase of nuclear matter might exist at high density, and might lie lower in energy than the most common type of matter in a nucleus. The Bevelac seemed to be the ideal instrument with which to make and discover this new matter. If it existed and was more stable than ordinary matter, it would accrete ordinary matter and grow. Eventually it would become so massive that it would fall to the floor of the experimental hall and be easily

> observed. But what would stop it from eating the Earth? [Eating it entirely, that is to say, by converting it all into matter of the new type.] Knowledge of dense nuclear matter was so poor at the time that the possibility of this disaster was taken seriously. Meetings were held behind closed doors to decide whether the proposed experiments should be aborted. Experiments were eventually performed, and fortunately no such disaster has yet occurred.[59]

Whether there is a serious danger of either of the above kinds is not yet settled and perhaps cannot be, since our reasoning—in physics as in everything else—is always based upon assumptions, one of which may be wrong.[60]

My third Spengler question was why the civilization creates conditions that threaten its own existence. I believe this question has been largely answered in considering the value systems of industrial capitalism, science, and its technology. As Herman Broch might have put it:

> we have corporations dedicated to the accumulation of capital by any legal or even illegal means regardless of the undermining of the political and social infrastructure of society; technology that is relentlessly applied to reduce the labor time in production and services, regardless of the number of persons thrown into unemployment and the number of families wrecked or disrupted thereby; science that is dedicated to a form of knowledge that is increasingly dangerous and scientists who will tolerate no restriction on their freedom of research.

There is more that should be said about this, but I want to end with a reflection on the work of Albert Schweitzer. Schweitzer believed the intellectual class had failed in its obligation to provide a new humanistic Weltanschauung for Western civilization. There is certainly no question that such a worldview is needed. One that provides a holistic and systemic vision of human beings and human society as part of the natural world. One that makes human and civil values primary and industrial values secondary. But such a worldview cannot be simply constructed by an intelligensia and delivered *ex cathedra*. One reason is that the old worldview is deeply embedded in all the major and most of the minor social institutions, institutions on which people are dependent for their livelihood as well as their existence. So there must be a growing and widespread apprehension that the old worldview is no longer capable of engendering the kinds of knowledge that are vitally needed, no longer providing explanations that really seem to explain, and no longer capable of providing justifications except for things that ought no longer to be justified.

This was not the situation when Schweitzer wrote; science, for example, still had far to go in seeking the ultimate building blocks of the physical world; law had far to go in developing individual rights, the global development of individual nations had hardly begun, and medicine had only begun to exploit the germ theory of disease. All this and much else continued to legitimize philosophical individualism, the culturally *a priori* premise that only individual things exist. And that being the case, we cannot hold the intelligensia responsible for what they could not have done.

Appendix I: How Democratic is the Constitution?

The Case of Voting Rights

KURT NUTTING

Introduction: The Motivations for Reconceptualizing Electoral Rights

THERE IS WIDESPREAD AGREEMENT that something is deeply wrong with American politics, a something that cannot be fixed merely by changing the individuals who occupy public office.[1] Large numbers of people believe that the government is more responsive to powerful interests than to ordinary citizens; and the popularity of this belief has remained at a very high level since the late 1960s.[2] It is in this context that I want to reexamine the ways we think of voting and political participation.

There are several reasons for reconsidering the present legal and philosophical understandings of political rights generally and voting rights in particular. First, as many commentators have pointed out, at the conceptual level there is ambiguity and uncertainty in many areas of the law of electoral rights.[3] Moreover, at a more philosophical level, voting is said to be theoretically "paradoxical,"[4] and democracy itself internally inconsistent.[5] Democratic political theory may well profit from a more explicit consideration of the material and institutional conditions of democratic life, including such commonplace but philosophically unexplored phenomena as the processes of electoral campaigning, the role of political parties, and the act of voting.[6]

Some of the legal puzzles about voting are of very long standing indeed—for example, the difficulty of properly distinguishing between a (reasonable) "regulation" of the suffrage and an (unreasonable and hence unconstitutional) abridgment of it,[7] or of defining the limits of state power in reducing the influence of wealth on electoral politics.[8] Others are more recent—the application of free speech and equal protection analysis to state regulation of access to the ballot,[9] or the use of race-conscious remedies under the Voting Rights Act and the reapportionment decisions.[10]

Furthermore, a detailed examination of the legal institutions of American elections might give us insight into the truth of claims made about the fundamental nature of American law itself, the extent to which it exhibits a morally defensible content and the extent to which it responds not to ideologically neutral legal principles but to ideologically conservative or anti-democratic beliefs.[11] Electoral law is especially interesting in this respect because it is strategically central, due to the role of elections and elected officials in determining the rest of the law. Since elected legislators and executives make statutory and administrative law, and they appoint many of those judges who are not themselves elected officials, if there is a conservative or class skew in the law of electoral arrangements it makes a class skew elsewhere in the law nearly inevitable.

Doctrinal confusion aside, as a normative matter the present state of the institutions of electoral politics in the United States is clearly unsatisfactory, and the judicial understanding of electoral rights bears part of the responsibility for that. The campaign-finance decisions of the past twenty years, beginning with *Buckley v. Valeo*,[12] are perhaps the most glaring set of examples of unsatisfactory opinions over a long period of time in this area, but the ballot-access and minority voting-rights cases are not too far behind. One hope underlying this work is that a reconceptualization of political rights will make possible more satisfactory doctrine on this subject.

The doctrinal confusion stems in part, I believe, from the fact that the constitutional doctrine on the subject of political rights has grown up not as an organic and unified whole but as a set of separate and discrete subfields, disconnected from one another and uninformed by any real vision of what the constitutional framework of representative democracy must be. The constitutional right to vote should encompass the processes reasonably (not logically) necessary for representative democracy. The courts have categorized these processes under the headings of the rights of voters, the rights of candidates, the rights of candidates' supporters and financial contributors, and the rights of political parties. But this is confusing. These are issues about legal standing; but to see questions of standing as determining the content of the right is to tie these issues too closely to nineteenth-century individualist notions of common-law injury rather than to the more collective interests served by a system of democratic political rights. To put matters a bit too simply, the current constitutional law governing political rights is based on an extraordinarily apolitical conception of those rights.

This is connected to the normative grounds for dissatisfaction, the moral and political failings of the current state of election-law doctrine and of current

American democracy itself. Despite the enormous growth in political-rights doctrine at the federal level over the past generation, and the democratization of many aspects of American political life, to a great extent that doctrine, and our political life generally, has been shaped by people, including judges, who are relatively complacent about the current state of American political life. This complacency has led the courts and other political actors to downplay or overlook the merits of claims that in various ways the American electoral system has become rigid, unresponsive, and resistant to necessary changes.

The Content and Structure of Electoral Rights

Electoral Rights

In a representative government, those who make policy are, directly or indirectly, chosen through the means of popular elections. Electoral rights in a republic, thus, concern the rights people have in regard to this process of electing the government. In the theory of representative government, elections are the central (though by no means the exclusive) means by which the ruled are (potentially) able to control the rulers. The set of electoral rights structures the process of popular election, and so in any particular political system the ability of the ruled to control the rulers depends upon how the political rights have been formulated and how they can be exercised.[13]

At a formal level, we can begin analyzing a right by distinguishing between (1) questions about which interests are protected or guaranteed by possession of the right, or the *content* of the right (2) questions about how the right protects those interests, or the *structure* of the right, and (3) questions about who possesses the right, or the identity of the *right-holders*. I focus on (1) in the first half of this paper, and then note the mismatch between content and structure in regards to voting rights in the second half.

What Interests Do Electoral Rights Protect? The Content of Electoral Rights

To determine the content of the electoral rights, then, we begin with a truism of liberal political theory—ultimately, that the function of elections in a genuinely representative government[14] is to provide a mechanism through which (some or all of) the ruled can exercise control over the state's exercise of power. Only by winning an election may at least the most important officials secure the legal title to exercise the powers and privileges of office; in legal and political theory, the election serves to transfer legal and political power from the electorate (or, less precisely, the people) to the officials, and without an election the power may not be exercised.[15]

What is it about a system of elections that brings the delegation of power from electorate to officials potentially under the effective control of the electorate? How does (in the ideal, anyway) the electorate use elections to control the officials and policies of the government? An election in a modern polity is an enormously complex social phenomenon, but we can identify at least some of the aspects of electoral politics which operate to make control of the government possible.[16]

At a minimum, control of the government through a system of popular elections presupposes that the conditions under which the people form their judgments about policy and administration are relatively favorable to free and rational thought, so that the judgments made can be the best possible given the limitations of available knowledge, time, and energy; that the (actual and potential) lawmakers and administrators are able to make proposals in response to popular judgments; and that there are moral or material incentives for the (actual and potential) lawmakers and administrators to make such proposals. Voting rights should be, but too often are not, structured to create conditions under which these presuppositions are true. The right to vote, as the right which protects the people's ability to use elections to control the power of the state, is more than the bare "right to mark a piece of paper and drop it in a box,"[17] but is a right protecting the entire electoral process through which popular control over the state is exercised.[18]

The Interest in Rational Deliberation. How do elections (in the ideal if not actual case) produce these beneficial results? First, an election serves as the occasion for heightened public discussion and deliberation about the past and future course of public policy; the campaign preceding the actual vote gives shape and meaning to that act of choice. An election without a campaign beforehand is, in a very real sense, not a legitimate election at all. In a good campaign, voters and candidates participate in a many-sided examination of the state of public affairs. The importance of this discussion and deliberation underscores the function of free speech and a free press in a representative government, as Meiklejohn[19] and others have emphasized; without wide opportunities for discussion and deliberation the election will not be an expression of the electors' considered judgments but (all too often) of top-of-the-head prejudices (whose moral claims over the content of public policy, as a matter of the theory of representative government, are presumably less weighty). In one respect, then, electoral democracy is (or ideally ought to be) educational. We will refer to this function as *deliberative* or *rational*,[20] and American constitutional law has formally recognized its importance.[21]

The Interest in Political Competition. Second, an election serves to force candidates for public office to seek the electorate's votes on a competitive basis with other candidates, before they can exercise public power. That is, a candidate may exercise power only if the electorate judges that the operations of the government will be better with that candidate exercising power than they would be with any available alternative, all things considered. Just as consumer sovereignty in a free and competitive product market is said, by neoclassical microeconomic theory, to lead to continued improvements in the consumer's well-being through a ceaseless process of innovation spurred by competition for the consumer's money, so is popular sovereignty in a free and competitive electoral "market" said, by the theorists of public choice, to lead to continued improvements in the public's well-being through a ceaseless process of policy innovation spurred by competition for votes. In another respect, then, electoral democracy is akin to self-interested economics. We will refer to this function, for short, as *instrumental* or *competitive;*[22] and as with the deliberative function, the courts have explicitly recognized its importance.[23]

The Interest in Popular Consent. Third, in addition to the creation of a forum for popular discussion and deliberation on matters of public policy, and the creation of a competitive struggle for political power, a system of popular campaigns and elections is itself the public representation, in a ritualized form, of the status of the government as periodically legitimated by the participation of the people, on the one hand, and of the status of the voters, recognized as full and equal members of the polity, on the other.[24] Consent occurs on at least two levels: we consent (or not) to the authority of the Constitution generally, and we consent (or not) to the specific policies proposed by particular elected officials at a given time. Voting implicates consent at both of these levels. These public recognitions of the moral status of the government and its policies as ultimately resting on the wills of the members of a free and equal electorate are a further way in which elections are a popular mechanism for exercising control over the policies of the government.[25] We will refer to this political function, for short, as *legitimizing*, and this too is firmly a part of American constitutional law.[26]

The Interest in Self-Expression. And fourth, in voting people may have various non-instrumental goals in mind, which we may for brevity refer to as symbolic. They vote to make a point or express a moral conviction; to stand with, or against, others (for example, to express solidarity with others of their class, gender, ethnicity, or religious background); to defy those in authority; and so on. Furthermore, campaigns and elections are diverting and entertaining[27] as well as educational. We will refer to this function (or set of functions), for short, as *expressive* or *symbolic,*[28] and note that expression has merited recognition by the courts as a constitutionally weighty interest in voting.[29]

There is no suggestion here that this listing is by any means an exhaustive one, only that the four aspects of electoral politics are in fact significant and that paying attention to each of them will help us understand in greater depth what we do when we hold elections or set up a political system employing elections, and therefore what the role of voting rights is in a legal system.[30] If the rough outline of this account is correct, then the content of legal voting rights should be (at least in part) explicable in terms of the social and political functions of electoral politics. That is, political rights should at a minimum serve to protect and guarantee the deliberative/rational, instrumental/competitive, legitimizing, and expressive/symbolic aspects of popular voting.

The Constitutional Right to Vote

The Supreme Court has long held that the right to vote is "fundamental."[31] Under modern constitutional doctrine, in determining whether a state law or practice denying or abridging such a fundamental right to anyone should be struck down under the equal protection clause of §1 of the Fourteenth Amendment, the courts are supposed to "strictly scrutinize" the state's action and uphold it only if the state can show that the law is narrowly tailored and necessary to achieving a "compelling" state goal.[32] However, in practice the Supreme Court has not been entirely consistent in strictly scrutinizing legislation affecting the right to vote, and many commentators refer to the doctrinal confusion and inconsistencies in this area, speculating that perhaps the Supreme Court is tacitly employing a standard of review *sui generis* to election-law cases.[33]

The Disparate Sources of Constitutional Voting Rights

Voting rights have been at the center of American politics and law since the Revolution, and voting rights cases have been decided under a bewildering array of constitutional provisions and doctrines. We find various aspects of electoral participation protected under the guarantees of free speech, free press, assembly, and petition of the First Amendment;[34] under the equal protection and due process clauses of the Fourteenth Amendment, or under the "privileges or immunities" clause of the Fourteenth Amendment;[35] under the guarantee of universal male citizen suffrage for federal and state officers in §2 of the Fourteenth Amendment;[36] under the guarantee of popular choice of Congress under Article I and the Seventeenth Amendment;[37] under the bans on discrimination in the suffrage of the Fifteenth, Nineteenth, Twenty-Fourth, and Twenty-Sixth Amendments;[38] and under non-textual rights of free association and travel.[39] The courts might also have, but heretofore have not, decided voting-rights cases under the clause guaranteeing a republican form of government to the states, under the Ninth and Tenth Amendments' reservation of nonspecified rights to the people, or even under the abolition of slavery decreed by the Thirteenth Amendment.[40] With so much textual and doctrinal support, the Supreme Court has been able to declare with much confidence that "[t]he United States is a constitutional democracy."[41]

Some Current Issues in The Constitutional Law of Voting

Personal Registration as an Abridgment of the Right to Vote. In the final half of this article, I would like to apply this broader and more political conception of the right to vote to some specific legal schemes currently regulating American elections. I start with a set of laws affecting who may vote—that is, the laws establishing registration of voters prior to the day of the election as a mandatory precondition to casting a valid vote. I have said that one function of elections is to provide a forum in which the state's power can be seen as resting legitimately upon the popular will. An election by a narrow oligarchy alone is both a denial of full citizenship to those outside the ranks of the oligarchy and an illegitimate authorization of political power. Now, state constitutions typically contain provisions defining the suffrage;[42] some specifically recite that political power depends upon the will of the people,[43] and often specifically guarantee free and open elections.[44] It is a commonplace that once a constitution has specified the qualifications under which people may exercise a right, the legislature may not add further qualifications.[45] But with voting, 43 of the 50 states now[46] require that in addition to satisfying the substantive conditions, the prospective voter must also personally take the initiative to register as a voter with an official agency days or weeks in advance of the election.

Almost alone among democratic nations, in the United States the burden of registering to vote is placed upon the voter rather than upon the state;[47] perhaps not by coincidence, the United States also has one of the lowest levels of electoral participation among all the democracies.[48] The requirement that the potential voter take the effort to register a month or more ahead of the election serves to eliminate the least motivated people from the electorate. The effects of this almost surely are to reduce voter turnout, and to reduce it disproportionately among the least educated people;[49] for example, one study estimated that voter registration systems reduced total voter turnout in the 1972 presidential election by 9.1%.[50]

But voter registration laws which place the burden of registering on the voter are constitutional,[51] at least in the absence of overtly racially discriminatory administration, even if the operation of those laws predictably reduce the size of the eligible electorate significantly and reduce it along race and class lines,[52] and even if the operation of those laws predictably reduce the number of actual voters significantly and reduce it along race and class lines.[53] Although voter registration thus screens many lower-class people out of the electorate in advance of Election Day, the courts have not held that these systems of prior registration operate in an unconstitutional manner except when they have been explicitly aimed at eliminating a whole race of voters from the polls and have more-or-less succeeded in this goal of racial exclusion.[54] The contrast with the judicial treatment of First Amendment rights of free speech and free press, where prior restraint on the exercise of these rights is presumptively unconstitutional, is noteworthy.lv Political *speech* is given much greater legal protection than is electoral *action*, even though the moral legitimacy of the state presumably depends as much or more on the free and equal exercise of the franchise as on the free and equal exercise of our vocal cords. (I will say a bit more about this contrast between speaking and voting in a later section of this paper.)

Despite its obvious effects in reducing the overall level of voting in the population by very large amounts, registration to vote is not conceptualized by the courts as a denial or abridgment of the right to vote, not even a narrowly tailored abridgment justified by the needs of reducing fraudulent voting on some sort of balancing test employing an intermediate level of judicial scrutiny. Rather, it is merely a non-substantive "regulation" of voting, supposedly analogous to the viewpoint-neutral "time, place, and manner" restrictions permissible in regulating speech under the First Amendment,lvi and scrutinized only minimally. But voter registration is *not* viewpoint-neutral; the sharpness of the class skew induced in voter turnout as a result of registration requirements should, if the underlying constitutional values of constitutional democracy obtained in full, trigger judicial concern. It does not.

Oligopoly in the "Political Marketplace." Another important function of the set of political rights, as I noted earlier, is to protect the competitive structure of electoral politics.lvii In all modern representative governments in the economically advanced world organized at the level of the nation-state, the central mechanism promoting political competition has been the presence of at least two active political parties. For there to be electoral competition, there must at a minimum be at least the *possibility* that the incumbent group of office-holders can be removed in an election and replaced by a different group.[58]

Under what conditions will people generally be better off with a system of electoral competition? Or, to put it differently, what sort of competitive situation will produce the beneficial effects that justify such a system? We know a fair amount about this question by analogy with product markets; in neoclassical microeconomic theory the characteristics of perfect competition and the conditions under which perfect competition will lead to a social optimum have been specified in great detail.[59] In general, perfect competition means that no buyer or seller has any power to influence prices, quality, or quantity of output; this requires in turn that there be an indefinitely large number of buyers and sellers participating in the market.[60] A perfectly competitive market will result in a "social optimum" if, in addition, individuals are rational and knowledgeable, there are no spillover effects or "externalities" from markets, and so forth.[61]

Of course, no electoral system is a system which leads to perfect competition in the economist's sense. The number of elected executive and judicial officials at the national[62] or state levels,[63] or the number seats in Congress[64] or state legislatures,[65] is fairly small. There are not an indefinitely large number of competitors for each available elected office; for well-known reasons, rational individuals participating in an electoral system will cooperate and increase their chances of backing a winner by agreeing to support the same candidate, even if the chosen candidate's platform is (from the point of view of any particular voter) not the best one available. Where only one candidate can be elected, and the candidate with the greatest number of votes is declared the winner, there will be a strong "basic tendency" for competition to crystallize around two candidates, at least *ceteris paribus*.[66] A voter who doesn't join in voting for one of the two leading parties is frequently at risk of having the less desirable of those two parties winning the election.[67]

In a product market, competition limited to two sellers is referred to as "duopoly." The theory of duopolistic competition is much less precise, and much more controversial within the discipline of economics, than is the theory of perfect competition, so determining the conditions under which two-party competition will lead to socially beneficial outcomes is much more difficult than in the case of perfect competition.

In general, though, it is widely agreed that an oligopolistic or monopolistic product market will be less responsive to consumers than will a perfectly competitive product market. An oligopolistic or monopolistic seller in a product market has power vis-à-vis consumers to influence market outcomes (total sales, product quality, or prices). Often, oligopolists will replace competition in price with non-price competition of the sort typified by the use of advertising to create an image of the product.[69] Again by analogy, in an electoral market the "seller" of candidates or platforms will have some power vis-à-vis voters to influence electoral outcomes (winners and losers, candidate quality, or platform issues). To the extent a party has such power, to that extent the party will be complacent in its responses to popular needs and concerns. Like the oligopolist, the complacent political party may compete not by offering a genuinely superior product (a better platform and candidates, or superior policy proposals) but by using advertising to create a differentiated image for its candidates.

Although economists recognize that in the context of an oligopolistic product market *laissez-faire* is inappropriate, there is no general legal understanding of how excessive power in an oligopolistic electoral market might best be curbed. In part this reflects the pull of competing constitutional values. One standard response to oligopoly in product markets—trust-busting—is ruled out, since the duopolistic market structure is itself a product of the state and federal constitutional arrangements creating a unitary executive and legislative bodies elected by plurality vote from single-member districts; it is an unintended byproduct of the constitutional design which neither the courts nor, apparently, very many other people want to upset; the other standard sort of response, public regulation over the right of the party or its voting members to make its own choices (on the model of public-utility regulation under the theory of natural monopolies), is ruled out on freedom-of-association grounds. lxix But these are not the only responses possible to oligopoly, and the courts have tended to be as concerned with the parties' (and the states) desires for "stability" in the electoral process as with the electorate's right to replace an unresponsive old party with an improved one.[70]

Economists refer to the structural impediments to competition in oligopolistic product markets as "barriers to entry." These include: brand loyalty among consumers; exclusive legal rights over certain products or production techniques (e.g., patents, copyrights, and trademarks); preferential access to capital, labor, or product markets; and economies of large scale in production or distribution.[71]

Given the rationality of a strong tendency towards two-party competition where electoral competition is organized in single-member districts using plurality elections, what are the sources of duopolistic electoral power for a *given* political party?[72] Many of the barriers to entry in product markets have analogies in electoral systems.[73]

The first barrier, and probably the most important one, is that for many people voting for the candidates of a particular party is not a matter of considered judgment regarding the general interest, or even a judgment regarding individual interest, but of custom and habit, or party loyalty.[74] That such habits can implicate voting rights is apparent in the circumstances of electoral activity by racial minorities; in that context, courts have held that block voting along racial lines can justify remedial measures including race-conscious legislative reapportionment.[75]

Second, in most states the existing parties have reinforced their competitive position through their influence over legislative apportionment, in which a central goal has come to be the creation of noncompetitive districts;[76] moreover, the existing parties have protected their standings outright through state-imposed restrictions on the ability of new parties or independent groups to nominate candidates.[77]

Third, existing parties have an easier time raising campaign funds or recruiting candidates and campaign staff, because of their ongoing relationships with funding sources, technical experts in campaigning, pools of potential candidates, and so forth.[78]

Fourth, there are economies of scale in political campaigning, especially in technical support, advertising, and fundraising, such that a national campaign for 435 U.S. representatives (say) is almost surely typically less expensive than 50 separate state campaigns or 435 separate district campaigns would be. As of the beginning of 1996, the Democratic and Republican parties were the only political parties with permanent ballot status in all fifty states and the District of Columbia.[79]

Fifth, the major parties occasionally collude, explicitly or tacitly, to stifle competition, from independent or minor-party candidates or from one another. Historically, this has sometimes taken the form of an agreement of the major parties to run only one candidate when a strong minor-party candidate is in the race.[80] Or, it can take the form of an agreement not to compete for certain offices,[81] and allow each party to win some offices virtually without competition.[82]

And, finally, it should be mentioned that there are powerful pressures affecting the wider culture of American politics which give it a pronounced conservative tilt, and which therefore operate to undermine the legitimacy (and hence the competitiveness) of anti-corporate political movements in particular.[83]

The cumulative effects of these factors—party loyalty, partisan bias in legislative districting, restrictions on minor-party ballot access, and preferential access to campaign funds by major-party candidates, and so forth—means that many or most candidates for public office do not face serious competition in the general election.[84]

From the point of view of the political theory underlying our electoral system, one of the basic reasons for having elections for representatives is precisely to set up a competitive struggle for votes; it stands to reason, then, that in adjudicating challenges to the laws establishing an electoral system, one value should be to promote the conditions favoring vigorous competition.

Open competition in elections, in the context of single-member plurality elections,[85] is protected by such devices as: fair opportunities for political parties and independent groups to organize and nominate candidates for office; fair legislative districting;[86] fair opportunities for political parties and independent groups to present their platforms to the electorate and have them discussed; and fair opportunities for the voters to choose the candidates and platforms of any of the available parties or groups.

If, for whatever reasons, effective political activity requires that voters act through a party that is separate from the two political parties already established in the United States, then the system must—if it is to claim democratic legitimacy—freely allow the formation of one or more new political parties which can effectively compete for votes with the older parties, according to the relative merits and demerits of the parties' candidates and proposals. And the Supreme Court has specifically held that the constitution protects the right of the people freely to associate,[87] including their right to associate in political parties.[88] But even if the voters have a right to associate in political parties, that does not mean (the Supreme Court says) that the state must allow ballot access to any and all political parties in which the voters may wish to associate; it may restrict access only to parties that are not "frivolous" or to those demonstrating substantial popular support, if it decides that such restriction is necessary to avoid voter confusion or preserve the "integrity" of the electoral process.[89] In practice, therefore, the "right" to associate in political parties is a fairly weak one; the burden is not on the state to show that it can achieve its "compelling" ends in no other manner than by restricting the party's access to the ballot, but is rather on the party to show how the severity of the restriction on it is weightier than the state's goals.[90]

Alternatively, it might be thought that imposing substantive restrictions as to which parties' candidates can appear on the official ballot is equivalent to creating new qualifications for office; and if that were the case, substantive ballot access restrictions would be unconstitutional.[91] The Supreme Court has held that neither the states nor Congress may add to the constitutional qualifications for being a U.S. representative or senator[92]—or, presumably, president—which qualifications are limited to requirements of citizenship, state residency, minimum age, minimum period of citizenship, and nonparticipation in rebellion.[93]

With state ballot access laws, a political party's candidates will appear on the official ballot only if either that party's candidates received a certain number or percentage of the votes in the previous election, or if the party presents the election officials with evidence of support in the electorate, typically endorsing petitions signed by a certain number or percentage of voters.[94] Independent candidates face similar, although not always identical, requirements.[95] A party, and a candidate, without this will not appear on the ballot, and a party whose candidates are not on the ballot will (almost surely) not win political power for its principles.[96] Ballot access laws are expressly designed to screen out some parties and candidates from the official ballot; they are designed to narrow the choices available to the voter.[97]

However, the apparent inference from these facts and the current understanding of the qualifications clause—that substantive ballot access requirements are additional qualifications for office and therefore are in violation of the Constitution—does not follow, the Supreme Court has told us.[98] The mere fact that the state has set up a system whereby certain otherwise qualified candidates (for all practical purposes) cannot be elected to office does not mean that the state has added to the qualifications for holding the office.

The reason is that appearance on the official ballot is not a *necessary* condition for election to office; the voters are, for example, ordinarily free to write in the name of a candidate who does not satisfy the ballot access requirements.[99] True, hardly anyone has in fact been elected to Congress as a write-in candidate.[100] But these contingencies of practical politics are apparently, for the Supreme Court, irrelevant.

Having held that the legal in-principle availability of the write-in helps save ballot access requirements from unconstitutionality, one might think that the Supreme Court would be especially solicitous of the write-in, and would strike down ballot access requirements where write-ins are unavailable. But in 1992, the Court did the reverse; it held that the states need not make accommodations on the official ballot for casting write-in votes, nor (therefore) need write-ins be counted if cast.[101]

And finally, to round out this confusing picture, it needs only be added that when the Supreme Court considered the constitutionality of a state scheme to impose term limits on federal legislators by denying official ballot access to them after they had served a certain number of terms, it struck the term limits down under the qualifications clause. Now at least some ballot-access restrictions *do* violate the qualifications clause, in apparent reversal of part of the *Storer* decision; in the term-limits decision the Court explicitly rejected the view that the write-in functioned as a satisfactory alternative path to the ballot.[102]

We can summarize this part of our discussion by observing that the ballot-access and write-in decisions, taken as a whole, have not satisfactorily advanced the ideals of political competition, or of political deliberation, or of free political expression. The interest in political competition requires that each candidate and each party not have safe seats; short of proportional representation, this suggests that partisan and incumbent-protection gerrymandering not be given the deference they now have, and that minor parties be given a more realistic opportunity —including financial and technical resources—to offer candidates in competition to the major parties. Furthermore, minor parties which desire to support major-party candidates on occasion should not be put to a choice between supporting their preferred candidate and giving up their access to the official ballot,[103] a forced choice which has had the effect of significantly reducing both the numbers and the political strength of minor parties in the U.S. over the past 75 years,[104] but this is the effective result of the antifusion laws currently on the statute books of 45 states and the District of Columbia.[105] The interest in political deliberation requires that a range of viewpoints be heard, but in a system with only two parties the tendency will be for the parties to say what they believe the median voter would like them to say. This suggests that more viewpoints than two be given a place in the election campaign, and therefore on the ballot, and thus that ballot access requirements be significantly liberalized. And, finally, it is not too much to say that the interests in free expression and political legitimacy require that voters be free to cast a ballot for any eligible candidate, via write-in if necessary; to maintain otherwise is to place the voter in the position of choosing between sacrificing a fundamental constitutional right or being coerced into voting for a candidate whom the voter does not in fact favor.

Wealth and Voting. As the voter registration system serves to screen out certain potential voters from the active electorate, and the ballot access laws serve to screen out certain political parties from appearance on the official ballot, so does the campaign finance system function to screen out certain candidates from serious consideration from office. In all three cases, the screening is not viewpoint-neutral, as democratic principles might seem to require. In particular, the screening exhibits a sharp bias along class lines. If we begin with the goals of enhancing electoral competition, of fostering discussion about public policy, or of legitimizing the state's exercise of power, private financing of electoral politics has proved nothing short of a disaster.

From the point of view of reducing the potential of the lower classes to affect public policy, the most important single feature of the current system is undoubtedly the system by which we finance political activity. Where political activity is regarded as a private activity, to be financed by private funds, those with funds have in effect a private veto over what sort of political activity will occur. To oversimplify somewhat, we can think of private campaign funding as functioning as a preliminary screening device to eliminate from electoral contention any potential candidates who are not acceptable to those with private wealth.[106] This operates at several stages: a candidate for nomination who is unable to spend money will not receive the party nomination, and a party's nominee who is unable to spend money will not win a plurality in the general election.

To take a concrete example. An election for one of the eighty seats in the California assembly costs about $700,000 every two years. That's about $4 for every registered voter in each assembly district. Counting the general election only, and *excluding* the costs of the primary election, the average cost of a winning campaign for a challenger opposing an incumbent member of the California assembly in 1994 was $413,208.[107] To keep that in perspective, that's more than eleven times as much as the median California household earned in 1994; more than thirty-five times the yearly income for a family of three at the 1994 poverty line; and nearly forty-nine years of full-time work at the 1994 minimum wage.[108]

With these financial requirements for a political campaign, how does anyone run for an elective office, such as member of the California state assembly? A few, the very wealthy, can raise it from their own personal funds. In 1992, about 7% of the total amount given to state legislative candidates came from personal and family funds. Another 5% or so came in small contributions, $100 or less.[109] But for the rest of the needed funds, candidates must raise money from others, and raise it in very big chunks. Most of the people who contribute to political campaigns are wealthy, even very wealthy. About three-quarters of the $72 million spent on legislative races in California in 1992 came in contributions of at least $1000.[110] One-ninth of all contributions to state legislative races—$7.7 million—came from only *ten* contributors: the political action committees of the state medical association, the prison guards, the public school teachers, the trial lawyers, the real estate industry, the insurance industry, a single oil company (Arco), the dental association, the optometric association, and a group devoted to advancing a pro-business ideology.[111] Most—around three-fifths, in fact—of the money given to candidates for the state legislature comes not from individual persons, but from organizations with a particular stake in what happens in Sacramento.[112]

The government does have the power to limit the size of individual contributions to a campaign, and to require that the sources and amounts of contributions be disclosed to the public, but under *Buckley* and its progeny it does not have the power to limit contributions to political campaigns independent of any particular candidate's or party's campaign, nor may it limit the total amount of money that one may contribute to one's own campaign for office. Nor may it limit the total amount of money candidates may spend on their campaigns for office. While spending money does not, of course, guarantee election to public office, and the connection between spending and victory is by no means a simple one-to-one relation,[113] the ability to spend money on a campaign does have a very noticeable effect on the odds of winning an election for either federal[114] or state office.[115]

This system is not *simply* the inevitable result of mixing electoral democracy with corporate capitalism;[116] many capitalist democracies have campaign financing systems much different, and in many respects much more egalitarian, than that of the United States.[117] From the legal point of view, this system by which organized wealth sets the limits to political activity in the United States exists as a matter of absolute constitutional right. Under the Constitution as currently interpreted by the Supreme Court, the federal or state governments have no more power to limit this sort of influence of money on politics than they have to establish a state religion or abolish jury trials in criminal cases. An individual political candidate may spend unlimited amounts of money to be elected;[118] a corporation may similarly spend unlimited amounts of money to advance its interests in politics.[119]

Interestingly, while the voter registration system, which functions to *reduce* political participation, especially along lines of economic class, is upheld as a mere content-neutral regulation of the right to vote, the congressional attempts to regulate campaign spending, which plausibly *increase* the ability of lower-income groups to participate equally, have not been seen as regulations to preserve the effectiveness of the equal right to vote, nor as content-neutral "time, place, or manner" regulations of speech, but rather as substantive restrictions on the content of political speech. According to the Supreme Court, equalizing the voice of rich and poor in political campaigns amounts to censoring the voice of the rich.

The rationale for these rulings is interesting. The spending of money on a political campaign is constitutionally protected because, as the Supreme Court said in the case of *Buckley v. Valeo*, spending money in this way is a form of speech, and the freedom of speech is, as we know, protected from government interference by the First Amendment to the Constitution. Earlier I pointed out that (mere) talk is given more protection than the activity of voting, under the constitution as presently interpreted; now consider that spending money on politics, as a form of talking about politics,[120] is also given a higher level of constitutional protection than is voting.

A more straightforwardly ideologically conservative and inegalitarian rationalization for the present arrangements of American electoral politics could hardly be imagined. While this ruling has not lacked for criticism from the commentators,[121] it has lasted as a part of American constitutional law for over twenty years and the Supreme Court has not suggested that the decision has lost legal vitality. *Buckley* did leave an opening for restricting the power of money on campaigns; Congress could regulate spending under a voluntary system of public financing of election campaigns. Of course, Congress doesn't have to set up a public financing system at all (which it hasn't, except for the presidential election); no candidate has to accept public financing and thus can evade all spending limits quite legally (as, for example, Ross Perot did in his 1992 campaign); and the Supreme Court was careful to say that Congress could have the same respect for third parties as the states had to demonstrate in the ballot access cases—that is, not so little as to actually eliminate them from the ballot entirely, but not so much as to allow them to compete on equal, or even fair, terms with the major parties.[122] (The present system of public funding provides funds only to parties which receive 5% or more of the total popular vote nationwide.[123])

How better might we think of the constitutional law of campaign finance? I suggest that if we conceptualized the issues as concerned with the collective right to a free vote, and saw free speech as implicating the collective rights of public self-governance as well as individual rights of private expression, we would examine the interests at stake differently and the political dimensions of the disputes would become more clear; we would therefore be in a better position to reshape the system of political rights. First, for example, we might question whether private financing along current lines promotes or distorts public deliberation on political matters; hardly anyone without a vested interest in the status quo seriously maintains that the present system promotes deliberative processes. Instead, we have campaigns which are simplistic and overemotional, frequently ignoring substance for trivia.

Second, we might question whether private financing enhances political competition. Again, while this is a complicated empirical matter, available evidence suggests that the unequal availability of private money makes the competitive arena still more uncompetitive than it already is, giving a strong advantage to the better-financed candidate rather than to the better candidate.

And third, we might question whether campaigns financed as they now are enhance the perceived legitimacy of the elected government, or weaken it. It may be no coincidence that the rise of "capital-intensive" rather than "labor-intensive" political campaigns, based on the amassing of gigantic sums of money to spend on campaigning through television and other mass media rather than face-to-face contact, has paralleled the decline of popular participation in electoral politics,[124] so that the electorate has shrunk by more than a fifth since the election of John F. Kennedy in 1960.[125] Civic consciousness may not be fully compatible with a culture in which political issues are advertised in the same manner as are ordinary commodities, and surely the Constitution gives the people the power to protect their democracy from trivializing and commodification.[126]

Conclusion

If we begin with a vision of the right to vote as extending to all the "political processes leading to nomination or election,"[127] and with the vision of free speech and of the First Amendment articulated so powerfully by Meiklejohn, we are not driven to accept the legitimacy of restrictive voter-registration and ballot-access laws, nor forced to accept the logic underlying *Buckley* and thus to acquiesce in the present tawdry mess of our common political life. For on an understanding of free speech as (in part) constituting a democratic society, and of the equal right to vote as protecting the participation of all in the electoral processes, where the ability to speak is not a function of wealth, then the contradiction between speaking and democratic life dissolves. We can see, instead, the equal right to vote as encompassing the entire process of nomination, campaign, and election, and see that right as strong enough to protect the practices of popular participation from regulations which unnecessarily restrict deliberation, competition, legitimacy, and political expression. And this, I submit, is both preservative of a system of ordered liberty and truer to our democratic ideals.

Appendix II: The International Covenant on Economic, Social and Cultural Rights

Preamble

The States Parties to the present Covenant,

Considering that, in accordance with the principles proclaimed in the Charter of the United Nations, recognition of the inherent dignity and of the equal and inalienable rights of all members of the human family is the foundation of freedom, justice and peace in the world,

Recognizing that these rights derive from the inherent dignity of the human person,

Recognizing that, in accordance with the Universal Declaration of Human Rights, the ideal of free human beings enjoying freedom from fear and want can only be achieved if conditions are created whereby everyone may enjoy his economic, social and cultural rights, as well as his civil and political rights,

Considering the obligation of States under the Charter of the United Nations to promote respect for, and observance of, human rights and freedoms,

Realizing that the individual, having duties to other individuals and to the community to which he belongs, is under a responsibility to strive for the promotion and observance of the rights recognized in the present Covenant,

Agree upon the following articles:

Part I

Article 1

1. All peoples have the right of self-determination. By virtue of that right

they freely determine their political status and freely pursue their economic, social and cultural development.

2. All peoples may, for their own ends, freely dispose of their natural wealth and resources without prejudice to any obligations arising out of international economic co-operation, based upon the principle of mutual benefit, and international law. In no case may a people be deprived of its own means of subsistence.
3. The States Parties to the present Covenant, including those having responsibility for the administration of Non-Self-Governing and Trust Territories, shall promote the realization of the right of self-determination, and shall respect that right, in conformity with the provisions of the Charter of the United Nations.

Part II

Article 2

1. Each State Party to the present Covenant undertakes to take steps, individually and through international assistance and co-operation, especially economic and technical, to the maximum of available resources, with a view to achieving progressively the full realization of the rights recognized in the present Covenant by all appropriate means, including particularly the adoption of legislative measures.
2. The States Parties to the present Covenant undertake to guarantee that the rights enunciated in the present Covenant will be exercised without discrimination of any kind as to race, colour, sex, language, religion, political or other opinion, national or social origin, property, birth or other status.
3. Developing countries, with due regard to human rights and their national economy, may determine to what extent they would guarantee the economic rights recognized in the present Covenant to non-nationals.

Article 3

The States Parties to the present Covenant undertake to ensure the equal right of men and women to the enjoyment of all economic, social and cultural rights set forth in the present Covenant.

Article 4

The States Parties to the present Covenant recognize that, in the enjoyment of those rights provided by the State in conformity with the present Covenant, the

State may subject such rights only to such limitations as are determined by law only in so far as this may be compatible with the nature of these rights and solely for the purpose of promoting the general welfare in a democratic society.

Article 5

1. Nothing in the present Covenant may be interpreted as implying for any State, group or person any right to engage in any activity or to perform any act aimed at the destruction of any of the rights or freedoms recognized herein, or at their limitation to a greater extent than is provided for in the present Covenant.
2. No restriction upon or derogation from any of the fundamental human rights recognized or existing in any country in virtue of law, convention, regulations or custom shall be admitted on the pretext that the present Covenant does not recognize such rights or that it recognizes them to a lesser extent.

Part III

Article 6

1. The States Parties to the present Covenant recognize the right to work, which includes the right of everyone to the opportunity to gain his living by work which he freely chooses or accepts, and will take appropriate steps to safeguard this right.
2. The steps to be taken by a State Party to the present Covenant to achieve the full realization of this right shall include technical and vocational guidance and training programmes, policies and techniques to achieve steady economic, social and cultural development and full and productive employment under conditions safeguarding fundamental political and economic freedoms to the individual.

Article 7

The States Parties to the present Covenant recognize the right of everyone to enjoyment of just and favorable conditions of work which ensure, in particular:

(a) Remuneration which provides all workers, as a minimum, with:

  (i) Fair wages and equal remuneration for work of equal value without distinction of any kind, in particular women being guaranteed conditions of work not inferior to those enjoyed by men, with equal pay for equal work;

  (ii) A decent living for themselves and their families in accordance with the provisions of the present Covenant;

(b) Safe and healthy working conditions;

(c) Equal opportunity for everyone to be promoted in his employment to an appropriate higher level, subject to no considerations other than those of seniority and competence;

(d) Rest, leisure and reasonable limitation of working hours and periodic holidays with pay, as well as remuneration for public holidays.

Article 8

1. The States Parties to the present Covenant undertake to ensure:
   (a) The right of everyone to form trade unions and join the trade union of his choice, subject only to the rules of the organization concerned, for the promotion and protection of his economic and social interests. No restrictions may be placed on the exercise of this right other than those prescribed by law and which are necessary in a democratic society in the interests of national security or public order or for the protection of the rights and freedoms of others;
   (b) The right of trade unions to establish national federations or confederations and the right of the latter to form or join international trade-union organizations;
   (c) The right of trade unions to function freely subject to no limitations other than those prescribed by law and which are necessary in a democratic society in the interests of national security or public order or for the protection of the rights and freedoms of others;
   (d) The right to strike, provided that it is exercised in conformity with the laws of the particular country.
2. This article shall not prevent the imposition of lawful restrictions on the exercise of these rights by members of the armed forces or of the police or of the administration of the State.
3. Nothing in this article shall authorize States Parties to the International Labour Organization Convention of 1948 concerning Freedom of Association and Protection of the Right to Organize to take legislative measures which would prejudice, or apply the law in such a manner as would prejudice, the guarantees provided for in that Convention.

Article 9

The States Parties to the present Covenant recognize the right of everyone to social security, including social insurance.

Article 10

The States Parties to the present Covenant recognize that:

1. The widest possible protection and assistance should be accorded to the family, which is the natural and fundamental group unit of society, particularly for its establishment and while it is responsible for the care and education of dependent children. Marriage must be entered into with the free consent of the intending spouses.
2. Special protection should be accorded to mothers during a reasonable period before and after childbirth. During such period working mothers should be accorded paid leave or leave with adequate social security benefits.
3. Special measures of protection and assistance should be taken on behalf of all children and young persons without any discrimination for reasons of parentage or other conditions. Children and young persons should be protected from economic and social exploitation. Their employment in work harmful to their morals or health or dangerous to life or likely to hamper their normal development should be punishable by law. States should also set age limits below which the paid employment of child labour should be prohibited and punishable by law.

Article 11

1. The States Parties to the present Covenant recognize the right of everyone to an adequate standard of living for himself and his family, including adequate food, clothing and housing, and to the continuous improvement of living conditions. The States Parties will take appropriate steps to ensure the realization of this right, recognizing to this effect the essential importance of international co-operation based on free consent.
2. The States Parties to the present Covenant, recognizing the fundamental right of everyone to be free from hunger, shall take, individually and through international co-operation, the measures, including specific programmes, which are needed:
   (a) To improve methods of production, conservation and distribution of food by making full use of technical and scientific knowledge, by disseminating knowledge of the principles of nutrition and by developing or reforming agrarian systems in such a way as to achieve the most efficient development and utilization of natural resources;
   (b) Taking into account the problems of both food-importing and

food-exporting countries, to ensure an equitable distribution of world food supplies in relation to need.

Article 12

1. The States Parties to the present Covenant recognize the right of everyone to the enjoyment of the highest attainable standard of physical and mental health.
2. The steps to be taken by the States Parties to the present Covenant to achieve the full realization of this right shall include those necessary for:
   (a) The provision for the reduction of the stillbirth-rate and of infant mortality and for the healthy development of the child;
   (b) The improvement of all aspects of environmental and industrial hygiene;
   (c) The prevention, treatment and control of epidemic, endemic, occupational and other diseases;
   (d) The creation of conditions which would assure to all medical service and medical attention in the event of sickness.

Article 13

1. The States Parties to the present Covenant recognize the right of everyone to education. They agree that education shall be directed to the full development of the human personality and the sense of its dignity, and shall strengthen the respect for human rights and fundamental freedoms. They further agree that education shall enable all persons to participate effectively in a free society, promote understanding, tolerance and friendship among all nations and all racial, ethnic or religious groups, and further the activities of the United Nations for the maintenance of peace.
2. The States Parties to the present Covenant recognize that, with a view to achieving the full realization of this right:
   (a) Primary education shall be compulsory and available free to all;
   (b) Secondary education in its different forms, including technical and vocational secondary education, shall be made generally available and accessible to all by every appropriate means, and in particular by the progressive introduction of free education;
   (c) Higher education shall be made equally accessible to all, on the basis of capacity, by every appropriate means, and in particular by the progressive introduction of free education;

(d) Fundamental education shall be encouraged or intensified as far as possible for those persons who have not received or completed the whole period of their primary education;
(e) The development of a system of schools at all levels shall be actively pursued, an adequate fellowship system shall be established, and the material conditions of teaching staff shall be continuously improved.

3. The States Parties to the present Covenant undertake to have respect for the liberty of parents and, when applicable, legal guardians to choose for their children schools, other than those established by the public authorities, which conform to such minimum educational standards as may be laid down or approved by the State and to ensure the religious and moral education of their children in conformity with their own convictions.
4. No part of this article shall be construed so as to interfere with the liberty of individuals and bodies to establish and direct educational institutions, subject always to the observance of the principles set forth in paragraph 1 of this article and to the requirement that the education given in such institutions shall conform to such minimum standards as may be laid down by the State.

Article 14

Each State Party to the present Covenant which, at the time of becoming a Party, has not been able to secure in its metropolitan territory or other territories under its jurisdiction compulsory primary education, free of charge, undertakes, within two years, to work out and adopt a detailed plan of action for the progressive implementation, within a reasonable number of years, to be fixed in the plan, of the principle of compulsory education free of charge for all.

Article 15

1. The States Parties to the present Covenant recognize the right of everyone:
   (a) To take part in cultural life;
   (b) To enjoy the benefits of scientific progress and its applications;
   (c) To benefit from the protection of the moral and material interests resulting from any scientific, literary or artistic production of which he is the author;
2. The steps to be taken by the States Parties to the present Covenant to achieve the full realization of this right shall include those necessary

for the conservation, the development and the diffusion of science and culture.

3. The States Parties to the present Covenant undertake to respect the freedom indispensable for scientific research and creative activity.
4. The States Parties to the present Covenant recognize the benefits to be derived from the encouragement and development of international contacts and co-operation in the scientific and cultural fields.

Note: Parts IV and V of this Covenant have been omitted to save space; they deal with the reporting process, review by the Economic and Social Council of the United Nations, conditions for the Covenant coming into force as international law, and other related matters. The Covenant came into force in international law in 1976; as of October 1999, it has been signed but still not ratified by the U. S. Government.

Notes

Law Subversive of Democracy

1. *Congressional Record—Senate*, S 4783–4784, April 2, 1992.
2. This point has been well argued by Henry Shue, *Basic Rights: Subsistence, Affluence, and Foreign Policy*, Princeton, 1980.
3. *Disclosure of Corporate Ownership*, Committee on Government Operations, U.S. Senate, 93rd Congress, 1st session, December 27, 1973.
4. Op. Cit., p.127.
5. The classic study of the rise of the corporation is *The Modern Corporation and Private Property*, Adolf Berle and Gardiner Means, Columbia University, 1934. The authors called attention to the radical change in the rights of private property created by the modern corporate structure.
6. On trusts generally, cf. *Preface to the Law of Trusts*, Paul Haskell, Foundation Press, 1975; on dynastic trusts, cf. Ronald Chester, *Inheritance, Wealth, and Society*, Indiana University Press, 1982, esp. chapter 6.
7. Chester, op. cit., p.125; on total stock value, cf. *Broadening the Ownership of New Capital*, Joint Economic Committee, Staff Study, 94th Congress, 2nd session, June 17, 1976, p.7; on percentage of stock held by the top 6.1%, *Personal Wealth estimated from Estate Tax Returns*, Internal Revenue Service, Publication 482 (3–76), Supplemental Statistics of Income, 1972, pp.1,2.
8. Attorney General Olney's report is cited in *The History of the Sherman Law of the United States*, by A. H. Walker, N.Y., 1910, pp. 96,97.
9. Cf. *The Du Pont Dynasty*, by Gerard Colby, Lyle Stuart, 1984, p.31; Colby adds that the personal wealth of the family was estimated at 10 billion by Forbes Magazine.
10. The basic source for the glass, incandescent bulb, and radio monopolies is the Temporary National Economic Committee hearings of the late 1930s and early 1940s: *Investigation of Concentration of Economic Power*, Hearings before the TNEC on Public Resolution 113, Parts 2 and 3 (Patents), Part 3 (Cartels), and also Committee Monograph #31, *Patents and Free Enterprise*.

11. On Phoebus, the international incandescent electric lamp cartel, cf. G. W. Stocking and M. W. Watkins, *Cartels in Action: Case Studies in International Business Diplomacy*, N.Y. The Twentieth Century Fund, 1946.

The Right of Association

1. Quoted in Rice, Charles E., *Freedom of Association*, N.Y., 1962, p.38.
2. *Constitution of the Union of Soviet Socialist Republics*, Novosti Press Agency Publishing House, Moscow, U.S.S.R., 1982, p.33.
3. For a general history of dissidents and dissident organizations in recent times cf. Rubenstein, Joshua, *Soviet Dissidents*, Boston, 1980. On the struggle of independent trade unions, cf. Haynes, Victor and Semyonova, Olga, *Workers Against the Gulag*, London, 1979. There is also considerable material in *Prisoners of Conscience in the Soviet Union*, Amnesty International Publications, London, 1975, 2nd ed., 1980.
4. The Norris-La Guardia Anti-Injunction Act of 1932, 47 *Stat.* 70, makes it public policy of the United States that workers have "full freedom of association."
5. *NAACP v. Alabama*, 357 US 449, at 460.
6. Cf. Douglas, William O., "Stare Decisis," *The Record of the Association of the Bar of the City of New York*, Vol.4, May, 1949, pp.152–179.
7. The International Covenant on Civil and Political Rights was ratified by the United States on June 8, 1992.
8. For another version of the relation between freedom of speech and democracy, cf. Schauer, Frederick, *Free Speech: A Philosophical Inquiry*, Cambridge, 1982, pp.35–46.
9. An illuminating collection of essays on this subject is *The Case Against the Consititution: From the Antifederalists to the Present*, ed. by J.F. Manley and K.M. Dolbeare, M.E.Sharpe, N.Y., 1987
10. Useem, Michael, The Inner Circle: Large Corporations and the Rise of Business Political Activity in the U.S. and U.K., Oxford University Press, 1984, p.35.
11. I have used the GNP figures from Ruth Leger Savard's *World Military and Social Expenditures*, 1982, World Priorities, Virginia, 1982, Table II, p.27.
12. A brief survey of the history of incorporation law is given in Berle, A., and Means, G., *The Modern Corporation and Private Property*, N.Y., 1934, Bk.II, Ch.1.
13. *Liggett Co. v. Lee*, 288 US 517; Brandeis' dissent begins at 548.
14. A similar problem afflicted the early inheritance laws of the States; the wealthy moved their official residences from states with the tax to states without it, eventually prompting a Federal inheritance or estate tax. The history is to be found in William J. Shultz, *The Taxation of Inheritance*, Boston & N.Y., 1926.
15. Douglas, W.O., *op. cit.*, p. 155.
16. Santa Clara County v. Southern Pacific R. Co., 118 US 394 (1886).
17. Minneapolis R. Co. V. Beckwith, 129 US 26 (1889).
18. Douglas, W.O., *op.cit.*, p.155.
19. Cf. Note 4, above.
20. The Sherman Act: 15 USC 1, 26 Stat. 209, July 2, 1890.
21. U.S. v. E.C. Knight Co., 156 US 1 (1894).

22. *Ibid.*, at 12.
23. *Ibid.*, at 11.
24. *Ibid.*, at 45.
25. Moody, John, The Truth About the Trusts: A Description and Analysis of the American Trust Movement, N.Y., Moody Publishing Co., c.1904, xi ff., and p. 485.
26. On the growth of Trade Associations, cf. *National Trade and Professional Associations of the United States*, 26th ed., Columbia Books, Wash. D.C., 1983, Introduction, p. 6,7.
27. Standard Oil Co. of New Jersey v. United States, 221 US 1 (1911); United States v. American Tobacco Co., 221 US 106 (1911).
28. 221 US 1, at 83.
29. 221 US 1, at 83.
30. 221 US 1, at 105.
31. 221 US 106, at 192,193.
32. Goodwyn, Lawrence, *The Populist Movement*, Oxford University Press, 1978, p.vii.
33. The only justices who were not former corporation and railroad attorneys at the time of the Standard Oil Case were the Chief Justice, who was a wealthy Louisiana sugar plantation owner, and Oliver Wendell Holmes.
34. For example, Richard Olney, Attorney General under President Cleveland (and a former attorney for the Whiskey Trust), informed Congress in his annual report of 1893 that the Sherman Anti-Trust Act was misbegotten, as Congress cannot limit the right of state corporations or of citizens, in the acquisition, accumulation and control of property, and cannot make criminal the intents and purposes of persons in the acquisition and control of property which the states of their residence or creation sanction. Needless to say there was no rush in the Justice Department to bring indictments under the Sherman Act.
35. Cf. Friedman, Lawrence M., *A History of American Law*, Simon and Schuster, 1973, Part II, Chapter 1.
36. Cf. *Organized Labor and the Law*, Alpheus T. Mason, 1925, Duke University Press, Part II, "Common Law and Labor in the United States." Generally speaking, if an action could be shown to be harmful to others, i.e., the employer or the general public, then it was judged illegal, regardless of any harms to workers and their families that may have led to the action.
37. Quoted in Albert H. Walker, History of the Sherman Law of the United States of America, N.Y. 1910, p.3.
38. 55 Fed. Rep. 605, Feb. 28, 1893, at 640, 641.
39. 54 Fed. Rep. 994, March 26, 1893, at 996.
40. History of the Sherman Law of the United States of America, Albert H. Walker, N.Y., 1910, p.97.
41. Walker, *op. cit.*, pp. 97–103. The cases are *U.S. vs. Debs et al*, 64 Fed.Rep.274, and 158 U.S. 577.
42. *Loewe v. Lawlor*, 208 U.S. 274, at 301/302 (1908). Billings is wrong that Congress made the act to apply to both capital and labor, unless he meant that Congress wrote the Act in language that would permit its judicial extension to labor.
43. Taff Vale Ry.Co. v. Amalgamated Society, 1901, A.C. 406.
44. Clayton Anti-Trust Act, 38 Stat.730, 15 U.S.C.12 et seq.

45. *Duplex v. Deering* 254 U.S. 443, at 445.
46. *Duplex v Deering*, 254 U.S., at 487/488.
47. *The History of the American Working Class*, Anthony Bimba, N.Y., 1927, p.299. Quoted from the New York Times of April 1, 1922.
48. Ibid., p.304. Quoted from the New York *World* of July 10,1922.
49. Frankfurter, F., and Greene, N., *The Labor Injunction*, N.Y., 1932.
50. Norris-LaGuardia Act, March 23, 1932, 47 Stat. 70.
51. *Lauf v. E.G. Shinner & Co.*, 303 U.S. 323 (1938).
52. *U.S. v. Hutcheson*, 312 U.S. 219, at 231 (1941).
53. *Thornhill v. Alabama*, 310 U.S. 88 (1940).
54. Basil Rauch, *The History of the New Deal*, Capricorn Books, 1963, Chapter IV.
55. James B. Atleson, *Values and Assumptions in American Labor Law*, University of Massachusetts Press, 1983, p. 38/39.
56. Atleson, op. cit., p.38, quoting I. Bernstein, *The New Deal Collective Bargaining Policy*, U. of Calif. Press, 1950.
57. David Selvin, A Terrible Anger: The 1934 Waterfront and General Strikes in San *Francisco*, Wayne State U. Press, 1996, p.194. This and similar remarks were made at the Greek Theater in Berkeley on the second day of the strike.
58. The NIRA was declared unconstitutional in *Schechter Poultry Corp. v. U.S.*, 295 U.S. 495 (1935). The Court relied on a very narrow reading of the Commerce Clause, and also maintained that Congress was guilty of an unconstitutional delegation of power to the President in giving him the authority to enact the NIRA codes.
59. NLRB v. Jones & Laughlin Steel Corp., 310 U.S. 1 (1937).
60. NLRB v. Mackay Radio & Telegraph Company, 304 U.S. 333 (1938).
61. NLRB v. Fansteel Metallurgical Corp., 306 U.S. 240 (1939).
62. Taft-Hartley Act, Title I, Section 9(h), 61 Stat. 146.
63. Many examples are discussed in detail by Wendell Berge, an Assistant Attorney General of the United States, in *Cartels: Challenge to a Free World*, Public Affairs Press, 1946. Among those indicted under anti-trust law in 1942 were Bendix Aviation, Aluminum Company of America, Standard Oil Company (N.J.), General Electric, and E.I. du Pont de Nemours & Co.
64. 339 U.S.382 (1950).

Human Rights vs. Classical Liberalism

1. *Human Rights: A Compilation of International Instruments*, Vol. I, First Part, pp.1–49, United Nations, 1993. In pamphlet form, *The International Bill of Human Rights*, Department of Public Information, DPI/797-40669, United Nations, 1985.
2. Reporting requirements are required by each of the treaties; Article 40 in the case of the ICCPR, and Article 16 of the ICESCR.
3. A classic study is *The Growth of Philosophic Radicalism*, by Elie Halevy, English translation by A. D. Lindsay, Faber and Faber, London, 1928.

4. The principal figures here, of course, are William of Ockham and his school. A useful account is Gordon Leff's *The Dissolution of the Medieval Outlook: An Essay on Intellectual and Spiritual Change in the Fourteenth Century*, N.Y. Univ. Press, 1976.
5. The formula was challenged in the mid-eighteenth century by French Materialists, but did not disappear until much later.
6. The Labor Theory of Value has an application in ethics, as in principle (4) here, but also in the theory of prices. Regarding the latter Marx's redefinition of value in terms of socially necessary labor time was a key step in resolving the problems surrounding Smith's original formulation and those of successors. Cf. Dobb, M., *Theories of Value and Distribution Since Adam Smith*, Cambridge, 1973.
7. Another influential philosophical idea favoring democracy in the 18th century was John Locke's theory of the mind as a *tabula rasa*. Cf. Kenneth MacLean, *John Locke and English Literature of the Eighteenth Century*, N.Y., 1962, Book I.
8. The Universal Declaration of Human Rights included a right to own property alone and in association with others (Article 17). However, neither Covenant includes a right to own property, nor any of the rights I have referred to here as economic liberties.
9. How the Free Market is supposed to accomplish these goals is spelled out by Smith in Book I of the *Wealth of Nations*, esp. Chapters II, V, VI, and VII.
10. Cf. Gunnar Myrdal, *The Political Element in the Development of Economic Theory*, Harvard, 1954, for an extended examination of the conflation of morality with science in the history of economic theory.
11. Ibid., p. v.
12. John Bates Clark, *The Distribution of Wealth*, N.Y., Augustus M. Kelly, 1965, p. 111.
13. Adam Smith, *An Inquiry into the Nature and Causes of the Wealth of Nations*, Book I, Chapter VI, 1776; cp. also, Book I, Chapter VIII.
14. Various attempts to justify the return on capital as having a different basis than that proposed by Smith are critically examined in the first chapter of David Schweickart's *Against Capitalism*, Westview Press, 1996.
15. Cf., for example, the discussion in *A Theory of Property*, by Stephen R. Munzer, Ch.10, Cambridge University Press, 1990.
16. So Adam Smith, for example, regarded the sovereign, the army and navy, and "some of the most frivolous professions," such as churchmen, lawyers, physicians, men of letters, buffoons, musicians, etc., as unproductive laborers. *Wealth of Nations*, Bk. II, Ch. III.
17. This is not to say that one cannot discern and characterize various tendencies and their possible interactions; but that is far from the quantitative prediction of future states of a system.
18. The United States government has undertaken to manage the economic system since the establishment of the Federal Reserve System, and particularly since the passage of the Full Employment Act of 1946.
19. The U.N. assesses the implementation of human rights treaties through a periodic and public reporting process; cf. Part V. The U.S. government has tied aid to human rights, as the 1974 Foreign Assistance Act, Section 502B, advising the President to withhold security assistance from countries that are gross human rights violators.

20. See Appendix II, *The International Covenant on Economic, Social, and Cultural Rights*, esp. Articles 7 and 9.
21. Veblen, Thorstein, *The Theory of Business Enterprise*, New American Library, undated, p.13, 14.
22. David M. Kotz, *Bank Control of Large Corporations in the United States*, Univ. of Calif. Press, 1978, p. 30. The quotation is from Vincent P. Carosso, *Investment Banking in America: A History*, Cambridge, Mass., 1970, pp.40–41.
23. Kotz, op. cit., p 30, 31.
24. Senate Report No.25, pursuant to Senate Resolution 20 (80th Cong.), 81st Congress, 1st Session, January 31, 1949, p.13–19, reprinted in Hearings Before The Antitrust Subcommittee of the Committee on the Judiciary, House of Representatives, 84th Congress, 1st Session, Part III, Oct. 25–Dec. 9th, 1955.
25. For a detailed account of the organization and operation of the oil industry, *The Control of Oil*, by John M. Blair, Pantheon, 1977, is an unparalleled study.
26. Blair, op. cit., p.171
27. Testimony of Mr. Claude Wild, head of Gulf's Government Operations Division, Watergate Hearings, Nov.14, 1973.
28. Figures are derived from *National Trade and Professional Associations of the United States*, 26th edition, Columbia Books Inc., 1991.
29. Edward S. Herman, *Corporate Control, Corporate Power*, A Twentieth Century Fund Study, Cambridge Univ. Press, 1981, p.215.
30. Hearings of the Anti-Trust Subcommittee of the Committee on Judiciary, House of Representatives, 84th Congress, 1st session, Oct.25–Dec.9, 1955, Part III, Serial No.12, p. 2174.
31. Daniel R. Fusfeld, "Joint Subsidiaries in the Iron and Steel Industry, American Economic Association *Papers and Proceedings of the Seventieth Annual Meeting* (Philadelphia, 1958) pp.5867; quoted in John R. Munkirs, *The Transformation of American Capitalism: From Competitive Market Structures to Centralized Private Sector Planning*, M.E.Sharp Inc., N.Y., 1985.
32. Reported in Edward S. Herman, *Corporate Control, Corporate Power: A Twentieth Century Fund Study*, Cambridge, 1981, pp.206–7.
33. Neale and Goyder, *The Anti-Trust Laws of the U.S.A.: A Study of Competition Enforced by Law*, 3rd ed., Cambridge, 1980, p.327.
34. Herman, op. cit., p.204.
35. Committee on Finance U.S. Senate, "The Role of Institutional Investors in the Stock Market"; Briefing Material for the Subcommittee on Financial Markets, 93rd Congress, 1st Session, July 24, 1973, Appendix C, Table 2.
36. "The C.E.D.—What is it and Why?," by Robert A. Brady, *The Antioch Review*, Spring 1944, pp.21–46.
37. *An Adaptive Program for Agriculture*, Research and Policy Committee, CED, 1962, 4th printing, 1965, p.59.
38. Perelman, Michael, *Farming for Profit in a Hungry World: Capital and the Crisis in Agriculture*, Allenheld, Osman, and Co. Publishers, Inc., N. Jersey, 1977, p.84.
39. Craig, B.H., *Chadha: The Story of an Epic Constitutional Struggle*, Oxford Univ. Press, 1988, p.40/41, citing 1975 House Committee hearings on administrative rulemaking.

40. Perelman, op. cit., Chapters 9 and 10, pp. 79–103.
41. Ibid. p.4
42. The case was *Santa Clara County vs. Southern Pacific Railroad*, 118 U.S. 394, 1886. The decision was made without hearing argument and without explanation by the Court. It was perhaps considered the most expedient thing to do at the time, since corporations were becoming increasingly important to the economy and the constitution, of course, said nothing about them.
43. Field vs. Clark, 143 U.S. 649, at 692 (1892).
44. Cf. *Chadha: The Story of an Epic Constitutional Struggle*, by Barbara H. Craig, Oxford University Press, 1988. *Immigration and Naturalization Service vs. Chadha* (1983) was the case that led to the setting aside of over 200 legislative veto provisions in Congressional statutes.
45. A. M. Honore', "Ownership," in A. G. Guest, ed., *Oxford Essays in Jurisprudence* (*First Series*), Oxford Univ. Press, 1961, pp.107–47.
46. T. H. Green, *Principles of Political Obligation*, Section 214, in *The Works of Thomas Hill Green*, ed. R. Nettleship, Vol. II, London, 1885–88, p. 335 ff.
47. One intangible that is an exception to this point would be the proprietary right in the reputation of a business.
48. Henwood, Doug, *Wallstreet*, Verso, 1997, p.12.
49. Of course a stockholder who has millions of shares and thus a controlling interest in a corporation may have a seat and/or one or more representatives on a Board. The classic study of the rise of the corporation as well as its challenge to the classical theory of private property is that of A. A. Berle and Gardiner C. Means, *The Modern Corporation and Private Property*, Macmillan, N.Y., 1934.
50. Cf. Berle and Means, op. cit., Book IV; The dissolution of private property, they wrote, "destroys the very foundation on which the economic order of the past three centuries has rested." (p.8).
51. Percentages are from "Stock Ownership Patterns, Stock Market Fluctuations, and Consumption," by James M. Poterba and Andrew A. Samwick, *Brookings Papers on Economic Activity* 2, ed. Brainard and Perry, Brookings Institution, 1995.
52. This figure is based the 1995 total for "Households" given in Henwood, op. cit. p.331, less 4% (maximum) of this total that is represented by non-profit institutions. Cf. Table F.100, Households, Personal Trusts, and Nonprofit Organizations, *Guide to the Flow of Funds Accounts*, Federal Reserve Board, 1997.
53. Gerard Colby, *Du Pont Dynasty: Behind the Nylon Curtain*, Lyle Stuart, 1984, p.30.
54. For a survey of various positions on the question, cf. Schultz, William J., *The Taxation of Inheritance*, Riverside Press, Boston, 1926, Part II, Inheritance Tax Theory.
55. Letter to James Madison, September 6, 1789; quoted by William J. Schultz, *The Taxation of Inheritance*, Riverside Press, Boston, 1926.
56. Estate of Guthman (1954), 125 C.A.2d 408, 413. And cf. U.S. vs. Perkins, 163 U.S. 628, 1896.
57. Quote marks because they are *not* more efficient in energy use, in providing wholesome and nutritious food, in preventing the pollution of ground waters and rivers, in preserving the genetic heritage, etc. Cf. Pereleman, n21.

58. J. Franklin Jameson, *The American Revolution Considered as a Social Movement*, Princeton University Press, 1926, Chapter II, and Richard B. Morris, *The American Revolution Reconsidered*, Harper and Row, 1967, pp.77–81.
59. See Part III of the International Covenant appended to this paper.
60. The day before Eleanor Roosevelt resigned, the U.S. Secretary of State—John Foster Dulles—announced that the U.S. would not sign or ratify the Covenants. President Carter signed the Covenants in 1977, and the ICCPR was ratified on June 8, 1992.
61. Resolution of the sixteenth session, 1961/61: United Nations Development Decade: A Program for international economic co-operation, *A New International Economic Order: Selected Documents 1945–75*, UNITAR, undated, Vol. II, p.831.
62. Cf. *The People vs. Global Capital: Report of the International People's Tribunal to Judge the G-7*, Tokyo, July, 1993; Pacific Asia Resource Center (PARC), Japan, 1994.
63. Instruments of categories II and III have the status of international law; those of category IV have an advisory status, as the Declaration on the Rights of Disabled Persons, or the Code of Conduct for Law Enforcement Officials.
64. Of the major human rights treaties the U.S. has ratified the Covenant on Civil and Political Rights, the Convention Against All Forms of Racial Discrimination, and the Convention Against Torture and Other Cruel, Inhuman or Degrading Treatment or Punishment. By Article VI, Section 2 of the U.S. Constitution, this law has the same status in the United States as any statute passed by Congress.
65. Human Rights: A Compilation of International Instruments, Vol. I, Universal Instruments, Parts I and II, Center for Human Rights at Geneva; United Nations., N.Y., 1993.
66. United Nations Center for Human Rights, *Manual on Human Rights Reporting*, United Nations, 1991, p.40.
67. Op.cit., p. 70,72. On the relation of U.N. agencies to the reporting process, cf. A. G. Mower, *International Co-operation for Social Justice: Global and Regional Protection of Economic and Social Rights*, Greenwood Press, 1985, Chapters 4 and 5.
68. UNCTAD I (Geneva, 1964). *Proceedings*, vol. 1: *Final Act and Report*.
69. Op. cit., Annex B: Observations of Delegations. A history of the non-aligned movement may be found in A.W. Singham and Shirley Hume, *Non-Alignment in an Age of Alignments*, Lawrence Hill and Co., 1986.
70. U.N. General Assembly, Sixth Special Session, May 1, 1974; Moss and Winton, *A New International Economic Order*, Vol. II, UNITAR, p.893.
71. Ibid., Articles I-1-(a), II-1-(b), and V-(a).
72. U.N. General Assembly, 29th Session, December 12, 1974; Moss and Winton, Ibid. p. 901–906.
73. J. Lozoya, J. Estevez, R. Green, *Alternative Views of the New International Economic Order: A Survey and Analysis of Major Academic Research Reports*, Pergamon Press, 1979, p. vii.
74. Vienna Declaration, U.N. GAOR, World Conference on Human Rights, 48th Session., U.N.Doc. A/CONF.157/24 (Part) I 1993.
75. George W. Ball, "Cosmocorp: The Importance of Being Stateless," *Atlantic Community Quarterly*, Summer, 1968, pp.163–170.
76. Much of this history may be found in *50 Years is Enough: The Case Against the World Bank and International Monetary Fund*, ed. by Kevin Danaher, South End Press, 1994. But see

also *The People vs Global Capital: The G-7, TNCs, SAPs, and Human Rights*. Report of the International People's Tribunal to Judge the G-7, Tokyo, July 1993, Pacific Asia Resource Center, 1994.

77. This is the *Multilateral Agreement on Investments* (MAI), which has been negotiated in great secrecy by the 29 richer nations that belong to the Organization for Economic Cooperation and Development (OECD). It has fortunately been exposed as of this writing (July, 1998) and has been placed on hold as a result of massive opposition.
77. "The United Nations and the Corporate Agenda," attachment to a memo by David C. Korten to the President of the U.N. General Assembly, communicated to the author via E-mail, July, 1997.

Some Legal and Moral Consequences of Philosophic Individualism

1. *The International Bill of Human Rights, United Nations*, Department of Public Information, 1985: or *Human Rights: A Compilation of International Instruments*, United Nations, 1983, E.83, XIV.1.
2. Nominalism is sometimes used to mean the view that only individual things exist, but it is more often used for other related views, as the thesis that there are no real universals. The latter view has no immediate bearing on the subject of the paper. The emergence of the thesis that only individual things exist as a strong current in European intellectual life should be credited to William of Ockham and Ockhamist movement in the 14th century. Cf. Gordon Leff, *Paris and Oxford Universities in the Thirteenth and Fourteenth Centuries*, N.Y., 1968, pp.240–255.
3. The positive/negative distinction is discussed and criticized by Henry Shue in *Basic Rights: Subsistence, Affluence, and U.S. Foreign Policy*, Princeton, 1980.
4. Cf. William James, "Philosophical Conceptions and Practical Results," A lecture in Berkeley, California, August 26, 1898; in *The Writings of William James*, ed. J. J. McDermott, N.Y., 1967, and Hans Vaihinger, *The Philosophy of `As If'*, 1877 (English translation, 1911), for the view that metaphysical concepts are mere fictions. That metaphysical propositions are meaningless was argued by Rudolph Carnap in "Ueberwindung der Metaphysik durch Logische Analyse der Sprache," *Erkenntnis*, Vol. II, 1932. That there is really nothing left for philosophers to say, see the Epilogue (1925) to *The Foundations of Mathematics and other Logical Essays* by Frank P. Ramsey, ed. by R. B. Braithwaite, Routledge, 1931.
5. Philosophic Individualism was probably firmly rooted in the sciences only after the publication of Newton's *Principia Mathematica* in 1687; for this established the awesome fact that one could explain or predict the motions of the planets knowing only a few facts about each individual planet and a simple mathematical formula.
6. This view of society is stated or presupposed by a whole series of very influential writers from the late 18th century on, as James Mill, John Stuart Mill, Adam Smith, or Jeremy Bentham. Cf. e.g., Bentham, *The Principles of Morals and Legislation*, 1789, Chapter I, section IV.

7. *Santa Clara County v. Southern Pacific*, 118 U.S. 394, 1886.
8. *Lynch v. United States*, 292 U. S. 571, 577, 1934.
9. *Walton v. Cotton*, 60 U.S. 751,754, 19 Howard 355, 1856.
10. *Goldberg, Commissioner of Social Services of the City of New York v. Kelly et al*, 397 U.S. 254 (1970). Italics by Justice Black.
11. The Social Security Act was passed August 14, 1935; it was challenged in *Steward Machine Co. v. Davis*, 301 U.S. 548 (1936) and *Helvering v. Davis*, 301 U.S. 619 (1937).
12. *Cohens v.Virginia*, 19 U.S. 264; 6 Wheaton 411–412, 1821.
13. The Judiciary Act and its amendments are located in *Statutes at Large* as follows: 1789, 1 Stat 73; 1793, 1 Stat 333; 1794, 1 Stat 395; 1801, 2 Stat 89; 1808, 2 Stat 471.
14. *United States V. Lee*, 106 U.S. 198, 1882.
15. *Gibbons v. United States*, 75 U.S. 269, 275, 1868. This case is cited in K.C. Davis, *Administrative Law*, Vol. III, West Pub. Co., 1958, Chapter 25, "Tort Liability of Governmental Units," which provides a useful account of the sovereign immunity doctrine with references.
16. John Locke, *Two Treatises of Government*, ed. P. Laslett, Cambridge, 1960, p.314.
17. Ibid., p. 306.
18. James Mill, *An Essay On Government*, ed. C. Shields, Bobbs-Merrill, 1955, p. 49.
19. Ibid., p.49.
20. Adam Smith, *An Inquiry into the Nature and Causes of the Wealth of Nations*, Vol. I, ed. Cannan, Bk.I, Ch. VI, p.54.
21. Ibid., p.54,55.
22. Ibid., p.15, and cf. p. 78.
23. Ibid., p.34.
24. Cf. the essay on the history of the right of association in this collection.
25. Cf. *Selling Our Security:The Erosion of America's Assets*, Martin and Susan Tolchin, Alfred A. Knopf, N.Y., 1992.
26. For a defense of this strong form, cf. Buchler, Justus, *The Metaphysics of Natural Complexes*, N.Y., Columbia Press, 1966; Second ed., ed. Kathleen Wallace, SUNY, 1989.
27. On the rise and hegemony of the corporation, cf. Berle, Adolf, and Means, Gardner, *The Modern Corporation and Private Property*, Columbia Univ. Press, 1934. The Employment Act of 1946, establishing the Council of Economic Advisors to the President and the Joint Economic Committee of Congress, empowered the Federal government to, among other things..." promote maximum employment, production, and purchasing power." This Act, along with the National Security Act of 1947, can be said to mark the beginning of the third phase in the evolution of the productive system, a phase in which the State not only assumes a strong role in managing the economy, but becomes indispensable in maintaining it. The first theoretical notice of this phenomenon appears to have been Eugene Varga's *Changes in the Economics of Capitalism as a Result of the Second World War*, published in 1946 in the U.S.S.R., and resulting in Varga's exile to Hungary until Stalin's death in 1953. Cf. Jaffe, Philip J., *The Rise and Fall of American Communism*, Horizon Press, 1975, Chapter III.

28. An interesting account of the struggle over the Full Employment Act of 1946 may be found in *Congress Makes a Law: The Story Behind the Employment Act of 1946*, Columbia U. Press, 1950.
29. Cf. Bonger, Willem Adriann, *Criminalite' et conditions economique*, Amsterdam, 1905.
30. Cf. M. Harvey Brenner, Division of Operations Research and Department of Behavioral Sciences, Johns Hopkins University, "The Influence of the Social Environment on Psychopathology: The Historic Perspective," in *Stress and Mental Disorder*, ed. by Jas. E. Barrett et al, Raven Press, N.Y., 1979. Also presented as testimony to the Joint Economic Committee, Ninety-Sixth Congress, First Session, October 31, 1979, *Hearings on the Social Costs of Unemployment*.
31. On the devastating consequences of the most recent episode of combating inflation by the method of raising interest rates, cf. Greider, William, *Secrets of the Temple: How the Federal Reserve Runs the Country*, Simon and Schuster, N.Y., 1987, Part I. On the first episode of the practice following World War II, cf. Bertram Gross and Wilfred Lumer, *The Hard Money Crusade*, Public Affairs Institute, 1954.
32. The rough estimate of cancers caused by social policies (and industrial civilization *per se*) as against those caused by background radiation is computed from the information in Goffman, John, *Radiation and Human Health*, Pantheon Books, 1981. (Dr. Goffman is not responsible for the computation). Background radiation (cosmic and terrestrial) produces roughly 40 to 50 thousand cancers per year, and there are over 400,000 cancer deaths per year.

The Metaphysical Basis of Racism in Western Civilization

1. On methodological individualism, cf. Brodbeck, May, "Methodological Individualisms: Definition and Reduction" *Philosophy of Science*, 25, 1958.
2. cf. *Outcasts from Evolution: Scientific Attitudes of Racial Inferiority*, 1859–1900, John S. Haller, Jr., University of Illinois Press, 1971; McGraw-Hill, 1975.
3. *Webster's Ninth New Collegiate Dictionary*, Merriam-Webster, Mass.,1988, for example, states: "1: a belief that race is the primary determinant of human traits and capacities and that racial differences produce an inherent superiority of a particular race 2: racial prejudice or discrimination."
4. Sir William Lawrence, *Lectures on Physiology, Zoology, and the Natural History of Man*, Delivered at the Royal College of Surgeons, London, 1819, pp.125, 126; quoted in Thomas F. Gossett, *Race: the History of an Idea in America*, Southern Methodist University Press, 1963; Schocken Books, N.Y., 1969, p.56.
5. Haller, *op.cit.*, p.117.
6. Cf. M.F. Ashley Montague, *Man's Most Dangerous Myth: The Fallacy of Race*, Cleveland, 1964.

   Some states in the United States classified people as Black if their ancestry was one sixteenth Black. Duvalier, Dictator of Haiti for many years, informed a reporter—much to that gentleman's surprise—that there were large numbers of Whites on the island. Why? Because in Haiti anyone who is one tenth White is classified as White.

7. *Slaughter-House Cases*, 16 Wallace 36 (1873).
8. *U.S. v. Reese*, 92 U.S. 214 (1876).
9. *Civil Rights Cases*, 103 U.S. 3,26 (1883).
10. *Ibid.*, Justice Bradley at 25.
11. *Regents of the University of California v. Bakke*, 438 U.S. 265 (1978).
12. Civil Rights Act of 1964, Title VI, Nondiscrimination in Federally Assisted Programs.
13. 18 Cal. 3d 34, 55; 553 P. 2d 1152, 1166.
14. *Regents v. Bakke*, Opinion of Justice Powell, Part V-B, apparently joined by Burger, Rehnquist, Stevens, and Stewart.
15. The Great Depression is discussed in Maurice Dobb, *Studies in the Development of Capitalism*, International Pub., 1947, rev. ed. 1963, p.300 ff.
16. "The New School of Criminal Anthropology," Robert Fletcher, M.D., *The American Anthropologist*, Vol. IV, No.3, July, 1891, p.206.
17. Galton, Francis, *Hereditary Genius: An Inquiry into its Laws and Consequences*, 1952, Horizon Press, N.Y., p.1.
18. Mark B. Adams, *The Wellborn Science*, Oxford University Press, p. 5.
19. Cf. "The Politics of Eugenics," by Alyce C. Gullattee, in *Eugenic Sterilization*, ed. J. Robitsher, 1973, Charles Thomas, Illinois.
20. *Eugenic Sterilization*, Robitsher, Appendix 1, pp.118,119.
21. *Buck v. Bell*, 274 U.S. 200 (1927).
22. Robitscher, *op. cit.*, Appendix I.
23. Gullattee, *op. cit.*, p.87.
24. One study of teaching hospitals found that over fifty percent made sterilization a requirement for performing abortions on selected women: J. Eliot, R. Hall, R. Wilson, & C. Houser, "The Obstetrician's View," in *Abortion in a Changing World*, ed. R. Hall., Columbia Univ. Press, 1970. p.93.
25. An example is Alexander Tille, deputy director of the Organization of German Industrialists in Berlin; cf. Alfred Kelly, Darwin: *The Popularization of Darwinism in Germany, 1860–1914*, University of North Carolina Press, 1981, p.107.
26. Quoted in Richard Hofstadter, *Social Darwinism in American Thought*, rev. ed., Beacon Press, 1955, p. 180.
27. John Stuart Mill, *Principles of Political Economy*, Book IV, Chapter IV, Of the Tendency of Profits to a Minimum, London, 1848.
28. Gaetano Mosca, *Elementi di scienza politica*, 1896, Engl. trans. from the ed. of 1923, McGraw-Hill, 1939; Vilfredo Pareto, "Un applicazione di teorie sociologiche," *Revista Italiana di Sociologia*, 1901, trans. as *The Ruling Class*, Bedminster, 1968.
29. Andrew Dickson White, *A History of the Warfare of Science and Theology*, Reprinted by Peter Smith, 1978, Vol. I, p.1, 2.
30. Quoted in *The Life, Letters, and Labours of Francis Galton*, by Karl Pearson, Galton Professor, University of London, Volume IIIA, Cambridge, 1930, p.91.
31. *Ibid.*, pp. 92, 93.
32. Cf. "The Race Hygiene Movement in Germany, 1904–1945" by Sheila F. Weiss, in *The Wellborn Science*, ed. Mark B. Adams, Oxford Univ. Press, 1990, p. 9.

33. Quoted in Jon M. Bridgman, *The Revolt of the Hereros*, University of California Press, 1981, p.62.
34. Haller, *op.cit.*, p.36, and Chapter I.
35. *Ibid.*, p. 63, pp. 164–168.
36. A very persuasive and non-individualistic explanation of the difference between the industrial countries of the "North" and those of the "South" has been put forward by Jared Diamond, in his *Guns, Germs, and Steel: The Fates of Human Societies*, W. W. Norton, 1997.

The Decline of the West

1. Spengler, Oswald, *Der Untergang des Abendlandes*, Vol.I, *Gestalt und Wirklichkeit*, 1918, Vol.II, *Welthistorische Perspektiven*, 1922, Munich. English translation, *The Decline of the West*, Vol.I, *Form and Actuality*, 1926, Vol. II, *Perspectives of World History*, 1928, Alfred A. Knopf, New York.

   Schweitzer, Albert, *Kulturphilosophie*, Vol.I, *Verfall und Wiederaufbau der Kultur*, 1923; Vol. II, *Kultur und Ethik*, 1923. English translation, *The Philosophy of Civilization*, Vol. I, *The Decay and the Restoration of Civilization*, 1923; Vol. II, *Civilization and Ethics*, 1923.
2. Volume II of Schweitzer's work is concerned with the history of ethical theory in the modern period. Volume III, published much later, with his own philosophy of life.
3. The eight civilizations he distinguished were Egyptian, Ancient Semitic, Indian, Chinese, Mexican, Apollinian (Greco-Roman), Magian, and Western or "Faustian." Spengler developed his own terminology, which I have avoided since it requires explanation and adds nothing of substance. One usage should, however, be mentioned. 'Culture' was used by Spengler to refer to the early creative stages of a civilization, and 'civilization' for the later declining and sterile stages, presumably because 'Kultur' has a more honorific sense than than 'Zivilisation.' I have used the two terms interchangeably. A brief but useful essay on their history and use in various languages will be found in Fernand Braudel's *A History of Civilizations*, Bk.I, Ch.I, N.Y., 1993.
4. *Decline of the West*, Vol. I, p. 21.
5. Ibid., Vol. II, p. 119.
6. Ibid., Vol. II, p. 7, p. 113, and p. 127.
7. Ibid., Vol. II, p. 114.
8. Ibid., Vol. II, p. 130, 124.
9. Ibid., Vol. I, p. 32.
10. Ibid., Vol. I, pp. 32-39; Vol. II, p.494.
11. The first printing of the *Decline* sold out and was followed by two more printings, and within eight years the work had sold a hundred thousand copies. Cf. H. Stuart Hughes, *Oswald Spengler*, Transaction Publishers, 1992, p.65, p.89 (Originally published by Charles Scribners, 1952).
12. Spengler, O., *Selected Essays*, Henry Regnery, 1967, p.3, p.57. The essay "Prussianism and Socialism" was published in Munich in 1920.

13. Ibid., p. 131. Hughes plays down Spengler's blood and soil racial theory, fastening on minor points of difference between Spengler's view and Nazi Party views, and so misses—I believe—the profound influence of the Spenglerian *Weltanschauung* in the rise of Nazism.
14. I have used the term 'racialism' here to mean the use of race as a fundamental premise on which to base explanations; while this is characteristic of Spengler's work, racism—in the sense of a theory or attitude of superiority of one race over others—is not. On the other hand, one can draw one's own conclusion regarding the outcome of a combination of racialism with advocacy of imperialism.
15. A. Schweitzer, *The Decay and the Restoration of Civilization*, 2nd ed., 1932, p.v.
16. Schweitzer, A., *Verfall und Wiederaufbau der Kultur*, Verlag C.H.Beck, Munchen, 1972, p.28. (Author's translation)
17. Schweitzer, A., *The Decay and the Restoration of Civilization*, London, 1932, pp. 24–25.
18. Much of this is in *The Decay and Restoration of Civilization*; however, Schweitzer also discusses the matter in other publications and letters. The best references are found in *The Ethical Mysticism of Albert Schweitzer* by Henry Clark, Beacon Press, 1962, Ch. 2.
19. Schweitzer, A., *The Decay and Restoration of Civilization*, London, 1932, p.4.
20. Ibid., pp.1–14.
21. John Locke, Baruch Spinoza, George Berkeley, and G.W.F.von Leibniz are philosophers who worked out or attempted to work out a consistent worldview; the Logical Positivist movement of the early 20th century probably marks the abandonment of the same as a primary concern of philosophy.
22. The last quarter of the 19th century produced a number of attacks on traditional philosophy and its metaphysics, from the camp of Neo-Kantianism (as Vaihinger's *Philosophy of As If*), Pragmatism (as William James), and Positivism (as Ernst Mach's *Analysis of Sensation*). The history of biblical criticism was explored by Schweitzer in his *Vom Reimarus zu Wrede*, 1906; English translation as *The Quest of the Historical Jesus*, 1910, London.
23. For example, the British Idealist movement produced several attempts to provide a philosophical basis for ethics: F.H. Bradley's *Ethical Studies*, 1876, or T.H.Green's *Prolegommena to Ethics*, 1883. These were followed by G.E.Moore's very narrow *Principia Ethica*, 1903, which laid the ground for the nadir of ethical studies, the Emotivist theory of the 1930's. Cf. Ayer, A., *Language, Truth, and Logic*, 1936, or Stevenson, C.L., "The Emotive Meaning of Ethical Terms," *Mind*, Vol. XLVI, 1937, pp.14-31.
24. These ideals have been actualized in the International Bill of Human Rights developed by the United Nations and coming into force as international treaty law in 1976.
25. The legal system, for example, consists of the federal and state institutions that create law, federal and state court systems and their related organizations of judges and lawyers, the federal and state correctional systems, police agencies, and so forth.
26. This is the ideology of Classical Liberalism, stemming from Adam Smith, and outlined in "Human Rights versus Classical Liberalism" in this volume.

27. An extended discussion of the transformational character of modern science and its techno-logies can be found in the posthumously published work of Robert A. Brady, *Organization, Automation, and Society*, Univ. of Calif. Press, 1961. I believe this work would be better known if it had been given the title the author intended: *The Logic of the Technological Substratum*.
28. The term 'industrialism,' going back to 1831, is defined as social organization in which industry, esp. large-scale industry is dominant. So it does not cover the institutional triad that is the core of the social system, nor does it include the associated culture. On the dynamic nature of the system, Part I of the *Communist Manifesto* is a masterpiece of description of the transformative effects of capitalism in its early stages, written before the term 'capitalism' came into use.
29. Bruno Bettleheim, "Individual and Mass Behavior in Extreme Situations," *Journal of Abnormal and Social Psychology*, 38, 4 (October, 1943).
30. I do not mean to deny, in speaking of two value systems antithetical to one another, that there are values found in both systems; loyalty may be one of these.
31. For important parts of this value system, see "Human Rights versus Classical Liberalism" in this volume.
32. Cornell University was the first secular university in the United States, and its founding in 1870 created a storm of protest.
33. See the "Right of Association" in this volume.
34. Hermann Broch, *Die Schlafwandler*, c1931/32; published as *The Sleepwalkers: A Trilogy*, trans. by W. and E. Muir, Pantheon Books, 1947. The quotation is from the sixth essay on the disintegration of values, p.445-6.
35. *Man and Technics: A Contribution to a Philosophy of Life*, Oswald Spengler, Alfred Knopf, 1932, Ch.12. p.90 ff.
36. Quoted in Patricia Hynes, *The Recurring Silent Spring*, Pergamon, 1989, p.7.
37. Cf. *Deadly Deceit: Low Level Radiation, High Level Cover-Up*, J.Gould and Benjamin Goldman, N.Y. 1990, p.96
38. An extensive account of the "peaceful" uses of nuclear explosives is in *Nuclear Dynamite: The Peaceful Nuclear Explosions Fiasco*, by Trevor Findlay, Pergamon Press, 1990.
39. Quoted in *Nuclear Dynamite: The Peaceful Nuclear Explosions Fiasco*, Trevor Findley, Pergamon Press, 1990, p.172.
40. For such people, retirement is very dangerous; it is psychologically equivalent to dying.
41. See "The Right of Association" in this volume. The political dimension of economic power is found its effect on the social system and on the governance of the same. Keep in mind that capital, at bottom, is the power to organize human labor.
42. Cf. *Networks of Power: Corporate TV's Threat to Democracy*, Dennis W. Mazzocco, South End Press, 1994. For a discussion of the role of communications monopolization on a global scale, *Communication, Commerce, and Power: The Political Economy of America and the Direct Broadcast Satellite, 1960-2000*, Edward A. Comer, St. Martin's Press, Inc., 1998.
43. On the book publishing industry, Cf. *The Business of Books: How International Conglomerates Took Over Publishing and Changed the Way We Read*, Andre' Schiffrin, Verso, 2000.

44. The Washington Post, for example, reports that Beltsville High Point high school made $72,438.53 from the Mid-Atlantic Coca Cola Bottling Co., Inc., and $26,277.49 from Monumental Vending Co. *Wash. Post*, Feb.26, 2001.
45. This is not to mention the economic assault on the family as an institution over the past 20 years, or the consequences on the family of the so-called "war" on drugs.
46. Futurologists, of course, try to guess what technologies will be developed, so as to tell us "what life will be like" in the future, if there is one.
47. "Science for Sale," David Noble, *Thought and Action:The NEA Higher Education Journal*, Vol. XVI No.2, Fall 2000, p.18,19.
48. David Dickson, *The New Politics of Science*, Pantheon, 1984, Chapters 5 and 6.
49. There is an extensive literature on cost/benefit analysis; two early critiques cited by Dickson are Ashford, Nicolas, "The Limits of Cost-Benefit Analysis in Regulatory Decision-Making," *Technology Review*, May, 1980, and Steven Kelman, "-Cost-Benefit Analysis: An Ethical Critique," *Regulation*, Jan./Feb., 1981.
50. This is the estimate of the Nuclear Regulatory Commission, Federal Register, July 30, 2001. It is undoubtedly a very conservative estimate. The present administration in Washington (Geo. W. Bush) apparently favors the recommissioning of these plants.
51. Joseph A. Tainter, *The Collapse of Complex Societies*, Cambridge Univ. Press, 1988.
52. This pattern may be aborted by the introduction of a new paradigm with a new set of general laws.
53. Tainter, op.cit., p. 101.
54. Tainter, op.cit., p. 114.
55. Tainter, op.cit., p.118/119.
56. Tainter, op.cit. p. 38.
57. Catherine Caufield's *Multiple Exposures: Chronicles of the Radiation Age*, London and New York, 1989, provides a fascinating history of these technologies.
58. Alice Stewart et al, "Preliminary Communication: Malignant Disease in Childhood, and Diagnostic Irradiation in-Utero," *Lancet* 2:447. 1956. John Gofman, *Radiation from Medical Procedures in the Pathogenesis of Cancer and Ischemic Heart Disease: Dose Response Studies with Physicians per 100,000 Population*, Committee for Nuclear Responsibility, San Francisco, 1999.
59. Quoted in John Leslie, *The End of the World: The Science and Ethics of Human Extinction*, Routledge, London, 1996, p. 123.
60. Hans Bethe noted that there could still be a danger of a chain reaction with nuclear weapons of an entirely different type, designed to produce much higher temperatures. *Bulletin of the Atomic Scientists*, June 1976, quoted in Leslie, above. Concerning the earth-eating dense matter, it has been argued by E. Farhi and R.L Jaffe that the same result could occur if there were negatively charged strange-quark matter, the which can only be shown to exist through experiment. Leslie, op.cit., p. 123–127.

Appendix I: How Democratic is the Constitution?

For Delivery To: Department of Philosophy Colloquium, San Francisco State University, San Francisco, California, November 1, 1996. (Added footnote material regarding 1996 elections and 1996–1997 Supreme Court term, 1996–1997). © 1996 Kurt Nutting; Additional material © 1997 Kurt Nutting.

1. This paper is taken from a larger work in progress, provisionally entitled ELECTORAL POLITICS AND SOCIAL JUSTICE: DEMOCRACY, THE LAW, AND AMERICAN POLITICAL PARTIES. A briefer version was presented to a colloquium of the Department of Philosophy at San Francisco State University on November 1, 1996. Some references were added or updated in November 2001. I discuss some related issues in Nutting, *Voting, Democratic Political Action, and the Public Good*, in ANATOLE ANTON, MILTON FISK, AND NANCY HOLMSTROM, EDS., NOT FOR SALE: IN DEFENSE OF PUBLIC GOODS, at 299–321 (2000). The most important legal decision over the past several years on the law of voting rights is not discussed in this paper, however. I make a few comments on the United States Supreme Court's decision in Bush v. Gore, 531 U.S. 98 (2000), focussing on their unstated presuppositions, in NUTTING, *Legal Practices and the Reason of the Law*, ARGUMENTATION (forthcoming 2002). The election, and the court judgment which decided it, was shocking on many levels. First, it was shocking that the candidate who received the highest number of votes for President was not elected (the first time this had happened since 1888, and only the fourth time in U.S. history). Second, it was shocking that the candidate who, in all probability, received the highest number of votes in one state (Florida) did not receive that state's electoral votes. Third, it was shocking that the Supreme Court should have forbidden the state of Florida from making a determination about which candidate had carried the state's vote. Fourth, it was shocking that this refusal to count several tens of thousand ballots occurred in the name of equally protecting the legal right to vote. And, fifth, it was shocking that all of this should have prompted so little outcry, and such feeble attempts to guarantee that these events never recur, by abolishing the indirect-vote arrangement of the electoral college and by reforming the mechanics of registering voters, and of casting and counting ballots.. The scholarly and journalistic literature analyzing the 2000 presidential election and Bush v. Gore is already quite extensive, a year after the decision, and will undoubtedly swell further; for a sampling, see SAMUEL ISSACHAROFF, PAMELA S. KARLAN, AND RICHARD H. PILDES, WHEN ELECTIONS GO BAD: THE LAW OF DEMOCRACY AND THE PRESIDENTIAL ELECTION OF 2000 (rev. ed. 2001) AND CASS R. SUNSTEIN AND RICHARD A. EPSTEIN, EDS., THE VOTE: BUSH, GORE, AND THE SUPREME COURT (2001).
2. The National Election Study has asked respondents in each election year from 1964 through the present whether they thought the government was run for "a few big interests" or "for all." In 1964 64% said for all, 29% said for a few big interests. In 1972 38% said for all, 53% said for a few big interests; in 1984, 39% said for all but 55% said for a few big interests. By 2000, 35% said for all, 61% said for a few big interests. See UNIVERSITY OF MICHIGAN, CENTER FOR POLITICAL STUDIES, NATIONAL ELECTION STUDY: GUIDE TO PUBLIC OPINION AND ELECTORAL BEHAVIOR 1952–2000, at Table 5A.2 (computer file September 3, 2001, accessed on the

Internet November 2, 2001 at <http://www.umich.edu/~nes/nesguide/toptable>).

3. See, e.g., LAURENCE H. TRIBE, AMERICAN CONSTITUTIONAL LAW § 13–20, at 1106 (2d ed. 1988): "as a pronouncement of doctrine under the equal protection clause, [the result of the decisions in the ballot access cases] is positively delphic."
4. For a summary of this debate, see "The Paradox of Voting," in DENNIS C. MUELLER, PUBLIC CHOICE II: A REVISED EDITION OF PUBLIC CHOICE, at 348–369 (1989).
5. Various alleged inconsistencies are raised in, e.g., Richard Wollheim, *A Paradox in the Theory of Democracy*, in PETER LASLETT AND W. G. RUNCIMAN, EDS., PHILOSOPHY, POLITICS AND SOCIETY (SECOND SERIES), at 71–87 (1962); and KENNETH J. ARROW, SOCIAL CHOICE AND INDIVIDUAL VALUES (Cowles Foundations for Research in Economics at Yale University Monograph 12; 2nd ed. 1963; originally published 1951).
6. A venerable radical anarchist tradition, of which in the United States the Wobblies have perhaps been the most prominent exponents, has dismissed the potential of electoral and legislative action. If voting could change anything, it is sometimes argued, it would be illegal. One of the conclusions of this paper is that this conditional comes uncomfortably close to the truth, though not in the way the Wobblies have believed; because voting *can* change things, it has in fact been very tightly confined by the law, if not made outright illegal. See the comment by one Wobbly, Father Thomas J. Hagerty, who said at the organizing convention of the I.W.W. in 1905, "The ballot box is simply a capitalist concession. Dropping pieces of paper into a hole in a box never did achieve emancipation of the working class, and in my opinion it never will," quoted in JOYCE L. KORNBLUH, ED., REBEL VOICES: AN I.W.W. ANTHOLOGY at 12 (1964); and MELVYN DUBOFSKY, WE SHALL BE ALL: A HISTORY OF THE INDUSTRIAL WORKERS OF THE WORLD at 83 (2nd ed. 1988). See also the discussions of nonelectoral democracy in the works cited *infra*, at note 15. Nothing said here is meant to imply that nonelectoral and nonparliamentary politics is unimportant, or even necessarily less important than electoral; only that electoral politics is important and (incidentally) that it is as philosophically complex as such forms of nonelectoral politics as (say) civil disobedience.
7. For example, in the leading case of Capen v. Foster, 29 Mass. (12 Pickering) 485, 23 Am. Dec. 632 (1832), a requirement that otherwise-eligible electors be registered before they are allowed to vote was held to be a reasonable regulation of the electoral process and not an additional qualification for voting. In other states, however, requirements that voters register in advance of the election were held to be unconstitutional abridgments or impairments of the right to vote. See, e.g., Page v. Allen, 58 Pa. (8 Smith) 338 (1868), and Daggett v. Hudson, 3 N.E. 538, 43 Ohio St. 548 (1885). For relevant textual provisions, compare PA. CONST., art. III, § 1 (1838), under which Page v. Allen was decided, and PA. CONST., art. VIII, § 1 (1873), with PA. CONST., art. VIII, § 1 (amendment adopted November 5, 1901, specifically authorizing the legislature to enact voter registration laws as a precondition for voting); the texts are reprinted in FRANCIS NEWTON THORPE, COMP. AND ED., 5 THE FEDERAL AND STATE CONSTITUTIONS, COLONIAL CHARTERS, AND OTHER ORGANIC LAWS OF THE STATES, TERRITORIES, AND COLONIES NOW OR HERETOFORE FORMING THE UNITED STATES OF AMERICA, at 3108, 3138, and 3152 (H. Doc. 357, 59th Cong., 2d

Sess., 1909). More recent cases upholding registration requirements include Blue v. State ex rel. Brown, 206 Ind. 98, 188 N.E. 583 (1934) and Beare v. Briscoe, 498 F.2d 244 (5th Cir. 1974). The still-standard account of the history of voter registration in the United States is in JOSEPH P. HARRIS, REGISTRATION OF VOTERS IN THE UNITED STATES (Institute for Government Research Studies in Administration, 1929); this research was the basis for NATIONAL MUNICIPAL LEAGUE, THE COMMITTEE ON A MODEL VOTER REGISTRATION SYSTEM, MODEL VOTER REGISTRATION SYSTEM (4th ed. 1954; 1st ed. 1927). Much of this history has now been told by ALEXANDER KEYSSAR, THE RIGHT TO VOTE: THE CONTESTED HISTORY OF DEMOCRACY IN THE UNITED STATES (2000). Most states put the burden of registering to vote on the voter, whereas in most other advanced democracies the burden of assembling a list of the eligible voters is on the election authorities. See RICHARD J. CARLSON, VOTER REGISTRATION SYSTEMS IN CANADA AND WESTERN EUROPE (1974). The claim that voter registration laws do in fact inhibit voting, and do so in a way that has a much greater impact on those of lower socio-economic class and on members of racial minorities, has been argued vigorously in the past thirty years. Some authorities believe this was one of the central motivations behind the passage of such laws. For empirical evidence on the effects of voter registration laws, see, e.g., Kelley, Ayres, and Bowen, *Registration and Voting: Putting First Things First*, 61 *Amer. Pol. Sci. Rev.* 359 (1967); RAYMOND E. WOLFINGER AND STEVEN J. ROSENSTONE, WHO VOTES? (1980); Erikson, *Why Do People Vote? Because They Are Registered*, 9 AMER. POL. Q. 259 (1981); for a summary as well as a discussion of the "original intent," see FRANCES FOX PIVEN AND RICHARD A. CLOWARD, WHY AMERICANS DON'T VOTE (1989), updated as *Why Americans Still Don't Vote: And Why Politicians Want It That Way* (2000). A constitutional challenge to restrictive voter registration laws based on such findings is offered in James, *Voter Registration: A Restriction on the Fundamental Right to Vote*, 96 YALE L.J. 1615 (1987); see also Quinlivan, *One Person, One Vote Revisited: The Impending Necessity of Judicial Intervention in the Realm of Voter Registration*, 137 U. PENN. L. REV. 2361 (1989). In 1993 Congress adopted a scheme for more uniform voter registration procedures nationwide, effective no later than January 1, 1996; see the provisions of the National Voter Registration Act of 1993, Pub.L. 103–31, 107 Stat. 77, now codified at 42 U.S.C. § 1973gg *et seq.*, constitutionality upheld in Association of Community Organizations for Reform Now v. Edgar, 56 F.3d 791 (7th Cir. 1995), and Voting Rights Coalition v. Wilson, 60 F.3d 1411 (9th Cir. 1995). The 1993 statute, so-called "motor voter" because it mandated voter registration through such state agencies as motor vehicle departments, aimed at making it easier for people to register, but it did not eliminate any state requirement for registration prior to election day. It is perhaps worthy of note that the NVRA was enacted only after a prolonged struggle in the U.S. Congress to ease voter registration requirements nationwide, lasting from 1970 until 1993. It had been the target of four filibusters in the U.S. Senate, and once was passed by both houses of Congress only to be vetoed by the president. Probably the key events precipitating national interest in reform of the registration laws were the publication of the REPORT OF THE PRESIDENT'S COMMISSION ON REGISTRATION AND VOTING (Scammon Commission Report) (November 1963) and two reports of the DEMOCRATIC NATIONAL

COMMITTEE, FREEDOM TO VOTE TASK FORCE, THAT ALL MAY VOTE (1969), and REGISTRATION AND VOTING IN THE STATES (1970) (Clark task force reports). For details of the progress of the federal legislation to final passage, see CONGRESSIONAL QUARTERLY, 3 CONGRESS AND THE NATION: 1969–1972, at 1006 (1973); 4 CONGRESS AND THE NATION: 1973–1976, at 986, 1000–1001 (1977); 5 CONGRESS AND THE NATION: 1977–1980, at 940–941 (1981); 8 CONGRESS AND THE NATION: 1989–1992, at 871, 893–894 (1993); and 9 CONGRESS AND THE NATION: 1993–1996, at 804, 807–809 (1997). Its operation is discussed in FEDERAL ELECTION COMMISSION, THE IMPACT OF THE NATIONAL VOTER REGISTRATION ACT OF 1993 ON THE ADMINISTRATION OF ELECTIONS FOR FEDERAL OFFICE (biennial, 1995–present).

8. Compare the discussion of the influence of wealth on electoral politics in Ex parte Yarbrough (The Ku-Klux Cases), 110 U.S. 651, 4 S.Ct. 152 at 159–160 (1884), with the discussion in Buckley v. Valeo, 424 U.S. 1, esp. at 25–30 (1976).
9. The leading case on access to the general-election ballot is Williams v. Rhodes, 393 U.S. 23 (1968). See also Jenness v. Fortson, 403 U.S. 431 (1971); Storer v. Brown, 415 U.S. 724 (1974); Anderson v. Celebrezze, 460 U.S. 780 (1983); Munro v. Socialist Workers Party, 479 U.S. 189 (1986); and Norman v. Reed, 502 U.S. 279 (1992).
10. See United Jewish Organizations of Williamsburgh v. Carey, 430 U.S. 144 (1977); Reno v. Shaw, 509 U.S. 630 (1993) (Shaw I); Miller v. Johnson, 515 U.S. 900 (1995); Shaw v. Hunt, 517 U.S. 899 (1996) (Shaw II); Bush v. Vera, 517 U.S. 952 (1996); Abrams v. Johnson, 521 U.S. 74 (1997); Hunt v. Cromartie, 526 U.S. 541 (1999) (Cromartie I); and Hunt v. Cromartie, 532 U.S. 234 (2001) (Cromartie II).
11. That legal decisions should be (though are not always) derived from "neutral" principles of law is the claim of Wechsler, *Toward Neutral Principles of Constitutional Law*, 73 Harv. L. Rev. 1 (1959). The view that the correct interpretation of a legal text requires that it be seen as maximally consistent with the best theory of political morality is defended in the essays of RONALD DWORKIN, TAKING RIGHTS SERIOUSLY (1978) and DWORKIN, A MATTER OF PRINCIPLE (1985). The view that American law contains an irreducibly ideological component is prominent in the writings of proponents of the critical legal studies movement. On CLS, see, e.g., ALLAN C. HUTCHINSON, ED., CRITICAL LEGAL STUDIES (1989); MARK KELMAN, A GUIDE TO CRITICAL LEGAL STUDIES (1987); ROBERTO MANGABEIRA UNGER, THE CRITICAL LEGAL STUDIES MOVEMENT (1986); *DAVID KAIRYS, ED.*, THE POLITICS OF LAW: *A PROGRESSIVE* CRITIQUE (3rd ed. 1998); but cf. ANDREW ALTMAN, CRITICAL LEGAL STUDIES: A LIBERAL CRITIQUE (1990). Accounts of American constitutional law from a critical perspective are offered by MARK TUSHNET, RED, WHITE, AND BLUE: A CRITICAL ANALYSIS OF CONSTITUTIONAL LAW (1988), and DAVID KAIRYS, WITH LIBERTY AND JUSTICE FOR SOME: A CRITIQUE OF THE CONSERVATIVE SUPREME COURT (1993). Both proponents and opponents are represented in *Critical Legal Studies Symposium*, 36 STAN. L. REV. 1 (1984).
12. Buckley v. Valeo, *supra* note 8.
13. By a wide margin, respondents to the National Election Study surveys say that elections make the government pay attention to what people think. (In 2000, 44% said elections make the government pay attention "a good deal," while 13% said

elections made the government pay attention "not much." In 1964, these figures were, respectively, 65 and 7%.) See NATIONAL ELECTION STUDY, GUIDE TO PUBLIC OPINION AND ELECTORAL BEHAVIOR 1952–2000, *supra* note 2, at Tables 5C.2, 5C.2.1.

There is a fair amount of difference between people on racial and class lines; whites are more optimistic about the role of elections than are blacks, and greater levels of optimism are generally correlated with higher socioeconomic status. See NATIONAL ELECTION STUDY: GUIDE TO PUBLIC OPINION AND ELECTORAL BEHAVIOR 1952–2000, *supra* note 2, at Tables 5C.2, 5C.2.1.

14. It should go without saying that this carries with it no suggestion that any particular government is in fact genuinely representative in the appropriate sense. Clearly, not all elected governments are under the electorate's control in any meaningful sense of the word. The present discussion is at the level of the theory of the ideal type, which I briefly sketch before applying it to particular electoral systems in order to construct a critique.

15. As noted earlier, *supra* note 6, there is a long-standing non-electoral tradition in democratic thought, going back to the Greeks. From the time of classical Athens until at least the late eighteenth century direct democracy was thought to be the most authentic variety of democracy. Aristotle, for example, remarks that "the appointment of magistrates by lot is thought to be democratic, and the election of them oligarchic." ARISTOTLE, THE POLITICS, at 1294b7–9 (Book IV, ch. 9) (*Cambridge Texts in the History of Political Thought*, J. Barnes trans., S. Everson ed. 1988; orig. written c. 335–322 B.C.) The Athenian assembly, the *ecclêsia*, was open to all adult male Athenians. Non-electoral arrangements short of universal participatory democracy also date back at least to fifth-century Athens; the Athenian Council of Five Hundred, the *boulê*, which served as a sort of agenda-setting executive committee for the assembly, was chosen by lot rather than by election, for example. And juries, noted by the Athenians and by Tocqueville to be the democratic element in a judicial system otherwise dominated by a legal elite, are in the United States to this day chosen from a pool assembled by a random process. See, on the Athenian assembly and council, R. K. SINCLAIR, DEMOCRACY AND PARTICIPATION IN ATHENS 17–23, 65–73 (1988); DAVID STOCKTON, THE CLASSICAL ATHENIAN DEMOCRACY 26–29 (1990); on the selection of Athenian jurors by lot, see MOGENS HERMAN HANSEN, THE ATHENIAN DEMOCRACY IN THE AGE OF DEMOSTHENES: STRUCTURE, PRINCIPLES, AND IDEOLOGY, at 97 (J. A. Crook trans., 1991); on the nineteenth-century American jury, see Alexis de Tocqueville, *1 Democracy in America* 280–287 (P. Bradley ed. 1945; originally published 1835–1840). A brief defense of selection of public officials by lot rather than by election is given in ANDREW LEVINE, THE GENERAL WILL: ROUSSEAU, MARX, COMMUNISM, at 98–99 (1993) [**xxx** to the Social Contract, & to some con law authority on the jury panel]

16. By "control" of the government is meant, at least, that the government's actions and inactions more-or-less systematically *correspond* to popular judgments about policy and administration *because* those are the popular judgments.

17. South v. Peters, 339 U.S. 276 at 279 (1950) (Justice Douglas, dissenting), cited in Reynolds v. Sims, 377 U.S. 533, at 555–556, n. 29 (1964).

18. As the Supreme Court said, approvingly citing the words of the Voting Rights Act, "voting includes 'all action necessary to make a vote effective.' " See Allen v. State Board of Elections, 393 U.S. 544 (1969), citing the Voting Rights Act of 1965, Pub. L. 89–110, tit. I, § 14, 79 Stat. 445, current version codified at 42 U.S.C. § 1973l (c) (1) (1993).
19. That the protection of political speech is at the core of the free-speech and free-press clauses of the First Amendment is the argument given its classical form in Meiklejohn, *Free Speech and Its Relation to Self-Government*, a 1948 essay reprinted in ALEXANDER MEIKLEJOHN, POLITICAL FREEDOM: THE CONSTITUTIONAL POWERS OF THE PEOPLE at 1–89 (1960). See also New York Times Co. v. Sullivan, 376 U.S. 254, esp. at 269, 273 (1964); Kalven, *The New York Times Case: A Note on "The Central Meaning of the First Amendment,"* 1964 THE SUPREME COURT REVIEW 191 (P. Kurland ed.); and (by the author of the Times v. Sullivan opinion) Brennan, *The Supreme Court and the Meiklejohn Interpretation of the First Amendment*, 79 Harv. L. Rev. 1 (1965). An understanding of the relation between the broadcast media and the First Amendment focusing more on the deliberative interests of the audience than on the financial or expressive interests of news media owners can be found in Red Lion Broadcasting Co. v. Federal Communications Commission, 395 U.S. 367 (1969), although the reach of this view was limited in such cases as Columbia Broadcasting System, Inc. v. Democratic National Committee, 412 U.S. 94 (1973). The focus on political speech and deliberation is also prominent in, for example, the concurrence by Justice Brandeis in Whitney v. California, 274 U.S. 357 (1927).
20. The emphasis on deliberation as a part of democratic and republican institutions has a very long pedigree, going back to the Greeks and to the republican theorists of the Italian renaissance as well as to the theorists of classical liberalism. A summary account of the functioning of the *ecclêsia*, the assembly of the Athenian *polis* under the democracy, is in STOCKTON, *supra* note 15, at 67–84. HANNAH ARENDT, THE HUMAN CONDITION at 26 (1958) emphasizes the role of discussion in the Greek *polis* and in the political thought deriving from it: "To be political, to live in a *polis*, meant that everything was decided through words and persuasion and not through force and violence." For the classic texts which have inspired recent thought on this matter, see especially the following: Pericles, *Pericles' Funeral Speech*, quoted in THUCYDIDES, HISTORY OF THE PELOPONNESIAN WAR, at 115–123 (Bk. II, ch. 4) (Penguin Classics; R. Warner trans. 1954; oration originally delivered c. 430 B.C.; history originally written c. 400 B.C.); ARISTOTLE, THE POLITICS, *supra* note 15, esp. at 1297b16–1299a2 (Bk. IV, ch. XIV); NICCOLÒ MACHIAVELLI, DISCOURSES ON THE FIRST TEN BOOKS OF TITUS LIVIUS, in THE PRINCE AND THE DISCOURSES, esp. at 258–266 (Bk. I, chs. LVII-LVIII) (Modern Library; C. Detmold trans. 1950; originally completed c. 1517); JOHN LOCKE, THE SECOND TREATISE OF GOVERNMENT: AN ESSAY CONCERNING THE TRUE ORIGINAL , EXTENT, AND END OF CIVIL GOVERNMENT, Book II of TWO TREATISES OF GOVERNMENT, esp. at 371–372 (ch. XIII, § 156) (Cambridge Texts in the History of Political Thought; P. Laslett ed. 1988; originally published 1690); DAVID HUME, *Of the Liberty of the Press*, in POLITICAL ESSAYS, at 3–7 (The Library of Liberal Arts; C. Hendel ed. 1953; originally published 1752); JEAN-JACQUES ROUSSEAU, ON SOCIAL CONTRACT OR PRINCIPLES OF POLITICAL RIGHT, in ROUSSEAU'S

POLITICAL WRITINGS: DISCOURSE ON INEQUALITY, DISCOURSE ON POLITICAL ECONOMY, ON SOCIAL CONTRACT (Norton Critical Editions in the History of Ideas; J. Bondanella trans., A. Ritter and J. Bondanella eds. 1988; originally published 1762); IMMANUEL KANT, THE METAPHYSICS OF MORALS, Part I: THE METAPHYSICAL ELEMENTS OF JUSTICE (The Library of Liberal Arts; J. Ladd trans. 1965; originally published 1797); TOCQUEVILLE, DEMOCRACY IN AMERICA, *supra* note 15; KARL MARX, CRITIQUE OF HEGEL'S DOCTRINE OF THE STATE, in EARLY WRITINGS, esp. at 185–194 (The Marx Library; R. Livingstone and G. Benton trans. 1975; originally written 1843); and JOHN STUART MILL, ON LIBERTY (Hackett Classics; E. Rapaport ed. 1978; originally published 1859). Some more recent discussions of deliberation and its role in democratic governance, out of a rapidly expanding literature, are in Bessette, *Deliberative Democracy: The Majority Principle in Republican Government*, in HOW DEMOCRATIC IS THE CONSTITUTION? at 102–116 (American Enterprise Institute Studies No. 294; R. Goldwin and W. Schambra eds. 1980); Elster, *The market and the forum: three varieties of political theory*, in FOUNDATIONS OF SOCIAL CHOICE THEORY at 103–132 (Studies in Rationality and Social Change series; J. Elster and A. Hylland eds. 1986); Manin, *On Legitimacy and Political Deliberation*, 15 POL. THEORY 338 (1987); Cohen, *Deliberation and Democratic Legitimacy*, in THE GOOD POLITY: NORMATIVE ANALYSIS OF THE STATE (A. Hamlin and P. Pettit eds., 1989); JAMES S. FISHKIN, DEMOCRACY AND DELIBERATION: NEW DIRECTIONS FOR DEMOCRATIC REFORM (1991); Miller, *Deliberative Democracy and Social Choice*, 40 POL. STUDS. 54 (1992); Estlund, *Making truth safe for democracy*, and Copp, *Could political truth be a hazard for democracy?* in THE IDEA OF DEMOCRACY, at 71–117 (D. Copp, J. Hampton, and J. Roemer eds. 1993); Estlund, *Who's Afraid of Deliberative Democracy? On the Strategic/Deliberative Dichotomy in Recent Constitutional Jurisprudence*, 71 TEX. L. REV. 1437 (1993); Galston, *Taking Aristotle Seriously: Republican-Oriented Legal Theory and the Moral Foundation of Deliberative Democracy*, 82 CALIF. L. REV. 329 (1994); JOSEPH M. BESSETTE, THE MILD VOICE OF REASON: DELIBERATIVE DEMOCRACY AND AMERICAN NATIONAL GOVERNMENT (American Politics and Political Economy Series 1994); AMY GUTMANN AND DENNIS THOMPSON, DEMOCRACY AND DISAGREEMENT (1996); and MICHAEL J. SANDEL, DEMOCRACY'S DISCONTENT: AMERICA IN SEARCH OF A PUBLIC PHILOSOPHY (1996). At a philosophical level this literature implicitly owes much to the writings of two philosophers, an American liberal, JOHN RAWLS, A THEORY OF JUSTICE (1971), and POLITICAL LIBERALISM (1993), and see also the early *Outline of a Decision Procedure for Ethics*, 50 PHIL. REV. 177 (1951); and a German Marxist, JÜRGEN HABERMAS, LEGITIMATION CRISIS (orig. German ed. 1973; T. McCarthy trans. 1975), MORAL CONSCIOUSNESS AND COMMUNICATIVE ACTION (orig. German ed. 1983; C. Lenhardt and S. Nicholsen trans. 1990), THE STRUCTURAL TRANSFORMATION OF THE PUBLIC SPHERE: AN INQUIRY INTO A CATEGORY OF BOURGEOIS SOCIETY (orig. German ed. 1962; T. Burger and F. Lawrence trans. 1989), JUSTIFICATION AND APPLICATION: REMARKS ON DISCOURSE ETHICS (orig. German ed. 1991; C. Cronin trans. 1993), and BETWEEN FACTS AND NORMS: CONTRIBUTIONS TO A DISCOURSE THEORY OF LAW AND DEMOCRACY (orig. German ed. 1992; Studies in Contemporary German Social Thought series, W. Rehg trans. 1996). Habermas' work on this topic is discussed in, e.g., SEYLA BENHABIB AND FRED DALLMAYR, EDS., THE COMMUNICATIVE ETHICS CONTROVERSY (Studies in Contemporary German Social Thought Series 1990), and

CRAIG CALHOUN, ED., HABERMAS AND THE PUBLIC SPHERE (Studies in Contemporary German Social Thought Series 1992). Discussions of Rawls's most recent work, in which the notion of "public reason" plays a central role, are in *Symposium on John Rawls*, 105 ETHICS 4 (1994) and *Symposium on Political Liberalism*, 94 COLUM. L. REV. 1813 (1994). Rawls and Habermas discuss the relations between their respective projects in Habermas, *Reconciliation through the Public Use of Reason: Remarks on John Rawls's Political Liberalism*, 92 J. PHIL. 109 (1995), and Rawls, *Reply to Habermas*, 92 J. PHIL. 132 (1995). The current understanding of "deliberative" democracy has also taken much from the traditions of civic republicanism, communitarianism, and participatory democracy in political theory and in the history of political practice, but the recent theorists of deliberative democracy have tended to emphasize the epistemic and legitimating functions of deliberation rather than the self-development emphasis found in much of the participation literature. On participatory democracy, as so construed, see especially THOMAS JEFFERSON, *Letter to Samuel Kercheval* (July 12, 1816), in THE PORTABLE THOMAS JEFFERSON, at 552–561 (Viking Portable Library; M. Peterson ed. 1975); JOHN STUART MILL, CONSIDERATIONS ON REPRESENTATIVE GOVERNMENT, at 4–74 (ch. III) (Gateway ed. 1962; originally published 1861); KARL MARX, THE CIVIL WAR IN FRANCE: ADDRESS OF THE GENERAL COUNCIL, in 3 POLITICAL WRITINGS: THE FIRST INTERNATIONAL AND AFTER, esp. at 208–218 (The Marx Library; D. Fernbach ed. 1974; originally published 1871); JOHN DEWEY, THE PUBLIC AND ITS PROBLEMS, esp. at 206–210 (1927); STUDENTS FOR A DEMOCRATIC SOCIETY, THE PORT HURON STATEMENT, excerpted in THE NEW LEFT: A DOCUMENTARY HISTORY, at 163–182 (M. Teodori ed. 1969; originally published 1962); ARNOLD S. KAUFMAN, THE RADICAL LIBERAL—THE NEW POLITICS: THEORY AND PRACTICE, at 56–75 (ch. 5) (1968); ROBERT A. DAHL, AFTER THE REVOLUTION? AUTHORITY IN A GOOD SOCIETY (1970); CAROLE PATEMAN, PARTICIPATION AND DEMOCRATIC THEORY (1970); C.B. MACPHERSON, THE LIFE AND TIMES OF LIBERAL DEMOCRACY, esp. at 93–115 (ch. V) (1977); JANE J. MANSBRIDGE, BEYOND ADVERSARY DEMOCRACY (1980); and ROBERT A. DAHL, DILEMMAS OF PLURALIST DEMOCRACY: AUTONOMY VS. CONTROL (Yale Studies in Political Science No. 31, 1982). The participatory democracy literature overlaps substantially with the related literature, mainly from anarchist and socialist sources, about employee control of workplaces, economic democracy, and market socialism. See, e.g., TERRENCE E. COOK AND PATRICK M. MORGAN, EDS. PARTICIPATORY DEMOCRACY (1971); C. GEORGE BENELLO AND DIMITRIOS ROUSSOPOULOS, EDS., THE CASE FOR PARTICIPATORY DEMOCRACY: SOME PROSPECTS FOR RADICAL DEMOCRACY (1971); GERRY HUNNIUS, G. DAVID GARSON, AND JOHN CASE, EDS., WORKERS' CONTROL: A READER ON LABOR AND SOCIAL CHANGE (1973); JAROSLAV VANEK, ED., SELF-MANAGEMENT: ECONOMIC LIBERATION OF MAN (Penguin Modern Economics Readings 1975); ROBERT A. DAHL, A PREFACE TO ECONOMIC DEMOCRACY (1985); JULIAN LE GRAND AND SAUL ESTRIN, EDS., MARKET SOCIALISM (1989); Bowles and Gintis, *A political and economic case for the democratic enterprise*, in THE IDEA OF DEMOCRACY, *supra*, at 375–399. A literature in philosophy, political science, and sociology calling itself "communitarian," and inspired in part by Aristotle and the Italian republicans, as well as Hegel, denying the sort of atomistic individualism which is often said to lie at the heart of liberal political theory, is represented by such works as MICHAEL J. SANDEL, LIBERALISM AND THE LIMITS OF

JUSTICE (1982) and ROBERT N. BELLAH, RICHARD MADSEN, WILLIAM M. SULLIVAN, ANN SWIDLER, AND STEVEN M. TIPTON, HABITS OF THE HEART: INDIVIDUALISM AND COMMITMENT IN AMERICAN LIFE (1985); discussions are in, e.g., MICHAEL J. SANDEL, ED., LIBERALISM AND ITS CRITICS (Readings in Social and Political Theory series 1984), and DAVID RASMUSSEN, ED., UNIVERSALISM VS. COMMUNITARIANISM: CONTEMPORARY DEBATES IN ETHICS (1990). The analysis of the individualism of liberal and liberal democratic political theory is found in C. B. MACPHERSON, THE POLITICAL THEORY OF POSSESSIVE INDIVIDUALISM: HOBBES TO LOCKE (1962). Recent historical work on republicanism includes especially BERNARD BAILYN, THE IDEOLOGICAL ORIGINS OF THE AMERICAN REVOLUTION (1967); GORDON S. WOOD, THE CREATION OF THE AMERICAN REPUBLIC, 1776–1787 (1969); J.G.A. POCOCK, THE MACHIAVELLIAN MOMENT: FLORENTINE POLITICAL THOUGHT AND THE ATLANTIC REPUBLICAN TRADITION (1975); and EDMUND S. MORGAN, INVENTING THE PEOPLE: THE RISE OF POPULAR SOVEREIGNTY IN ENGLAND AND AMERICA (1988). Republicanism has enjoyed something of a revival in the world of legal scholarship in recent years as well. See, e.g. (in a large and growing literature), Michelman, *The Supreme Court, 1985 Term—Foreward: Traces of Self-Government*, 100 HARV. L. REV. 4 (1986); *Symposium: The Republican Civic Tradition*, 97 YALE L. J. 1493 (1988); CASS R. SUNSTEIN, THE PARTIAL CONSTITUTION (1993).

21. As a matter of law, the deliberative aspect of electoral politics is acknowledged in, e.g., Buckley v. Valeo, *supra* note 8, 424 U.S. at 92–93, and Illinois State Board of Elections v. Socialist Workers Party, 440 U.S. 173, 186 (1979) ("an election campaign is a means of disseminating ideas as well as attaining political office").

22. The emphasis on permanent competition among self-interested individuals as a crucial element in maintaining the institutions of a republic goes at least as far back as 1788, to Madison's famous discussion of factions. See especially THE FEDERALIST No. 10 (J. Madison). It is not clear, however, that Madison had in mind *electoral* competition *within* districts, as opposed to competition within legislative assemblies. The classic works using the model of individually self-interested market behavior developed in economic theory to explain features of political behavior include: JOSEPH A. SCHUMPETER, CAPITALISM, SOCIALISM AND DEMOCRACY, at 269–283 (3d ed. 1950); ARROW, SOCIAL CHOICE AND INDIVIDUAL VALUES, *supra* note 5; DUNCAN BLACK, THE THEORY OF COMMITTEES AND ELECTIONS (1958); ANTHONY DOWNS, AN ECONOMIC THEORY OF DEMOCRACY (1957); and MANCUR OLSON, THE LOGIC OF COLLECTIVE ACTION: PUBLIC GOODS AND THE THEORY OF GROUPS (Harvard Economic Studies No. 124; 2nd ed. 1971). A brief summary of Downs' work was first published in ANTHONY DOWNS, *An Economic Theory of Political Action in a Democracy*, 55 J. POL. ECON. 135 (1957). In contrast to the deliberative democracy literature, in which the voters' processes of forming judgments are given central place, the public-choice literature, like the neoclassical microeconomic literature from which it derives, generally understands voting, like other acts of choice, as an expression of exogenously given and unchanging preferences about which nothing further can be said. See, e.g., ROBIN FARQUHARSON, THEORY OF VOTING, at 6 (1969); MICHAEL DUMMETT, VOTING PROCEDURES, at 31–32 (1984); such views are criticized in DAVID M. ESTLUND, THE THEORETICAL INTERPRETATION OF VOTING (unpublished Ph.D. dissertation, Department of Philosophy, University of Wisconsin—Madison, 1986). An

extremely useful work connecting the literature of deliberation with that of economic competition is ALBERT O. HIRSCHMAN, EXIT, VOICE, AND LOYALTY: RESPONSES TO DECLINE IN FIRMS, ORGANIZATIONS, AND STATES (1970), which offers the classic discussion of "voice" in institutions as contrasted with "exit."

23. "Competition in ideas and governmental policies is at the core of our electoral processes and of the First Amendment freedoms." Williams v. Rhodes, *supra* note 9, 393 U.S. at 32. As a matter of law, the competitive struggle aspect of electoral politics is also emphasized in such cases as Storer v. Brown, *supra* note 9, 415 U.S., esp. at 735, Davis v. Bandemer, 478 U.S. 109 (1986), and Burdick v. Takashi, 504 U.S. 428 (1992).
24. Empirical examinations of the determinants of political participation are in, e.g., LESTER W. MILBRATH AND M. L. GOEL, POLITICAL PARTICIPATION: HOW AND WHY DO PEOPLE GET INVOLVED IN POLITICS? (2nd ed. 1977), and in STEVEN J. ROSENSTONE AND JOHN MARK HANSEN, MOBILIZATION, PARTICIPATION, AND DEMOCRACY IN AMERICA (New Topics in Politics Series 1993).
25. The social contract tradition is given its classic formulations in LOCKE, THE SECOND TREATISE OF GOVERNMENT, *supra* note 20; JEAN-JACQUES ROUSSEAU, ON SOCIAL CONTRACT, *supra* note 20; and IMMANUEL KANT, THE METAPHYSICS OF MORALS, Part I, *supra* note 20. The modern exposition of the social contract is, of course, in JOHN RAWLS, A THEORY OF JUSTICE, *supra* note 20. See also JOSEPH TUSSMAN, OBLIGATION AND THE BODY POLITIC (1960); MICHAEL WALZER, OBLIGATIONS: ESSAYS ON DISOBEDIENCE, WAR, AND CITIZENSHIP (1970); and Pitkin, *Obligation and Consent*, in PETER LASLETT, W. G. RUNCIMAN, AND QUENTIN SKINNER, EDS., PHILOSOPHY, POLITICS AND SOCIETY (FOURTH SERIES) at 45–85 (1972). For the social and intellectual background of consent theory, see, e.g., GEORGE H. SABINE, A HISTORY OF POLITICAL THEORY (3rd ed. 1961).
26. The legitimizing aspects of electoral politics are emphasized in the reapportionment cases, such as Wesberry v. Sanders, 376 U.S. 1, at 17–18 (1964), and Reynolds v. Sims, *supra* note 17, 377 U.S. at 555, 562 (1964). The need to avoid corruption and to assure the integrity of the government, which are presumably closely connected to political legitimacy, is acknowledged in Buckley v. Valeo, *supra* note 8. And, of course, see the Declaration of Independence (1776).
27. As George Marshall, army chief of staff during World War II, said, admiringly, of Franklin Roosevelt, "the leader in a democracy has to keep the people entertained." Quoted in ERIC LARRABEE, COMMANDER IN CHIEF: FRANKLIN DELANO ROOSEVELT, HIS LIEUTENANTS, AND THEIR WAR, at 9 (1987).
28. See Fiorina, *The Voting Decision: Instrumental and Expressive Aspects*, 38 J. POL. 390 (1976); and see also Note, *Expressive Voting*, 68 N.Y.U.L. REV. 330 (1993).
29. As a matter of law, the expressive aspects of the vote are acknowledged in, e.g., Socialist Labor Party v. Rhodes, 290 F. Supp. 983 (S.D. Ohio 1968), *modified and aff'd sub nom.* Williams v. Rhodes, *supra* note 9, and Illinois State Board of Elections v. Socialist Workers Party, *supra* note 21, 440 U.S. at 184 ("By limiting the choices available to voters, the State impairs the voters' ability to express their political preferences").
30. I do not offer, here or elsewhere, a unified "theory" of voting which identifies the essential or necessary and sufficient attributes of a valid vote in a system of elec-

toral politics. My goal is more modest: to offer a set of descriptions and normative claims which are part of our more naive understanding of voting and elections; this phenomenology of voting and elections is offered as part of the data which should be accommodated by a legal right to vote. My understanding of philosophical method in this regard is influenced by the anti-essentialism expressed in LUDWIG WITTGENSTEIN, PHILOSOPHICAL INVESTIGATIONS (G.E.M. Anscombe trans., 3rd ed. 1958), and by the method of reflective equilibrium developed in RAWLS, A THEORY OF JUSTICE, *supra* note 20.

31. See Yick Wo v. Hopkins, 118 U.S. 356, 370 (1886); see also the National Voter Registration Act of 1993, discussed *supra* note 7, § 2 (a) (1), codified at 42 U.S.C. § 1973gg (a) (1) (1994) ("The Congress finds that—(1) The right of citizens of the United States to vote is a fundamental right.").
32. Such a standard of review for legislation affecting fundamental rights or for legislation employing a "suspect classification" such as race stands in contrast to the minimal scrutiny applied in regard to other legislation, in which the court merely determines if the law has some conceivable basis in reason. Compare the standard of review employed in, e.g., Korematsu v. United States, 323 U.S. 214, at 216 (1944), with that in Williamson v. Lee Optical of Oklahoma, 348 U.S. 483, at 487–488 (1955). The classic formulation of the two standards of review is in United States v. Carolene Products Co., 304 U.S. 144, 154 n.4 (1938). In more recent years the courts have adopted so-called intermediate standards of judicial review, in which legislation affects "important" if not "fundamental" rights or interests, or employs a "quasi-suspect" classification such as gender or illegitimacy. See, e.g., Craig v. Boren, 429 U.S. 190 (1976).
33. See, e.g., TRIBE, AMERICAN CONSTITUTIONAL LAW, *supra* note 3, § 13–20, at 1110.
34. U.S. CONST., amend. I ("Congress shall make no law…abridging the freedom of speech, or of the press; or the right of the people peaceably to assemble, and to petition the Government for a redress of grievances"). See, e.g., Williams v. Rhodes, *supra* note 9, which applied the First Amendment to a state restriction on ballot access through the due process clause of the Fourteenth Amendment.
35. U.S. CONST., amend. XIV, § 1 ("No state shall make or enforce any law which shall abridge the privileges or immunities of citizens of the United States; nor shall any State deprive any person of…liberty, or property, without due process of law; nor deny to any person in its jurisdiction the equal protection of the laws"). The right to vote for national officers is a privilege or immunity of national citizenship under Twining v. New Jersey, 211 U.S. 78, at 97 (1908). That the right to vote for state officers is a fundamental right under the equal protection clause was the rationale of Harper v. Virginia State Board of Elections, 383 U.S. 663 (1966), and Bullock v. Carter, 405 U.S. 134 (1972). The right to vote is a liberty so fundamental that its denial or abridgment violates the due process clause of the Fourteenth Amendment, according to U.S. v. Texas, 252 F. Supp. 234, 236 (W. D. Tex. 1966), *aff'd mem.* 384 U.S. 155 (1966).
36. U.S. CONST., amend. XIV, § 2 ("...But when the right to vote at any election for the choice of electors for President and Vice President of the United States, Representatives in Congress, the Executive and Judicial officers of a state, or the

members of the Legislature thereof, is denied to any of the male inhabitants of such State, being twenty-one years of age, and citizens of the United States, or in any way abridged, except for participation in rebellion, or other crime, the basis of representation therein shall be reduced in the proportion which the number of such male citizens shall bear to the whole number of male citizens twenty-one years of age in such State"). Judicial enforcement of this provision was, however, denied in Saunders v. Wilkins, 152 F.2d 235 (4th Cir. 1945), *cert. den.* 328 U.S. 870 (1946). See also Lampkin v. Connor, 239 F.Supp. 757 (D.D.C.), *aff'd* 360 F.2d 505 (1965).

37. See U.S. CONST., art. I, § 2 ("The House of Representatives shall be composed of Members chosen every second Year by the People of the several States, and the Electors in each State shall have the qualifications requisite for Electors of the most numerous Branch of the State Legislature."); U.S. CONST., amend. XVII ("The Senate of the United States shall be composed of two Senators from each State, elected by the people thereof.... The electors in each State shall have the qualifications requisite for electors of the most numerous branch of the State legislatures"). Under article I, § 2, "The right to vote for members of the Congress of the United States...has its foundation in the Constitution of the United States," as well as in state law, according to Ex parte Yarbrough, *supra* note 8, 110 U.S. at 653; cf. U.S. v. Classic, 313 U.S. 299, at 315, 321 (1941). In U.S. v. Aczel, 219 F. 197 (D. Ind. 1915), the right to vote for U.S. senators was held to be derived from the U.S. Constitution; requiring the payment of a poll tax as a precondition for voting was said to constitute an additional qualification for voting for senators in Forssenius v. Harman, 235 F. Supp. 66 (E.D. Va. 1964), *aff'd on other grounds*, after ratification of the Twenty-Fourth Amendment, 380 U.S. 529 (1965).

38. U.S. CONST., amend XV, § 1 ("The right of citizens of the United States to vote shall not be denied or abridged by the United States or by any State on account of race, color, or previous condition of servitude"); U.S. CONST., amend. XIX, § 1 ("The right of citizens of the United States to vote shall not be denied or abridged by the United States or by any State on account of sex"); U.S. CONST., amend. XXIV ("The right of citizens of the United States to vote in any primary or other election for President or Vice President, for electors for President or Vice President, or for Senator or Representative in Congress, shall not be denied or abridged by the United States or any State by reason of failure to pay any poll tax or other tax"); U.S. CONST., amend. XXVI, § 1 ("The right of citizens of the United States, who are eighteen years of age or older, to vote shall not be denied or abridged by the United States or by any State on account of age").

39. The freedom to associate for the advancement of political beliefs, derived by implication from the First Amendment guarantees of free speech and assembly, was said to be constitutionally protected in National Association for the Advancement of Colored People v. Alabama ex rel. Patterson, 357 U.S. 449 (1958); the scope of this freedom extends to protection for joining or forming political parties and nominating candidates for office, under Kusper v. Pontikes, 414 U.S. 51 (1973), Cousins v. Wigoda, 419 U.S. 477 (1975), Democratic Party v. Wisconsin ex rel. LaFollette, 450 U.S. 107 (1981), and subsequent cases.

Durational residency requirements for voting were said by the Supreme Court to impermissibly infringe on the (nontextual) constitutional right of interstate travel in Dunn v. Blumstein, 405 U.S. 330 (1972).

40. See U.S. CONST., art. IV, § 4 ("The United States shall guarantee to every State in this Union a Republican Form of Government..."); U.S. CONST., amend. IX ("The enumeration in the Constitution, of certain rights, shall not be construed to deny or disparage others retained by the people"); U.S. CONST., amend. X ("The powers not delegated to the United States by the Constitution, nor prohibited by it to the States, are reserved to the States respectively, or to the people"); U.S. CONST., amend. XIII, § 1 ("Neither slavery nor involuntary servitude...shall exist within the United States, or any place subject to their jurisdiction"). In Luther v. Borden, 48 U.S. (7 How.) 1 (1849), the Supreme Court held that disputes arising under the guarantee clause were nonjusticiable under the political question doctrine, which still seems to be the view under Pacific States Tel. & Tel. Co. v. Oregon, 223 U.S. 118 (1912) and Baker v. Carr, 369 U.S. 186 (1962). Political rights have been said to be included within the scope of the Ninth and Tenth Amendments, in, e.g., United Public Workers v. Mitchell, 330 U.S. 75, 94–95 (1947). The Supreme Court has said that the Thirteenth Amendment established and decreed "universal civil and *political* freedom throughout the United States," U.S. v. Stanley (Civil Rights Cases), 109 U.S. 3 at 20 (1883) (emphasis added), which might naturally be thought to include the suffrage.
41. Smith v. Allwright, 321 U.S. 649, at 664 (1944); see also Reynolds v. Sims, *supra* note 17, 377 U.S. at 554–555 ("The Constitution of the United States protects the right of all qualified citizens to vote").
42. For example, the Iowa constitution of 1857, as amended, provides that "Every citizen of the United States of the age of twenty-one years, who shall have been a resident of this state...and of the county in which he claims his vote...shall be entitled to vote at all elections...." IA. CONST., art. II, § 1, reprinted in COLUMBIA UNIVERSITY, LEGISLATIVE DRAFTING RESEARCH FUND, 3 CONSTITUTIONS OF THE UNITED STATES: NATIONAL AND STATE (1993)
43. The constitution of Arizona (1912) provides that "All political power is inherent in the people..." ARIZ. CONST., art. II, § 2, reprinted in 1 CONSTITUTIONS OF THE UNITED STATES: NATIONAL AND STATE (1993), *supra* note 42.
44. For example, the constitution of Colorado (1876) provides that "All elections shall be free and open..." COLO. CONST., art. II, § 5, reprinted in 2 CONSTITUTIONS OF THE UNITED STATES: NATIONAL AND STATE (1992), *supra* note 42.
45. This would seem to be one of the principles underlying Powell v. McCormick, 395 U.S. 486 (1969). See a much older expression of a very similar principle in THOMAS M. COOLEY, A TREATISE ON THE CONSTITUTIONAL LIMITATIONS WHICH REST UPON THE LEGISLATIVE POWER OF THE STATES OF THE AMERICAN UNION, at 99 and n. 3 (7th ed. 1903).
46. Current voter registration requirements are summarized in 33 THE BOOK OF THE STATES: 2000–2001, at 169–170 (Table 5.6) (2000). North Dakota does not require voters to register. Six other states—Idaho, Maine, Minnesota, New Hampshire, Wisconsin, and Wyoming—allow voters to register on election day. ID.

In 1998, however, these seven states collectively had only 5.7% of the total citizen population of voting age in the United States (about 10,510,000 in a voting-age citizen population of 183,451,000, according to U.S. Census Bureau estimates).

47. See Powell, *Voting Turnout in Thirty Democracies: Partisan, Legal, and Socio-Economic Influences*, a 1980 paper reprinted in RICHARD G. NIEMI AND HERBERT F. WEISBERG, EDS., CONTROVERSIES IN VOTING BEHAVIOR, 34–53, at 38–39 (2nd ed. 1984). It should be noted that even under the NVRA or motor-voter statute, discussed *supra* note 7, voter registration requirements in the U.S. continue to place the burden of registration on the voter rather than on the state; motor-voter lightens the burden but does not, as Canada and most western European democracies do, shift it elsewhere.
48. Cross-national comparisons are not precise, but rough figures are possible. In 153 elections between 1968 and 1989 in 24 economically advanced democracies other than the U.S., voter turnout for elections to the lower house of the national legislature averaged 82.48% of the eligible electorate. Each nation had at least four elections over this period. The countries are Australia, Austria, Belgium, Canada, Denmark, Finland, France, Germany, Greece, Iceland, Ireland, Israel, Italy, Japan, Luxembourg, Malta, The Netherlands, New Zealand, Norway, Portugal, Spain, Sweden, Switzerland, and the United Kingdom. Greece, Portugal, and Spain had free elections beginning only in the mid-1970s; the other 21 had free elections throughout this period. The nation-by-nation data, from which this average was calculated, is in THOMAS T. MACKIE AND RICHARD ROSE, COMPS., THE INTERNATIONAL ALMANAC OF ELECTORAL HISTORY (3d ed. 1991). The comparable U.S. figures, covering six presidential and five off-year elections from 1968 through 1988, are 51.85% (presidential election years) and 39.48% (off-year elections). ID., at tables 25.15b and 25.16b. On average, therefore, turnout for U.S. House elections was only 56% as high as the level of turnout in comparable legislative elections in the other 24 democracies.
49. See, e.g., RAYMOND E. WOLFINGER AND STEVEN J. ROSENSTONE, WHO VOTES? supra note 7, at 79; Wolfinger, *Improving Voter Participation*, in PAUL E. FRANK AND WILLIAM G. MAYER, EDS., WHAT TO DO: RECOMMENDATIONS FOR IMPROVING THE ELECTORAL PROCESS (forthcoming); FRANCES FOX PIVEN AND RICHARD A. CLOWARD, WHY AMERICANS DON'T VOTE (1989).
50. See WOLFINGER AND ROSENSTONE, *supra* note 7, at 75–76 (Table 4.2).
51. See Capen v. Foster, *supra* note 7, and the materials discussed there.
52. From a constitutional point of view, the fact that registration operates to reduce turnout in an indirect rather than a direct fashion should not matter; as the Supreme Court noted when it struck down the Oklahoma voter registration law which replaced the law employing the "grandfather clause," but in effect perpetuated the effects of the clause, the Constitution forbids "sophisticated as well as simple-minded modes of discrimination," and bans "onerous procedural requirements which effectively handicap exercise of the franchise," Lane v. Wilson, 307 U.S. 268, at 275 (1939); see also Gomillion v. Lightfoot, 364 U.S. 339, at 342 (1960). (The original Oklahoma law employing a grandfather clause was struck down in Guinn v. U.S., 238 U.S. 347 (1915).) For the November 1992 presiden-

tial election, in a Census Bureau survey 74.01% of white citizens of voting age, 67.23% of black citizens of voting age, 58.52% of Hispanic citizens of voting age, and 57.01% of Asian or Pacific Island citizens of voting age, reported that they were registered to vote. Of voting-age citizens living in families—which was 74.49% of the total population of voting-age citizens—50.06% of those with family incomes under $5000 reported they were registered to vote, but 73.58% of those with family incomes from $20,000 to $24,999, and 87.32% with family incomes of $50,000 or more, reported being registered voters. Similar results, of higher registration rates as socio-economic status rises, obtain when the population is stratified by education level or occupation; such results have been reported quite consistently since the Census Bureau surveys began in 1964. See U.S. DEPARTMENT OF COMMERCE, BUREAU OF THE CENSUS, VOTING AND REGISTRATION IN THE ELECTION OF NOVEMBER 1992, at 4–5 (Table 2), 55 (Table 12), and 71 (Table 17) (Current Population Report P20–466, 1993). People interviewed by the Current Population Survey overreported their own voting by about 5%, compared to official tabulations of the vote cast; registration may also be overreported. ID., at v, and n. 1. Since registration in advance of the election is in most (43 out of 50) states a necessary precondition to voting, the race and class skew in registration will predictably result in a race and class skew in actual voting.

53. Available evidence demonstrates overwhelmingly that voter turnout in American elections at all levels exhibits a strong race, age, and class bias. The importance of the class skew in American voting patterns is emphasized in Burnham, *The Changing Shape of the American Political Universe*, 59 AMER. POL. SCI. REV. 7 (1965), reprinted in WALTER DEAN BURNHAM, THE CURRENT CRISIS IN AMERICAN POLITICS, at 25–57 (1982). A standard treatment of the skew is in SIDNEY VERBA AND NORMAN H. NIE, PARTICIPATION IN AMERICA: POLITICAL DEMOCRACY AND SOCIAL EQUALITY (1972). See also AMERICAN BAR ASSOCIATION, SPECIAL COMMITTEE ON ELECTION REFORM, THE DISAPPEARANCE OF THE AMERICAN VOTER: A SYMPOSIUM ON DECLINING VOTER PARTICIPATION (1978). Middle-aged whites from the middle and upper classes are much more likely to register and vote than are those who are young, who are members of racial and ethnic minorities, or who are working class or lower class. When first enfranchised, women voted less frequently than did men, but gender disparities in voting have now disappeared. In the 1996 presidential election, 52.8% of men and 55.5% of women reported having voted. BUREAU OF THE CENSUS, VOTING AND REGISTRATION IN...1996, *supra* note 52, at 2–3 (Table 1). While racial disparities in voting have declined markedly since the Second World War, in the 1996 presidential election blacks were still only nine-tenths as likely to vote as whites; Hispanics, and Asians and Pacific Islanders, were less than half as likely to vote as whites; 45% of Asians and Pacific Islanders, 44% of persons of Hispanic origin, 53% of non-Hispanic blacks, and 61% of non-Hispanic white citizens of voting age reported having voted. ID., at 5 (Table 4). Those under 21 years of age were only about three-fifths as likely to vote as those 21 and over; about 31.2% of those under 21, and 55.6% of those 21 and over, reported having voted in the 1996 presidential election. ID., at 5 (Table 2). Class differences in voting, as reflected in differences in voting at different educational, occupational, or income levels, are

also striking; high school graduates are less than three-fourths as likely to vote as were those with four years or more of college. In 1996, of those with less than an eighth grade education, 29.9% reported voting; 49.1% of high school graduates did so; and 72.6% of those with a bachelor's degree or higher reported voting. ID., at 34 (Table 7). Those employed as operators, fabricators, or laborers were less than three-fifths as likely to vote as were those employed as managers or professionals; of those employed as operators, fabricators, or laborers, only 38.2% reported having voted in 1996, while of those employed as professionals or managers, 70.2% reported having voted that year. ID., at 51 (Table 11). People with family incomes less than $15,000 in 1996 were only about half as likely to vote as were those with family incomes $75,000 or more; of those whose family income was under $15,000, 36.2% reported voting in 1996, while of those whose family income was $75,000 or more, 73.6% reported voting. ID., at 55 (Table 12). This class skew is much greater than that obtaining in the nineteenth-century America electorate, and much greater than that obtaining in the electorates of other economically advanced democracies. See also the discussion in SIDNEY VERBA, NORMAN H. NIE, AND JAE-ON KIM, PARTICIPATION AND POLITICAL EQUALITY: A SEVEN-NATION COMPARISON (1978), esp. ch. 10. Non-voting is placed in the context of the median-voter hypothesis in Garvey, *The Theory of Party Equilibrium*, 60 AMER. POL. SCI. REV. 29 (1966). It is surely plausible that the class skew of the electorate translates itself into a decided class skew in the making and administering of public policy.

54. See Davis v. Schnell, 81 F.Supp. 872 (S.D. Ala. 1949), *aff'd* 336 U.S. 933 (1949); Louisiana v. U.S., 380 U.S. 145 (1965). A finding of a racially discriminatory intent is required in order to establish a violation of the Fifteenth Amendment, according to City of Mobile, Alabama v. Bolden, 446 U.S. 55 (1980). These issues as applied to voter registration laws are discussed in James, *Voter Registration*, *supra* note 7. Similarly, imposing literacy tests on prospective voters has not been found to be unconstitutional, absent a racially discriminatory intent, Lassiter v. Northampton County Board of Elections, 360 U.S. 45 (1959), although such tests have been suspended nationwide by an act of Congress since 1970. Voting Rights Act Amendments of 1970, § 6, Pub. L. 91–285, 84 Stat. 315, codified as amended at 42 U.S.C. § 1973aa (1993), held a constitutional exercise of congressional powers under § 5 of the Fourteenth Amendment (and, by one justice, of § 2 of the Fifteenth Amendment as well) in Oregon v. Mitchell, 400 U.S. 112 (1970). Congress had earlier suspended the use of literacy tests in some jurisdictions with especially low rates of voting; see the Voting Rights Act of 1965, § 4, *supra* note 18, 79 Stat. 438, codified as amended at 42 U.S.C. § 1973b (1993), held constitutional in Katzenbach v. Morgan, 384 U.S. 641 (1966).

55. Under the doctrine of "prior restraint," a state law which attempted to require that, in order to speak or publish a newspaper, one must register as a qualified speaker or publisher thirty days in advance of speaking or publishing, would face a "heavy presumption against its constitutional validity," and the state would need to show both that it is attempting to avoid a serious harm and that it has no less restrictive method of avoiding that harm. Quote from Bantam Books, Inc., v.

Sullivan, 372 U.S. 58, 70 (1963); see also Near v. State of Minnesota ex rel. Olson, 283 U.S. 697 (1931) and New York Times Co. v. United States, 403 U.S. 713 (1971) (the Pentagon Papers case). The analogy between the protections afforded to speaking and voting was noted by Judge Thornberry in his decision striking down the Texas poll tax for participation in state elections; taxing voting is no more acceptable than taxing speech, he concluded. See U.S. v. Texas, *supra* note 35, 252 F. Supp. at 254.

56. See Cox v. New Hampshire, 312 U.S. 569, 574 (1941).
57. "Competition must be the central value of election law." Gottlieb, *Election Reform and Democratic Objectives*, 9 YALE L. & POL'Y REV. at 213 (1991).
58. This position is associated most prominently with the work of Schumpeter, *supra* note 22. Schumpeter sees the main benefit of electoral competition, which he equates with "democracy" by definition, as the avoidance of a tyrannical ruling elite because any such elite could be replaced by a competing party. Most theorists who analyze political competition in the terms of economic competition go beyond Schumpeter's rather pessimistic assessment of the potential of democratic elections to control policy and believe that under at least some favorable conditions competition will allow the electorate to control the content of (some if not all) public policies as well as the membership of the governing elites—in particular, that the policies adopted (or, perhaps, retrospectively approved) will be those judged best by the "median voter." The median voter hypothesis comes from the economist Harold Hotelling. See Hotelling, *Stability in Competition*, 39 ECON. J. 41 (1929). The ideas were refined in Lerner and Singer, *Some Notes on Duopoly and Spatial Competition*, 45 J. POL. ECON. 145 (1937); Smithies, *Optimum Location in Spatial Competition*, 49 J. POL. ECON. 423 (1941); and DOWNS, *supra* note 22, at 115–141. On the "median voter hypothesis," compare the summary in MUELLER, PUBLIC CHOICE II, *supra* note 4, at 180–193 (1989), with the argument in THOMAS FERGUSON, GOLDEN RULE: THE INVESTMENT THEORY OF PARTY COMPETITION AND THE LOGIC OF MONEY-DRIVEN POLITICAL SYSTEMS, at 377–415 (Appendix) (1995).
59. That this comparison is *merely* an analogy should be clear from the fact that whereas neoclassical economists are agreed that, e.g., firms are profit-maximizers, there is no parallel agreement in public-choice theory as to what it is that parties or candidates maximize. (Votes? Legislative seats? Influence over the political and legislative agenda?) See MUELLER, PUBLIC CHOICE II, *supra* note 4, at 179.
60. "Perfect competition occurs when no producer can affect the market price.... Perfect competition arises when there are a large number of small firms, each producing an identical product and each too small to affect the market price." PAUL A. SAMUELSON AND WILLIAM D. NORDHAUS, ECONOMICS, at 476 (12th ed. 1985).
61. The "optimum" conditions of production and exchange in product markets are examined in I.M.D. LITTLE, A CRITIQUE OF WELFARE ECONOMICS, at 129–165 (2nd ed. 1957) and J. DE V. GRAAFF, THEORETICAL WELFARE ECONOMICS, at 142–155 (1957).
62. Most obviously, the federal Constitution provides for only one President over a four-year term. While the numerous buyers in a product market can allocate their purchases between many sellers—not all buyers end up driving the same make of

car at any given time, or brushing with the same brand of toothpaste on any given morning—all voters in the United States end up with the same one President over a given time. The dominance of the two largest parties at this level is quite pronounced. Of course, no one but the nominees of the Republican and Democratic parties has been elected to the presidency and vice-presidency since the foundation of the Republicans in 1854, and only once (1912) has someone other than the Republican or Democratic nominee even been the runner-up. Over the span of 36 presidential elections from 1856 through 1996, minor parties and independent candidates averaged about 6.3% of the popular vote, leaving the Democrats and Republicans between them with about 93.7% of the total votes cast. The minor-party share has declined in the modern era; in the 17 presidential elections beginning with the 1932 election and running through the 1996 election, minor parties and independents have received, on average, about 4.2% of the total popular vote for president. The trend continued in the 2000 presidential election; the minor-party vote for president that year amounted to 3.9% of the total national vote. See U.S. HOUSE OF REPRESENTATIVES, CLERK, STATISTICS OF THE PRESIDENTIAL AND CONGRESSIONAL ELECTION OF NOVEMBER 7, 2000, at 73–74. Historically, the two-party organization of American electoral politics seems to depend upon the creation of the presidency as the most important elected office with the ratification of the Constitution in 1788; the Federalists and the (Democratic-) Republicans seem to have arisen as political parties out of the battle between Hamilton and Jefferson over the course of the Washington Administration's policies, as these two looked to Congress, and then to officials and voters in the states, for support. See, e.g., the account in NOBLE E. CUNNINGHAM JR., THE JEFFERSONIAN REPUBLICANS: THE FORMATION OF PARTY ORGANIZATION, 1789–1801 (1957).

63. As the federal constitution provides for only one President over a four-year term, so do each of the fifty state constitutions provide for only one Governor over a two- or four-year term. Although occasionally minor-party or independent candidates win election to governorships, this is relatively rare. From 1896 through 2001, the American states conducted 1737 regular elections for governor; the Democratic or Republican candidates won all but 22 (1.3%) of these, in 13 different states. Only six of these victories, in only four states, have come in the half-century-plus since World War II (Maine in 1974, 1994, and 1998; Alaska and Connecticut in 1990; Minnesota in 1998). Calculated from data in CONGRESSIONAL QUARTERLY, GUIDE TO U.S. ELECTIONS (4th ed. 2001). Likewise, the share of the total gubernatorial vote to minor-party and independent candidates is small. Taking the most recent (as of the end of 2000) election for the governorship in each of the fifty states (eleven states in 2000, three in 1999, thirty-four in 1998, and two in 1997), Democrats received 45.1% of the nationwide total, Republicans received 50.2%, and independent or minor-party candidates received 4.7%. Calculated from data in RICHARD M. SCAMMON, ALICE V. MCGILLIVRAY, AND RHODES COOK, COMPS. AND EDS., AMERICA VOTES 23: A HANDBOOK OF CONTEMPORARY AMERICAN ELECTION STATISTICS 1997–1998, at 2 (1999), and SCAMMON, MCGILLIVRAY, AND COOK, COMPS. AND EDS., AMERICA VOTES 24: A HANDBOOK OF CONTEMPORARY AMERICAN ELECTION STATISTICS 1999–2000, at 2 (2001).

64. The 535 members of both houses of the federal Congress, and most (although not all) of the 7424 members of the 99 houses of the state legislatures, are elected from single-member districts, in which (as with single executives) the tendency is more-or-less inexorably towards two competitors for each seat. (Single-member congressional districts were first required by federal law in the act of June 25, 1842, ch. 47, 5 Stat. 491, and have been required in all states, without exception, since 1967 (Act of December 14, 1967, Pub. L. 90–196, 81 Stat. 581); the requirement is currently codified at 2 U.S.C. § 2c (1993).) Multi-member state legislative districts are not, *per se*, violations of the equal protection clause under the one-person, one-vote doctrine, but they may be challenged under the Voting Rights Act if they have a disparate impact on the voting strength of protected minorities or under the Fifteenth Amendment if they are aimed at reducing the voting strength of protected minorities. See Whitcomb v. Chavis, 403 U.S. 124 (1971); White v. Regester, 412 U.S. 755 (1973); City of Mobile v. Bolden, *supra* note 54; Voting Rights Act Amendments of 1982, Pub.L. 97–205, § 3, 96 Stat. 134, currently codified at 42 U.S.C. § 1973 (a) (1993); Thornburg v. Gingles, 478 U.S. 30 (1986). Just as the presence of a unitary executive seems to produce a tendency towards a two-party system, so apparently does the presence of a single-member district system for electing legislators, such as members of the U.S. Congress. In the 72 congresses elected from the formation of the Republican Party in 1854 through the election of the 105th Congress in 1996, the Democrats and Republicans were the two largest parties in each one; only 402 of the 27,398 representatives (about 1.5%) who began those congresses were seated as members of minor parties or as independents. The rest were Democrats or Republicans. Moreover, the dominance of the major parties has grown more pronounced in the twentieth century. From the beginning of the New Deal (the 73rd Congress, elected in 1932) through the 105th Congress (elected in 1996), only 53 of the 14,323 representatives (about 0.4%) who began those 33 congresses were seated as members of minor parties or as independents. (Vacancies are excluded from these calculations.) See the tabulation in the GUIDE TO U.S. ELECTIONS, *supra* note 63. Minor parties or independents received, on average, only 4.2% of the national vote for representative in the general elections from 1894 through 1996, and only 2.4% from 1932 through 1996. Only once in the twentieth century—on the occasion of the 1912 progressive/conservative split in the Republican party—has the non-Democratic and non-Republican vote for U.S. House exceeded 10% of the national total. The nationwide House vote in the 2000 election, for example, was 47.7% Democratic, 48.1% Republican, and 4.2% (including 0.3% of the total vote cast for major-party candidates on minor-party lines) for minor-party and independent candidates. Congressional vote totals 1894–1940 calculated from the data in INTER-UNIVERSITY CONSORTIUM FOR POLITICAL AND SOCIAL RESEARCH, CANDIDATE NAME AND CONSTITUENCY TOTALS, 1788–1988 (Computer file ICPSR 0002; 4th ICPSR ed. 1990); 1942–2000 from U.S. HOUSE OF REPRESENTATIVES, CLERK, STATISTICS OF THE CONGRESSIONAL ELECTION (quadrennial 1942–1998) and STATISTICS OF THE PRESIDENTIAL AND CONGRESSIONAL ELECTION (quadrennial 1944–2000).

65. The state legislatures exhibit a similar pattern to that noted above for Congress. Following the 1998 elections, the state legislatures included 3944 Democrats (52.5%), 3543 Republicans (47.2%), and 16 independents or minor-party members (0.2%), with five vacancies. Following the 1996 elections, the state legislatures included 3875 Democrats (52.5%), 3476 Republicans (47.1%), and only 20 others, including vacancies (0.3%); following the 1994 elections, the 7366 state legislators (there were nine vacancies) included 3838 Democrats (52.1%), 3508 Republicans (47.6%), and 20 from minor parties or independents (0.3%). (The 49 members of Nebraska's unicameral legislature, elected on a non-partisan basis, are excluded from these totals.) Figures on the partisan composition of state legislatures are from U.S. DEPARTMENT OF COMMERCE, BUREAU OF THE CENSUS, STATISTICAL ABSTRACT OF THE UNITED STATES 1998, at 286 (Table 469) (120th ed. 2000). Recent popular vote totals for each state's legislative races are not readily available, but results from two large states with long histories of active and well-established third parties may be illuminating. The statewide vote for the California state assembly (the lower house of the state legislature) in 1996 was 49.4% Democratic and 46.3% Republican, with only the remaining 4.3% or so spread among minor party and independent candidates. In 1994 the statewide assembly vote was distributed 48.1% Democratic, 48.9% Republican, and 3.0% for all other candidates; and in 1992 it was 51.7% Democratic, 42.9% Republican, and 5.4% for candidates from the other four parties, independents, and write-ins. In New York state, the statewide vote for the state assembly in 1996 was 55.5% for Democratic candidates, 42.5% for Republican candidates, and 2.0% for minor-party or independent candidates; in 1994 it was 50.5% for Democratic candidates, 47.4% for Republican candidates, and 2.0% for minor-party or independent candidates; and in 1992 it was 53.7% cast for Democratic candidates, 43.5% cast for Republican candidates, and 2.8% cast for minor-party or independent candidates. (Totals for Democrats and Republicans in New York include 9.0% of the total vote in 1996, 7.8% in 1994, and 7.2% of the total vote in 1992 cast for major-party candidates as nominees of minor parties.) California election figures calculated from STATE OF CALIFORNIA, SECRETARY OF STATE, STATEMENT OF VOTE: NOVEMBER 5, 1996, PRESIDENTIAL GENERAL ELECTION (1996); STATEMENT OF VOTE: NOVEMBER 8, 1994 GENERAL ELECTION (1994); and STATEMENT OF VOTE: GENERAL ELECTION NOVEMBER 3, 1992 (1992). New York figures calculated from NEW YORK STATE, BOARD OF ELECTIONS, 1996 GENERAL ELECTION VOTE (1996); NEW YORK STATE GENERAL ELECTION VOTE: NOVEMBER 8, 1994 (1994); and NEW YORK STATE GENERAL ELECTION VOTE: NOVEMBER 3, 1992 (1992).

66. See MAURICE DUVERGER, POLITICAL PARTIES: THEIR ORGANIZATION AND ACTIVITY IN THE MODERN STATE at 228 (Barbara and Robert North, trans.; 3d English ed. 1964). See also Duverger at 217: "...the simple-majority single-ballot system favours the two-party system....this approaches...a true sociological law." See also the explanation of a two-party system in terms of single-member districts in E.E. SCHATTSCHNEIDER, PARTY GOVERNMENT, at 69–80 (American Government in Action Series, 1942). And for a summary account of the literature, see generally Riker, *The*

Two-party System and Duverger's Law: An Essay on the History of Political Science, 76 AMER. POL. SCI. REV. 753 (1982); MUELLER, PUBLIC CHOICE II, *supra* note 4, at 220–222.

67. In a free and open election for a single office, such as a single executive or a legislator in a single-member district, where the voters' preferences have a "single-peaked" structure across a single dimension (such as the familiar left-to-right political spectrum), this instrumental rationality will ultimately result in elections between only two candidates or parties. A two-party arrangement will, on these assumptions, characteristically result in both parties—if they are rational and have the relevant knowledge of the voters' preferences—seeking the vote of the "median voter" in the distribution. See BLACK, *supra* note 22, at 18; MUELLER, PUBLIC CHOICE II, *supra* note 4, at 64–66. Another way of stating this point is that the platform of the majority winner in a two-party race has matched up more closely with the (pre-existing) preferences of a majority of the voters. See DOWNS, AN ECONOMIC THEORY OF DEMOCRACY, *supra* note 22, at 64.

68. Economists have traditionally used "concentration ratios" to express the degree of power in product markets. It is the share of output accounted for by the four (or eight) largest firms; "where the 4 leading producers account for as much as half (or possibly even less) of the industry's output they will undoubtedly be acutely conscious of one another's reactions to any competitive moves," and thus have some ability to influence the market. JOHN M. BLAIR, ECONOMIC CONCENTRATION: STRUCTURE, BEHAVIOR AND PUBLIC POLICY, at 7 (1972). Obviously, in virtually every American electoral district, the "two-party concentration ratio" would be over 50%; in fact, it is typically well over 90%. In the November 1992 general election, an election in which minor parties were more active than in any other for the preceding twenty years, parties other than Democrats or Republicans received a total of about 4% of the total valid votes for U.S. Representative, giving a two-party concentration ratio of around 95.84%. The four-party concentration ratio—adding the totals for the Libertarian party and the New York Conservative Party, the two largest minor parties that year, to those for the Democrats and Republicans—would be 97.06% of the votes received. In the November 1994 and November 1996 elections, minor parties were slightly less important. The two major parties shared 96.83% of the nationwide congressional vote in 1996, and 96.24% in 1994; the four-party share of the vote was 97.85% in 1996 and 98.22% in 1994. In only four of the 435 House districts in 1996 did the share of the vote for the top two candidates fall below 90% (the two races won by independents, Missouri's eighth and the at-large seat in Vermont, plus the fourth district in Indiana and the nineteenth district in New York, which had strong showings by Libertarian and Conservative candidates, respectively). If we take the number of *seats* held rather than the number of *votes* received, the two-party concentration ratio in the U.S. House at the beginning of each of the last five congresses, from 1993 through 2001, was between 99.54 and 99.77%. Party vote calculated from figures in U.S. HOUSE OF REPRESENTATIVES, CLERK, STATISTICS OF THE PRESIDENTIAL AND CONGRESSIONAL ELECTION OF NOVEMBER 3, 1992, at 85–86 (1993); RICHARD M. SCAMMON AND ALICE V. MCGILLIVRAY, COMPS. & EDS., AMERICA VOTES 20: A HANDBOOK OF CONTEMPORARY AMERICAN ELECTION STATISTICS 1992, at 244–245 (1993) (for candi-

dates elected in 1992 Louisiana House primaries); CLERK, U.S. HOUSE OF REPRESENTATIVES, CLERK, STATISTICS OF THE CONGRESSIONAL ELECTION OF NOVEMBER 8, 1994, at 47–48 (1995); FEDERAL ELECTION COMMISSION, FEDERAL ELECTIONS 94: ELECTION RESULTS FOR THE U.S. SENATE AND THE U.S. HOUSE OF REPRESENTATIVES, at 71–72 (1995) (for candidates elected in 1994 Louisiana House primaries); U.S. HOUSE OF REPRESENTATIVES, CLERK, STATISTICS OF THE PRESIDENTIAL AND CONGRESSIONAL ELECTION OF NOVEMBER 5, 1996, at 81–82 (1997); and FEDERAL ELECTION COMMISSION, FEDERAL ELECTIONS 96: ELECTION RESULTS FOR THE U. S. PRESIDENT, THE U.S. SENATE AND THE U.S. HOUSE OF REPRESENTATIVES, at 107–108 (1997) (for candidates elected in the 1996 Louisiana House primaries). These figures ignore the blank, void, and scattered vote (0.98% in 1996, 1.07% in 1994, and 1.33% of the total in 1992), and unopposed candidates in Florida and Louisiana in whose elections votes were not tallied (three Republicans and a Democrat in 1996, five Republicans and one Democrat in 1994, one Republican in 1992).

69. On the political party's right to autonomy under the freedom of association guaranteed by the First Amendment, see, e.g., California Democratic Party v. Jones, 529 U.S. 803 (2000); Eu v. San Francisco County Democratic Central Committee, 489 U.S. 214 (1989); Tashjian v. Republican Party of Connecticut, 479 U.S. 208 (1986), and Democratic Party of the United States v. Wisconsin ex rel. LaFollette, 450 U.S. 107 (1981).

70. This is perhaps most evident in Storer v. Brown, *supra* note 9. In a democratic republic, it should not need repeating, the stability of the constitutional order is best assured by ensuring that the government remains responsive to popular need, not by resisting such changes as will accommodate new popular needs. See, e.g., Justice Brandeis' famous concurrence in Whitney v. California, *supra* note 19, or Justice Jackson's opinion in West Virginia State Board of Education v. Barnette, 319 U.S. 624 (1943).

71. See, e.g., JOE S. BAIN, BARRIERS TO NEW COMPETITION: THEIR CHARACTER AND CONSEQUENCES IN MANUFACTURING INDUSTRIES (1956). Note especially the discussion at 114–117 (product differentiation advantages, including brand loyalty); at 144–147 (absolute cost advantages, including legal rights and imperfections in the markets for productive factors, such as investible funds); at 53–56 (economies of large scale).

72. That is, that there will be strong tendency towards a two-party arrangement under the conditions of American political life—plurality elections, unitary executives and single-member-district legislators—is one thing. That these two parties will be Republicans and Democrats in particular is another. See Williams v. Rhodes, *supra* note 9, 393 U.S. at 32, where the Court explicitly refers to the position of the Democrats and Republicans under restrictive ballot access laws as "a permanent monopoly."

73. The analogy between entry barriers to product markets and entry barriers to forms of political competition is made explicitly by THOMAS R. IRELAND AND MARILYN J. IRELAND, *The Political Arena: Revolution in the Barriers to Entry*, 1970 LAW & THE SOC. ORD. 213. A more recent comparison, focussing on the decision permitting state regulation of corporate spending on political campaigns in Austin v.

Michigan Chamber of Commerce, 494 U.S. 652 (1990), is in Cole, *First Amendment Antitrust: The End of Laissez-Faire in Campaign Finance*, 9 YALE L. & POL'Y REV. 236 (1991). The Supreme Court addressed this issue in Williams v. Rhodes: "New parties struggling for their place must have the time and opportunity to organize in order to meet reasonable requirements for ballot position." Williams, *supra* note 9, 393 U.S. at 32.

74. On average, about 74% of voters in the ten presidential elections from 1956 through 1992 voted for the candidate of the party with which they identified, and, similarly, around 75% of voters in the nineteen congressional elections from 1956 through 1992 voted for their party's candidate for representative. During this same period, the number of voters not identified with either party averaged only about 7%. See NORMAN J. ORNSTEIN, THOMAS E. MANN, AND MICHAEL J. MALBIN, VITAL STATISTICS ON CONGRESS 1993–1994, at 67–68 (Table 2–17) (1993). In 1996 77% voted for their party's candidate for U.S. representative and 80% for their party's presidential candidate. See ORNSTEIN, MANN, AND MALBIN, VITAL STATISTICS ON CONGRESS 1997–1998, at 74–75 (Table 2–19) (1998). This suggests that party identity plays a fairly important role in most people's voting decisions. The classic social-scientific study of party loyalty, emphasizing its role in American politics during the 1940s and 1950s, is ANGUS CAMPBELL, PHILIP E. CONVERSE, WARREN E. MILLER, AND DONALD E. STOKES, THE AMERICAN VOTER, especially at 121, 146–147 (1960). See also Campbell and Miller, *The Motivational Basis of Straight and Split Ticket Voting*, 51 AMER. POL. SCI. REV. 293 (1957), and the discussion of ticket-splitting between presidential and House candidates in MILTON C. CUMMINGS JR., CONGRESSMEN AND THE ELECTORATE: ELECTIONS FOR THE U.S. HOUSE AND THE PRESIDENT, 1920–1964, at 28–55 (1966). The apparent weakening of party affiliation in the 1960s and early 1970s is a theme of NORMAN H. NIE, SIDNEY VERBA, AND JOHN R. PETROCIK, THE CHANGING AMERICAN VOTER, at 49 (enlarged ed. 1979). Differing conclusions about the effects of partisan identification over the more recent past are offered in MARTIN P. WATTENBERG, THE DECLINE OF AMERICAN POLITICAL PARTIES 1952–1992 (1993) and BRUCE E. KEITH, DAVID B. MAGLEBY, CANDICE J. NELSON, ELIZABETH ORR, MARK C. WESTLYE, AND RAYMOND E. WOLFINGER, THE MYTH OF THE INDEPENDENT VOTER (1992). Wattenberg points out that by 1980, only 43% of those surveyed said that they always voted for the same party's presidential candidate, a drop of 19% from the 1956 figure. Wattenberg, *supra*, at 20. On the other hand, even with a strong third-party candidacy in the presidential race, in 1992 78% of all voters voted for the same party for President and U.S. representative; in the 2000 election, 82% did. On average, 80% of the voters voted for the candidates of the same party for these two offices in the thirteen presidential-year elections from 1952 through 2000. See NATIONAL ELECTION STUDY, NES GUIDE TO PUBLIC OPINION AND ELECTORAL BEHAVIOR 1952–2000, *supra* note 2, at Table 9B.2. Looking at the issue from a different angle, we can get a rough idea of the strength of party habit over voting decisions in a relatively pure form by considering that in 1986 right-wingers associated with cult leader Lyndon LaRouche won the Democratic nominations for several minor state executive offices in Illinois. The Democratic gubernatorial nominee, former U.S. Senator Adlai Stevenson III, refused to run

with the LaRouche supporters, resigned his nomination, and instead ran as the candidate of a newly-created third party. Although the ballot contained only a blank space for governor in the Democratic column, nearly 7% of the Illinois electorate still voted Democratic for governor. (The Illinois ballot allowed straight-ticket voting with a single mark.) See Cook, *LaRouche and His Followers: Angry, Noisy and Persistent*, 44 CONG. Q. WEEKLY REP. 742–745 (April 5, 1986); *Outlook—Illinois—Senate: The LaRouche Factor*, 44 CONG. Q. WEEKLY REP. 2422 (October 11, 1986). Some of the details of Stevenson's legal battle to remain on the ballot without the Democratic nomination can be traced in Stevenson v. State Board of Elections, 638 F.Supp. 547 (N.D. Ill. 1986), *aff'd*, 794 F.2d 1176 (7th Cir. 1986). For vote totals and the number of straight-ticket votes cast, see STATE OF ILLINOIS, STATE BOARD OF ELECTIONS, STATE OF ILLINOIS: OFFICIAL VOTE CAST AT THE GENERAL ELECTION NOVEMBER 4, 1986 (1986). Similarly, in 1980, through a fortuitous combination of circumstances, a state leader of the Ku Klux Klan won by a narrow plurality a Democratic nomination for the U.S. House in California. Although state and local party officials disavowed his candidacy and urged voters to vote for the Republican candidate, the Klansman still received 13.4% of the vote, which is almost surely much larger than the level of support for the platform of the Klan among the electorate of that district. See *House Outlook—California*, 38 CONG. Q. WEEKLY REP. 2998–2999 (October 11, 1980); Richardson, *The bloody infighting among the Klans of California*, 11 CAL. J. 357–358 (September 1980); STATE OF CALIFORNIA, SECRETARY OF STATE, STATEMENT OF VOTE: GENERAL ELECTION, NOVEMBER 4, 1980, at 12 (1981).

75. See Thornburg v. Gingles, *supra* note 64 (racial bloc voting which minimized ability of protected racial minority to elect candidates it supported would be element supporting claim under § 2 of Voting Rights Act as amended).
76. See White v. Weiser, 412 U.S. 783 (1973); Karcher v. Daggett, 462 U.S. 725 (1983) (avoiding contests between incumbents a legitimate criterion in congressional redistricting).
77. The disparities between the established parties and new parties can be demonstrated using a concrete example. To run as an *independent* candidate for the U.S. House in California, one must show support (as demonstrated by signatures on a nominating petition) from at least 3% of the registered voters in that congressional district as of the preceding general election. CAL. ELEC. CODE § 8400 (West Special Pamphlet 1996). For example, to run for Congress in the 1996 general election, an *independent* candidate in the Forty-Third Congressional District (Riverside County) must have collected the valid signatures of 8018 registered voters from that district. But a candidate for the nomination of the *Democratic* or *Republican* parties for the same office must collect "not less than 40 nor more than 60" signatures on a nomination paper, a requirement less than one-half of one percent as great. CAL. ELEC. CODE § 8062 (b) (West Special Pamphlet 1996). To run a statewide slate of 52 congressional candidates, therefore, an independent group would need to collect a minimum of 441,714 signatures from registered voters; to do the same thing, one of the two major parties needs to collect between 2080 and 3120 signatures. For registration as of the 1994 general election, statewide and by congressional district, see STATE OF CALIFORNIA, SECRETARY OF STATE, REPORT OF

REGISTRATION: OCTOBER 1994, at 2 (state total), and 27 (congressional district 43). A party in California *attains* official status—and therefore has its primary nominees automatically placed on the general election ballot—by having at least 1% of the number of voters in the preceding gubernatorial election register as affiliated with that party, CAL. ELEC. CODE § 5100 (b) (West Special Pamphlet 1996), or at least 10% of the number of voters in the preceding gubernatorial election must sign a petition for the party to participate in the next primary election, CAL. ELEC. CODE § 5100 (c) (West Special Pamphlet 1996). For the 1996 and 1998 elections, this amounts to 89,006 registrants as members or 890,060 petition signatures. For a political party to *retain* official status, at least one of its candidates for a statewide office at the preceding gubernatorial election must have received at least 2% of the vote, which currently translates to having received in the 1994 election a minimum of 163,756 votes for state treasurer, the statewide office with the lowest turnout that year, or more in races for offices with higher turnout, up to 173,307 votes cast for governor. See STATE OF CALIFORNIA, SECRETARY OF STATE, STATEMENT OF VOTE: NOVEMBER 8, 1994 GENERAL ELECTION, at vii (new party requirements) and at 1–42 (votes for candidates voted on statewide) (1994); Cal. Elec. Code § 5100 (a) (West Special Pamphlet 1996) (2% of vote for statewide candidate to retain party status). It must also have retained the affiliation of registered voters equal to one-fifteenth of one percent of the registered voters in the state, which for the 1996 primary was 9683 voters. CAL. ELEC. CODE § 5101 (West Special Pamphlet 1996); STATE OF CALIFORNIA, SECRETARY OF STATE, STATEMENT OF VOTE: MARCH 26, 1996 PRIMARY ELECTION, at ix (1996). Of course, candidates for nomination in a direct primary must still win a plurality of the votes in the primary to appear on the general-election ballot. CAL. ELEC. CODE §§ 15400, 15450 (West Special Pamphlet 1996). This is not an insignificant barrier to the general-election ballot. On the other hand, it is not as difficult as it may seem, since in many districts party nominations are essentially uncontested. In 1996, for example, 35 Democratic and 25 Republican candidates for their parties' congressional nominations (out of 52 nominations available in each party) were completely unopposed. Most of the rest won nomination easily; only six Democratic and four Republican nominees had margins of victory lower than 10%. See STATEMENT OF VOTE: MARCH 26, 1996 PRIMARY ELECTION, *supra*, at 23–32. These figures are not untypical of recent experience; in the 19 direct primary elections from 1960 through 1996, the median number of candidates for a Democratic congressional nomination was 1.9111, and for a Republican nomination it was 1.7907 per seat. That is, in both parties fewer than half the nominations had even nominal primary contests. The median Democratic nominee received 81.07% of the vote in his or her primary; the median Republican nominee received 82.24%. Only 12.17% of Democratic nominees, and 9.68% of Republican nominees, had victory margins under 10% of the total vote. Figures calculated from candidate vote totals in STATE OF CALIFORNIA, SECRETARY OF STATE, STATEMENT OF VOTE: PRIMARY ELECTION (biennial; 1960–1996). It remains only to point out that in general elections from 1960 through 1996 California elected 816 members of Congress, 815 of them the official nominees of the Democratic or Republican parties (the lone exception was a

Republican who, having narrowly lost a primary bid, then ran a successful write-in campaign in the general election against the primary winner). On average, over that time a bit more than 2% of the state's vote for members of Congress in general elections went to independent or minor-party candidates. For the partisan composition of state congressional delegations from the 87th through the 105th Congresses, see U.S. CONGRESS, OFFICIAL CONGRESSIONAL DIRECTORY (biennial; 1961–1997); for the partisan division of the state's congressional vote over the same period, see the relevant editions of U.S. HOUSE OF REPRESENTATIVES, CLERK, STATISTICS OF THE PRESIDENTIAL AND CONGRESSIONAL ELECTION and STATISTICS OF THE CONGRESSIONAL ELECTION, *supra* note 64.

78. At the presidential level, this preferential access to capital by the existing parties has been codified into law by the provisions of the Federal Election Campaign Act (FECA) Amendments of 1974, which provides partial federal funding to a party receiving 5% or more of the presidential vote in the preceding election and full funding to a party receiving 25% or more of the presidential vote. Only the Democrats and the Republicans had received the five-percent minimum in the 1972 presidential election, and only they have received the minimum in all the elections since then (although independent candidates received 5% or more of the vote in 1980, 1992, and 1996, and were entitled to partial funding retroactively based on that showing). See the Federal Election Campaign Act of 1971, Pub.L. No. 92-225, 86 Stat. 3; the Federal Election Campaign Act Amendments of 1974, Pub.L. No. 93-443, 88 Stat. 1263, the Federal Election Campaign Act Amendments of 1976, Pub.L. No. 94-283, 90 Stat. 475, and the Federal Election Campaign Act Amendments of 1979, Public Law No. 96-187, 93 Stat. 1339. The law, as amended, is currently codified at 2 U.S.C. § 431 *et seq.*, 18 U.S.C. §§ 591, 600, 608–611, and 47 U.S.C. §§ 312, 315, 801 *et seq.* (1993). The constitutionality of the presidential election campaign fund was upheld in Buckley v. Valeo, *supra* note 8. It is worthy of note that on a model of electoral competition premised on rational self-interest, a party defending the interests of wealthy classes will have a further fundraising advantage over a party less devoted to those interests. See generally FERGUSON, *supra* note 58, especially the Appendix, at 377–415.

79. See Ballot Access News, May 28, 1996, at 4 (table showing that, as of publication date, no minor party had met the legal requirements for placing a presidential candidate on the general-election ballot in more than 31 of the 51 jurisdictions choosing presidential electors in 1996). A summary and analysis of current state ballot access requirements is in the work for the Federal Election Commission's National Clearinghouse on Election Administration by EDWARD D. FEIGENBAUM AND JAMES A. PALMER, BALLOT ACCESS (4 vols.; William C. Kimberling ed. 1988; vols. 2–4 rev. 1996). Current developments have been monitored every four weeks since June 1985 in a newsletter, Ballot Access News. Earlier studies of the state ballot access statutes are in AMERICAN CIVIL LIBERTIES UNION, MINORITY PARTIES ON THE BALLOT (1932); Note, *Limitations on Access to the General Election Ballot*, 37 COLUM. L. REV. 86 (1937); WILLIAM E. HANNAN, PROVISIONS OF THE LAWS OF THE VARIOUS STATES WITH RESPECT TO THE FORMATION OF A NEW POLITICAL PARTY (1938); AMERICAN CIVIL LIBERTIES UNION, MINORITY PARTIES ON THE BALLOT: A SURVEY OF RESTRICTIONS ON MINORITY

PARTIES, TOGETHER WITH RECOMMENDED LEGISLATION (1940; 2d rev. ed. 1943); Comment, *Legal Obstacles to Minority Party Success*, 57 YALE L. J. 1276 (1948); CONGRESSIONAL RESEARCH SERVICE, THE QUALIFICATION OF MINOR AND NEW PARTIES AND INDEPENDENT CANDIDATES FOR A PLACE ON THE GENERAL ELECTION BALLOT: A COMPILATION OF SUMMARIES OF STATE LAWS AND AN INTRODUCTORY ANALYSIS OF SELECTED COURT DECISIONS (1975); PAUL H. BLACKMAN, THIRD PARTY PRESIDENT? AN ANALYSIS OF STATE ELECTION LAWS (1976); the four-volume study for the Federal Election Commission by BRUCE W. ROBECK, JAMES A. DYER, AND HENRY J. WOODS, BALLOT ACCESS (Report No. FEC-CH-78-013, 1978); HEATHER HERNDON, BALLOT ACCESS: OPTIONS AND OBSTACLES (1992). The role of third parties in the American political system is discussed in DANIEL A. MAZMANIAN, THIRD PARTIES IN PRESIDENTIAL ELECTIONS (Studies in Presidential Selection series 1974) and STEVEN J. ROSENSTONE, ROY L. BEHR, AND EDWARD H. LAZARUS, THIRD PARTIES IN AMERICA: CITIZEN RESPONSE TO MAJOR PARTY FAILURE (1984; 2nd ed. 1996).

80. For example, when the Socialist Party was strong in many cities early in this century, Democrats and Republicans sometimes agreed to run a single candidate against the Socialist nominee. Victor Berger, who was elected to the U.S. House as a Socialist from Milwaukee by pluralities in three-way contests in 1910 and 1918, was defeated by a Republican in 1920 when the Democrats failed to field a candidate. Similarly, Vito Marcantonio, who was elected to the House from Harlem in 1948 on the American Labor ticket, by a plurality in a three-way contest, was defeated for reelection in 1950 by a Democrat who also had the Republican nomination. See ICPSR, CANDIDATE NAME AND CONSTITUENCY TOTALS, *supra* note 64.

81. In the context of product markets, an agreement between erstwhile competitors to concede certain portions of the market to one another is referred to as "market division." Market division agreements are illegal under § 1 of the Sherman Act. See U.S. v. Addyston Pipe & Steel Co., 85 F. 271 (6th Cir. 1898), *modified and aff'd* 175 U.S. 211 (1899); U.S. v. Topco Associates, 405 U.S. 596 (1972). The Sherman Antitrust Act is the Act of July 2, 1890, ch. 217, § 1, 26 Stat. 209, currently codified as amended at 15 U.S.C. § 1 (1993). For a brief discussion, see, e.g., LAWRENCE ANTHONY SULLIVAN, HANDBOOK OF THE LAW OF ANTITRUST, at 213–229 (1977).

82. The Republican Party in New York City did this formally in 1981 when it gave its mayoral nomination to the incumbent Democrat, Edward Koch. See New York City Board of Elections, *Statement and Return of the Votes for the Office of Mayor, Nov. 3 1981*; CHRIS MCNICKLE, TO BE MAYOR OF NEW YORK: ETHNIC POLITICS IN THE CITY, at 277–278 (1993). New York election law allows a non-member to enter a party primary only if the relevant party committee approves; typically, however, joint nominations involve a major-party candidate entering the primary of one of the state's minor parties, not a major-party candidate seeking the other major party's nomination, as Koch did. The operation of the New York state fusion statute is discussed and criticized in HOWARD A. SCARROW, PARTIES, ELECTIONS, AND REPRESENTATION IN THE STATE OF NEW YORK, at 55–79 (1983). For the statute itself, see Act of March 25, 1947, ch. 432, § 1, 1947 N.Y. Laws 954 (Wilson-Pakula Law), constitutionality upheld in Ingersoll v. Curran, 297 N.Y. 522, 74 N.E. 2d 465 (1947) (per curiam) and Ingersoll v. Heffernan, 297 N.Y. 524, 74 N.E. 2d 466 (1947) (per curiam);

the current version is codified at N.Y. Elec. Law § 6–120 (1978 & 1996 Cumulative Pocket Part). Where cross-nomination is not permitted, as it is under New York state law, noncompetition will simply amount to deliberate (or negligent) failure to nominate a candidate for a particular office, or failure to mount a serious campaign in support of the nominal candidate. Even at the level of elections for the U.S. House, this occurs with surprising frequency: in the 2000 elections, thirty-one districts (out of 435) had no Democratic candidate, and thirty-two had no Republican candidate. See the relevant issues of U.S. HOUSE, CLERK, STATISTICS, *supra* note 64.

83. See LOUIS HARTZ, THE LIBERAL TRADITION IN AMERICA: AN INTERPRETATION OF AMERICAN POLITICAL THOUGHT SINCE THE REVOLUTION (1955); Burnham, *The Changing Shape of the American Political Universe*, *supra* note 53. As Burnham points out, there is almost surely a connection between (a) the fact that the United States is the only advanced industrial democracy without a social-democratic or socialist party grounded in the working classes (b) the fact that the United States has one of the lowest rates of voter participation of any advanced industrial democracy, a low rate that is characterized by a pronounced skew away from participation by lower-class groups, and (c) the domination in American life of an ideology more individualist than in any other democracy, which may for brevity be referred to as "Lockean liberalism."

84. The median victory margin in the 435 House races held in 1996 was 27.76% of the total vote cast. The traditional threshold for a "safe" seat, a 10% margin of victory over the second-place finisher, was attained by 355 candidates (82% of the total). In 1996 261 of the 435 congressional races (60%) were won with a vote of 60% or more (that is, a margin over all opponents combined exceeding 20% of the vote); 103 of 435 (24%) were won with a vote of 70% or more (that is, a margin over all opponents combined exceeding 40% of the vote). In 1994, there had been even more noncompetitive congressional elections; 266 of 435 (61%) were won with a vote of 60% or more, and 136 (31%) were won with a vote of 70% or more. In 1992, the first election following the reapportionment consequent to the 1990 decennial census, 245 of the 435 congressional races (56%) were won with a vote of 60% or more; 94 of 435 (22%) were won with a vote of 70% or more. From 1956 through 1992, on average, 71% of all members of Congress facing reelection received 60% or more of the major-party vote. Similar findings seem to hold true at the state level. For example, in 1996 43 out of 80 assembly seats (54%) were won with a vote of 60% or more, and 18 of 80 (23%) were won with a vote of 70% or more. In 1994, 52 out of 80 (65%) were won with a vote of 60% or more, and 19 of 80 (24%) were won with a vote of 70% or more; in 1992 37 out of 80 (46%) of California state assembly races were won with a vote of 60% or more of the total vote, and 13 out of 80 (16%) were won with a vote of 70% or more. In New York state assembly elections, in 1996 88 of 150 (59%) won with margins of 20% or more over their major-party opponent, and 49 of 150 (33%) beat their opponent by 40% or more. in 1994, 90 out of 150 (60%) beat their major-party opponent by at least 20%, and 39 out of 150 (26%) beat their major-party opponent by at least 40%; and in 1992 77 out of

150 (51%) beat their major-party opponent by 20% or more, and 28 of 150 (19%) beat their major-party opponent by 40% or more. Percentages of the total vote for congressional candidates are in FEDERAL ELECTION COMMISSION, FEDERAL ELECTIONS 96 and FEDERAL ELECTIONS 94, *supra* note 68. and FEDERAL ELECTION COMMISSION, FEDERAL ELECTIONS 92: ELECTION RESULTS FOR THE U.S. PRESIDENT, THE U.S. SENATE AND THE U.S. HOUSE OF REPRESENTATIVES (1993); average votes for congressional candidates seeking reelection are given in ORNSTEIN ET AL, VITAL STATISTICS, *supra* note 74, at 61 (Table 2–10). California assembly percentages of the total vote in STATE OF CALIFORNIA, SECRETARY OF STATE, STATEMENT OF VOTE: NOVEMBER 3, 1992 (1992), STATEMENT OF VOTE: NOVEMBER 8, 1994 GENERAL ELECTION, and STATEMENT OF VOTE: NOVEMBER 5, 1996, PRESIDENTIAL GENERAL ELECTION (1996), *supra* note 65. New York state assembly margins for major-party candidates calculated from NEW YORK STATE GENERAL ELECTION VOTE: NOVEMBER 3, 1992, NEW YORK STATE GENERAL ELECTION VOTE: NOVEMBER 8, 1994, and 1996 GENERAL ELECTION VOTE, *supra* note 65.

85. Of course, various systems of proportional representation, at least in legislative elections, will tend to be more open to electoral competition in this respect. The present discussion does not address the debate over PR. For a recent defense of proportional representation, see DOUGLAS J. AMY, REAL CHOICES/NEW VOICES: THE CASE FOR PROPORTIONAL REPRESENTATION ELECTIONS IN THE UNITED STATES (1993). A legal argument is in Note [Low-Beer], *The Constitutional Imperative of Proportional Representation*, 94 YALE L. J. 163 (1984). There is no right under the Voting Rights Act and its amendments to legislative representation by any group, including a protected racial minority, in proportion to its share of the total population; see Voting Rights Act Amendments of 1982, *supra* note 64, current version codified at 42 U.S.C. § 1973 (b) (1994). An argument that remedies under the Voting Rights Act should include some employment of some kinds of proportional representation is offered in various of the essays in LANI GUINIER, THE TYRANNY OF THE MAJORITY: FUNDAMENTAL FAIRNESS IN REPRESENTATIVE DEMOCRACY (1994).

86. See Davis v. Bandemer, *supra* note 23 (redistricting plans that discriminate against political parties are justiciable, and may be unconstitutional under the equal protection clause).

87. NAACP v. Alabama ex rel. Patterson, *supra* note 39.

88. Cousins v. Wigoda, *supra* note 39.

89. The Supreme Court's use of concepts such as "frivolous" and "integrity" in these contexts is hardly viewpoint-neutral or apolitical. A candidacy is not judged as being frivolous according to the plausibility of its proposals as a response to currently pressing social problems (this, after all, is what the electorate is supposed to do at the polls, not what the judiciary is supposed to do on the bench; and it's not a test which, objectively speaking, every major-party candidate with automatic access to the ballot could pass, either). So ballot position for Richard Nixon (say) as the person to "preserve, protect, and defend" the Constitution, or to be placed in sole charge of the nation's thermonuclear arsenal, would not thought by the courts to be "frivolous." Rather, a frivolous candidacy is typically one which has no chance of electoral success, although given the partisan gerrymandering of legislative and congressional districts this epithet should also apply to major-party

candidates in many if not most congressional and state legislative races. See, e.g., the data presented in note 84, *supra*. Presumably, however, the Supreme Court would not maintain that a Republican in a safely Democratic district (or vice versa) is running a "frivolous" candidacy and need not be accorded ballot space. "Frivolity" in this context is a concept thus applying only to minor-party and independent candidates, although not to all such candidates. As to "integrity," the Supreme Court seemingly believes that if a person changes his party registration from Democrat to independent six months before the primary, the "integrity" of the electoral system would be compromised by allowing that person to run for office as an independent (the situation in Storer v. Brown, *supra* note 9). However, the "integrity" of the electoral system is seemingly *not* compromised—or at least not sufficiently to justify the government's efforts to regulate the situation—if a wealthy candidate decides to spend $6 million to win election as the mayor of the nation's second-largest city, or nearly $30 million in an attempt to buy a seat in the United States Senate, or $60 to $70 million to try to throw the Presidential election into the House of Representatives, as was the predictable effect of the ruling in Buckley v. Valeo, *supra* note 8. On frivolous candidacies, voter confusion, and electoral integrity, see, in addition to Storer, American Party v. White, 415 U.S. 767 (1974), and Burdick v. Takashi, *supra* note 23. On Nixon and The Bomb, note that in the summer of 1974, the secretary of defense gave orders that the armed forces were to accept no orders from the president without his countersignature, apparently to prevent Nixon from beginning a war to divert attention from his legal troubles (resolved only by United States v. Nixon, 418 U.S. 683 (1974), and Nixon's resignation from the presidency). See the account of this episode in J. ANTHONY LUKAS, NIGHTMARE: THE UNDERSIDE OF THE NIXON YEARS, at 760–761 (1976). On the integrity of the electoral system under the Buckley decision, note that Richard Riordan spent over $6 million to be elected mayor of Los Angeles in 1993 (Los Angeles Times, May 8, 1993, § B, p. 2, col. 2); Michael Huffington, called "such a complete cipher he gave empty suits a bad name" by his own campaign manager, spent about $30 million in an unsuccessful race for the U.S. Senate from California in 1994 (Los Angeles Times, November 13, 1994, § A, p. 1, col. 5; for the comments of Ed Rollins, Huffington's campaign manager, see Los Angeles Times, August 5, 1996, § A, p. 1, col. 4); Ross Perot spent over $60 million on his unsuccessful presidential race in 1992, which he admitted during his campaign would have the likely and unfortunate effect of creating an electoral-vote deadlock that would throw the election into the House for the first time since 1824 (Los Angeles Times, November 7, 1992, § A, p. 22, col. 1; Cook, *Perot's Retreat Sends Tremor Across Political Landscape*, 50 CONG. QUART. WEEKLY REP., at 2078–2079 (July 18, 1992); Galvin, *House Warily Dusts Off Rules on Choosing a President*, 50 CONG. QUART. WEEKLY REP., at 1420–1422 (May 23, 1992)). That wealthy individuals have a distinct advantage in being elected to public office might be shown in the fact that the 103rd Congress (1993–1995) included at least 28 millionaires, out of 100 members, in the Senate, and 50, out of 435 members, in the House of Representatives (Christian Science Monitor, October 24, 1994, p. 7, col. 1). In contrast, as of 1989, about two American households in a hundred—an estimated 2.3 million out of 93.3 million households—had net assets of a million dollars or more, and in 1992 the median net wealth for all American families was $52,200. Wealth data from U.S. DEPARTMENT OF COMMERCE, BUREAU OF THE CENSUS, MONEY INCOME OF HOUSEHOLDS, FAMILIES, AND PERSONS IN THE UNITED STATES: 1991, at 1 (Table 1) (Current Population Reports P60–180, 1992) (number of households in 1989); U.S. DEPARTMENT OF COMMERCE, BUREAU OF THE CENSUS, STATISTICAL ABSTRACT OF THE UNITED STATES 1995, at 486 (Table 757) (1995) (median family wealth in 1992); unpublished data from the 1989 Survey of Consumer Finances, sponsored by the Federal Reserve and other federal agencies (number of households with net worth of $1 million or more).

90. Anderson v. Celebrezze, *supra* note 9.
91. See Powell v. McCormick, *supra* note 45.
92. ID.; cf. also U.S. Term Limits, Inc. v. Thornton, 514 U.S. 779 (1995).
93. See U.S. CONST., art. I, § 2, cl. 2 (qualifications for representative); art. I, § 3, cl. 3 (qualifications for senator); art. I, § 6, cl. 2 (members of Congress may not hold other federal office); art. II, § 1, cl. 5 (qualifications for president); art. VI, cl. 3 (oath of office required of federal legislators and officers; religious tests barred); amend. XIV, § 3 (federal legislators and officers may not have participated in insurrection against U.S. after having taken oath as federal or state legislator or officer); amend. XXII (two-term limit on president).
94. See, for example, the discussion of the California ballot access scheme, *supra* note 77.
95. Again, the California scheme is illustrative. Since ballot access, at least to the primary election ballot, is so much simpler for candidates within an established party than for independents or candidates in an unofficial party, this system pretty clearly functions to encourage potential candidates to stay within the established parties; see the discussion *supra*, note 77.
96. The strength of the tendency to two-party competition may be shown from the following election results to the U.S. Congress. In the 42 years from the 1954 election to the present (through the 1996 election), covering 9,573 House races for full terms, only nine (0.094%) were won by independent candidates. Three of the winning independents later became Democrats and two Republicans, suggesting that strong independent candidacies in this context are often a response to splits within a major party rather than candidacies genuinely independent of the major parties. Over the same period, in 733 general elections for full-term U.S. Senate seats, four (0.546%) were won by candidates other than Democratic or Republican nominees (one by a Conservative supported by the Republican national administration, one by a former Democratic governor running a write-in campaign, and two wins by an incumbent Democratic senator turned independent). The congressional victories without major-party nominations since 1954 are: 1954, Strom Thurmond as senator from South Carolina; 1958, Dale Alford as representative from the Fifth District of Arkansas; 1970, James L. Buckley (Conservative) as senator from New York; 1970 and 1976, Harry F. Byrd Jr. as senator from Virginia; 1972, John J. Moakley as representative from the Ninth District of Massachusetts; 1980, Thomas Foglietta as representative from the Second

District of Pennsylvania; 1982, Ron Packard as representative from the Forty-Third District of California; 1990, 1992, 1994, and 1996, Bernard Sanders as representative from Vermont (at-large); 1996, Jo Ann Emerson as representative from the Eighth District of Missouri. Thurmond, Alford, Moakley, and Foglietta were reelected to subsequent terms as Democrats; Byrd had served a previous term as a Democrat. Packard was reelected to subsequent terms as a Republican. Buckley received the Republican nomination in his unsuccessful reelection bid. Emerson is the widow of the previous incumbent, a Republican, who died five months before the election, had run as a Republican to win the special election (held simultaneously with the general election she won as an independent) to fill the vacancy left by her husband's death, and joined the House Republican caucus at the beginning of the 105th Congress.

97. Restrictive ballot access thus reduces the potential competition to the established parties, and to the extent that voting is political expression, such a narrowing of choice functions almost as a sort of coerced speech, while it eliminates many viewpoints from the political discussion central to elections as forums for deliberation and constructs a mechanism for consent that secures votes for the candidates who form the government only at the cost of reducing the number of alternatives to voting for those candidates, which means that the "consent" we grant to a particular set of officials is not the result of fully voluntary choices and hence is not genuine consent. As Justice Jackson wrote in Barnette, *supra* note 70, "[c]ompulsory unification of opinion achieves only the unanimity of the graveyard.... We set up government by consent of the governed, and the Bill of Rights denies to those in power any legal opportunity to coerce that consent.... If there is any fixed star in our constitutional constellation, it is that no official, high or petty, can prescribe what shall be orthodox in politics, nationalism, religion, or other matter of opinion or force citizens to confess by word or act their faith therein." It would presumably violate the establishment-of-religion and free-exercise clauses of the First Amendment to prescribe a nondenominational Christian prayer, neutral as between Catholics and Protestants, in public schools. See Engel v. Vitale, 370 U.S. 421 (1962); Abington Township School District v. Schempp, 374 U.S. 203 (1963). But in the political context, it apparently does not violate the Constitution to prefer Democrats and Republicans over Socialists and Libertarians as to access to the official ballot.

98. The claim that any particular ballot access requirement establishes an additional qualification for office is "wholly without merit," because there are alternative routes to the ballot, Storer v. Brown, *supra* note 9, 415 U.S. at 746 n. 16. These alternatives, the Court pointed out, include write-ins. Storer, 415 U.S. at 736 n. 7. The Court had also mentioned the availability of the write-in, while upholding the Georgia ballot access scheme, in Jenness v. Fortson, *supra* note 9. The viability of this view as expressed in Jenness and Storer must now be in doubt, given the decision in Burdick, *supra* note 23, that states need not provide for write-in votes in general elections.

99. The original Australian ballot laws were challenged on constitutional grounds, as discriminating against minor parties and independent candidates, when they were

first adopted in the late 1880s and 1890s. Several courts specifically held that imposing restrictions on minor-party or independent access to the official ballot did not unconstitutionally restrict the right to vote, *provided* that write-in votes were permitted. See, e.g., Eaton v. Brown, 96 Cal. 371, 31 P. 250 (1892); State ex rel. Lamar v. Dillon, 32 Fla. 545, 14 So. 383 (1893); Sanner v. Patton, 155 Ill. 553, 40 N.E. 290 (1895); Bowers v. Smith, 111 Mo. 45, 17 S.W. 761 (1891); People ex rel. Bradley v. Shaw, 133 N.Y. 493, 31 N.E. 512 (1892); an early discussion of the legal issues is in Wigmore, *Ballot Reform: Its Constitutionality*, 23 AM. L. REV. 719 (1889).

100. The importance of access to the official ballot may be shown from the following election results to the U.S. Congress. In the 42 years from the 1954 election to the present (through the 1996 election), covering 9,573 House races for full terms, only three (0.031%) were won by write-in, two in opposition to the major-party candidates and a third as a Republican. Only one out of 733 (0.136%) Senate elections for full terms during this period was by write-in. On the post-1952 write-ins, see CONGRESSIONAL QUARTERLY, 10 CONGRESSIONAL QUARTERLY ALMANAC: 83RD CONGRESS, 2ND SESSION, at 714 (1954) (write-in victory by Strom Thurmond as senator from South Carolina); CONGRESSIONAL QUARTERLY, 14 CONGRESSIONAL QUARTERLY ALMANAC: 85TH CONGRESS, 2ND SESSION, at 726 (1958) (write-in victory by Dale Alford as representative from the Fifth District of Arkansas); 38 CONG. Q. WEEKLY REP. 3319–3320 (November 8, 1980) (write-in victory of Republican nominee Joe Skeen as representative from the Second District of New Mexico); 40 CONG. Q. WEEKLY REP. 2893 (November 20, 1982) (write-in victory of Ron Packard as representative from the Forty-Third District of California). Skeen and Packard won subsequent terms as the Republican candidate, with official ballot position; Alford won subsequent terms as a Democrat; Thurmond was reelected to a four-year and a six-year term as a Democrat and then to six terms as a Republican. In somewhat longer, but narrower, perspective, since California adopted the present scheme of direct primary nominations in 1913 (from the 1914 through the 1996 general elections), there have been a total of 1,250 regular general election races in the state for a seat in the U.S. House of Representatives. Only two (0.16%), one in 1930 and one in 1982, were won by a write-in candidate; in both cases, the write-in candidate was associated with the Republican Party prior to the election, ran as a Republican, and in fact served in the House as a Republican once elected. The 1930 write-in victory for the House in California was by Charles F. Curry Jr. in the Third District; he was the son of the previous Republican incumbent, who had died in office during his reelection campaign less than a month before the general election. Curry ran for reelection as a Republican in 1932, but lost. For the 1982 write-in success of Ron Packard, see *supra*, note 96.

101. Burdick v. Takushi, *supra* note 23. The Court's decision was somewhat qualified, relying in part on the fact that the state involved, Hawaii, had relatively unburdensome requirements for ballot access. Nonetheless, under the electoral system approved by the Supreme Court, there remains a (small but not empty) class of candidates who satisfy the constitutional qualifications for being a U.S. representative or senator , but who would be unable to satisfy the state's ballot access

requirements and yet be legally barred from winning election as write-in candidates. With respect to this class, it appears that Hawaii *has* added to the constitutional qualifications for these federal offices, in contradiction to the principles enunciated in Powell v. McCormick, *supra* note 45, and U.S. Term Limits v. Thornton, *supra* note 92. From the viewpoint of voting as a form of political expression, one might also question whether the denial of write-in space resulting from the decision in Burdick is consistent with the principles expressed in Wooley v. Maynard, 430 U.S. 705 (1977) (First Amendment establishes a right to "refrain from speaking") It might be thought a person could avoid the problem of "coerced speech" by abstaining from voting, but the availability of not owning an automobile did not save the requirement struck down in Wooley, which was the display of a motto on the state's automobile license plates. Presumably requiring someone to abstain from voting so that they not be coerced into speaking is at least as burdensome to one's rights as is requiring them to abstain from owning an automobile so that they not be coerced into speaking.

102. U.S. Term Limits, *supra* note 92, 514 U.S. 779, 116 S.Ct. at 1867–1868.

103. This is the dilemma faced by minor parties in most states, given that most states have enacted laws forbidding or severely restricting so-called "fusion" candidacies (i.e., joint nominations of the same candidate by two or more political parties) alongside their laws imposing strict requirements on party access to the official ballot. Before the introduction of the official or Australian ballot, two parties expressed their agreement on a common candidate simply by printing the candidate's name on the unofficial ballots the parties distributed to their voters; a common slate of candidate could either be printed on each party's separate ballot, or (if the parties agreed on an entire slate of candidates) the two parties could jointly print a single ballot under whatever common heading they wished. Once the official ballot was introduced and restrictions were put on which parties had automatic access to that ballot, a party had to nominate its candidates under its own name or else give up its automatic ballot access, and thus have to requalify for the ballot for the next general election. The more stringent the qualifications for ballot access were made, the larger the penalty placed on fusion nominations under a party name reflecting the fact of the fusion (e.g., "Democratic and People's"). Once the ballot access laws ruled out the possibility of easily forming and then dissolving multi-party coalitions from one election to the next, the parties interested in fusion then turned to the obvious alternative—each party running the jointly nominated candidates under its own name, so that each fusion candidate's name would appear separately on the ballot for each separate party's nomination. The state legislatures—typically under the control of parties which did not employ fusion tactics but whose political opponents did—then attempted to outlaw this version of fusion. The dilemma thus created is illustrated nicely by the political situation in Michigan during the mid-1890s. The Republican-controlled legislature passed an anti-fusion law in 1895, forbidding any candidate's name from appearing in more than one column of the party-column ballot, a law apparently aimed at the candidacy of one A. M. Todd, nominated by the Democrats, the People's party, the Union Silver party, and the Prohibition party,

who was running in a special election for a vacant seat in the U.S. House of Representatives against the Republican lieutenant governor, Alfred Milnes. The state Supreme Court upheld the law against a constititutional challenge; the four Republican justices voted in favor and the one Democrat dissented. See Todd v. Board of Election Commissioners of Kalamazoo [etc.] Counties, 104 Mich. 474, 62 N.W. 564, 64 N.W. 496 (1895), and the discussion in ARTHUR CHESTER MILLSPAUGH, PARTY ORGANIZATION AND MACHINERY IN MICHIGAN SINCE 1890, at 54–55 (Johns Hopkins University Studies in Historical and Political Science, Series XXXV, No. 1, 1917). The Democrats and two minor parties then formed a coalition in Michigan for the 1896 elections under a common name (the "Democratic-People's-Union Silver Party"), with a common slate of candidates and a single column on the ballot. MILLSPUAGH, *supra*, at 13. The election officials then ruled that the Democrats had abandoned their party name, and that other groups could run candidates on the Democratic column, which a splinter group of Democrats opposed to the liberal national and state tickets then did. If the state used the "party-column" form of ballot, in which each party's candidates are printed in a separate column, the antifusion statute would prohibit any candidate's name from appearing in more than one column. If the state used the "office-block" form of ballot, in which the names of all candidates for a particular office are printed together with the name of the party nominating them under the title of the office, the antifusion statute would prohibit the use of separate voting squares next to each party's name, or forbid the printing of more than one party's name next to the name of any candidate. With the adoption of the direct primary for party nominations, and the accompanying state regulation of the party nomination process, the states began to forbid fusion via the mechanism of forbidding candidates not affiliated with a party from running in that party's primary, the so-called anti-partyraiding laws, or by forbidding candidates from running in more than one party's primary, regardless of whether the party's own leadership, voters, or office-holders favored a fusion nomination or not. With only a few exceptions, by about 1920 virtually every state had adopted at least one of these antifusion devices, and fusion nominations became a thing of the past. In 1997 the Supreme Court held that state antifusion laws did not violate theconstitutional rights of free association. Timmons v. Twin Cities Area New Party, 520 U.S. 351 (1997). For the legal challenges to the state anti-fusion laws leading up to the Twin Cities decision, based on the constitutional right to freedom of association as applied to political parties, rather than upon the sort of constitutional right to vote sketched in this article, see Swamp v. Kennedy, 950 F.2d 383 (7th Cir. 1991); Twin Cities Area New Party v. McKenna, 73 F.3d 196 (8th Cir. 1996); Patriot Party of Allegheny County v. Allegheny County Department of Elections, 95 F.3d 253 (3d Cir. 1996), and the discussion of legal issues in Note [Kirschner], *Fusion and the Associational Rights of Minor Political Parties*, 95 COLUM. L. REV. 683 (1995) and Note, *Fusion Candidacies, Disaggregation, and Freedom of Association*, 109 HARV. L. REV. 1302 (1996).

104. As noted earlier, *supra* note 103, fusion was common in nineteenth-century American elections, and was used mainly by the minor parties of economic protest, like the Greenbackers and Populists, in alliance with the major party that

was, locally, the smaller of the two (typically, the Republicans in the South, the Democrats in the North and West). Its frequently successful use by the Populists seems to have been decisive in the motivations of those who supported passage of anti-fusion laws in several states. The earliest antifusion statutes were passed precisely in those states which formed the central battleground of the 1896 presidential campaign between the Democratic-Populist fusion and the Republicans—the states carved from the Northwest Territory and the states of the Great Plains. See, e.g., Argersinger, *"A Place on the Ballot": Fusion Politics and Antifusion Laws*, 85 AMER. HIST. REV. 387 (1980), reprinted in PETER H. ARGERSINGER, STRUCTURE, PROCESS, AND PARTY: ESSAYS IN AMERICAN POLITICAL HISTORY, 150–171 (1992). As noted above, the earliest antifusion laws were amendments to the state Australian ballot laws, and took the form of requiring that no candidate be named in more than one party's column, or allowed more than one voting square, on the ballot. By 1900 some 14 states and a territory had antifusion restrictions of these sorts (with another two states and a territory having used them for a time but repealing them by 1900), and by 1910 the total had reached 20 states and two territories, with another four states having used them earlier but repealing or judicially overturning the laws before 1910. Of the 22 states or territories enacting antifusion laws before 1910, all twelve states in the Old Northwest or on the Great Plains, and all three Pacific Coast states, had done so; but of the less-competitive states dominated by a single political party, none of the six New England states and only three of the eleven Southern states had done so. Relatively competitive states outlawed fusion first, on the whole. In the 16 states enacting some sort of antifusion law prior to 1900, for example, the absolute value of the median difference between Bryan and McKinley in the 1896 election was 11.1%; in the other 29 states participating in the 1896 election, the absolute value of the median difference between Bryan and McKinley in 1896 was 38.2%. Of the 16, the Republicans carried ten for their presidential ticket in 1896. Election statistics from ICPSR, CANDIDATE NAME AND CONSTITUENCY TOTALS, *supra* note 64; for the chronology of early antifusion laws, the main source is the tabulation of ARTHUR C. LUDINGTON, AMERICAN BALLOT LAWS, 1888–1910, at 12–83 (University of the State of New York Education Department Bulletin No. 448, 1911). The next wave of antifusion enactments came with adoption of direct primary laws; the ability of Progressives to capture Republican nominations seems to have the main "abuse" aimed at in this period, and the response was to amend the direct primary laws to require that no candidate be allowed to file for or win nomination in the direct primary election of any party but the candidate's own, or to require that no candidate be allowed to file for or win nomination in more than one primary election. By 1920 27 of the 37 states outside the South had either antifusion or anti-partyraiding laws, as did the territories of Alaska and Hawaii, and by 1940 30 of the 37, plus the two territories, had them. Four New England states, Connecticut, Maine, Rhode Island, and Vermont, did not restrict multiple nominations as late as 1940, nor did Delaware, New York, and California. Four of these seven states—Connecticut, Rhode Island, Delaware, and New York —were also the last four states outside the South which still used conventions rather than direct primaries for all party nominations for statewide offices. The bans on fusion were upheld by the courts in most states; see, e.g., Todd v. Board of Election Commissioners, *supra* note 103; State ex rel. Bateman v. Bode, 55 Oh. St. 224, 45 N.E. 195 (1896); State ex rel. Runge v. Anderson, 100 Wis. 523, 76 N.W. 482 (1898). Similarly, the anti-partyraiding laws were upheld in most states; see Socialist Party v. Uhl, 155 Cal. 776, 103 P. 181 (1909) and Gardner v. Ray, 154 Ky. 509, 157 S.W. 1147 (1913) In California and New York, however, the state courts overturned some anti-fusion laws on constitutional grounds. See Murphy v. Curry, 137 Cal. 479, 70 P. 461 (1902); In the Matter of Callahan, 200 N.Y. 59, 93 N.E. 262 (1910); In the Matter of Hopper v. Britt, 203 N.Y. 144, 96 N.E. 371 (1911), 204 N.Y. 524, 98 N.E. 86 (1912); In the Matter of Crane v. Voorhis, 257 N.Y. 298, 178 N.E. 169 (1931). The legal issues were discussed in Note, *Constitutionality of Discrimination on the Party-Column Form of Ballot*, 25 HARV. L. REV. 176 (1911), Note, *Constitutional Law—Elections—Right of a Candidate to Have His Name Appear More Than Once Upon the Ballot*, 80 U. PENN. L. REV. 591 (1932); Note, *Political Combinations in Elections*, 45 HARV. L. REV. 906 (1932), and Note, *The Constitutionality of Anti-Fusion and Party-Raiding Statutes*, 47 COLUM. L. REV. 1207 (1947); the political motivations and implications of the New York anti-fusion law were discussed in Bard, *The "Levy Election Law" of 1911 in New York*, 27 POL. SCI. Q. 36 (1912). An argument for permitting fusion, based on the function of minor parties as a sort of political "safety valve," is offered by DANIEL A. MAZMANIAN, THIRD PARTIES IN PRESIDENTIAL ELECTIONS (Studies in Presidential Selection series 1974). In one of the few states where legal fusion still survives, New York, fusion nominations have played a significant role in the state's politics throughout the twentieth century, and especially since the 1930s. The American Labor Party (1936–1954) and the Liberal Party (1944–present) have frequently nominated Democratic candidates; the Conservative Party (1962–present) has followed a parallel strategy of most often nominating Republican candidates. Since the strategy of the New York minor parties is, typically, to serve as the "balance of power" between the two major parties, they cannot allow their natural major-party ally to take their support for granted; all three have also run separate candidates, and on occasion Republican candidates have received American Labor or Liberal support while Democrats have sometimes won Conservative support. The statewide margin of victory was less than the number of votes provided to a major-party candidate by the minor-party ally in four of the sixteen presidential elections since 1936 (in 1940, 1944, 1960, and 1980); in three gubernatorial elections out of sixteen (in 1938, 1954, and 1994); and in six U.S. Senate elections out of 22 (in the regular elections for six-year terms in 1944, 1950, 1980, and 1992, plus special elections in 1938 and 1949; in addition, a minor party candidate won election to the Senate in 1970). Minor-party votes similarly provided the winning margin in the general election for 51 congressional candidates from 1936 through 1996, or in about 4% of all elections to the House from the state. Figures for presidential, gubernatorial, senatorial, and congressional elections in New York state 1936–1988 are from ICPSR, CANDIDATE NAME AND CONSTITUENCY TOTALS, *supra* note 64; for 1990–1994, from STATE OF NEW YORK, NEW YORK STATE BOARD OF ELECTIONS,

GENERAL ELECTION VOTE (biennial, 1990–1996). In New York City mayoral elections, minor-party votes for a fusion candidate have made the difference five times in the last eighteen (1933–2001) regular elections (in 1933, 1937, 1941, 1965, and 1993), and a minor-party candidate was elected mayor over major-party opposition in one regular election (in 1969) plus a special election (in 1950). Mayoral election statistics are from CITY OF NEW YORK, BOARD OF ELECTIONS, ANNUAL REPORT (quadrennial issues 1933–1969, plus issue of 1950), and unpublished data from the Board.

105. At the time of the Twin Cities decision in 1997, the statutes of at least four states explicitly allowed major and minor parties to "fuse" on a single candidate for important offices such as governor, state legislator, U.S. senator, or U.S. representative, under at least some circumstances: see CONN. GEN. STAT. ANN. §§ 9-253, 9-453t (West 1989 & Supp. 1996) [but, in light of party affiliation requirement for candidacy in party primaries, this would be permissible only for candidates endorsed by a major party at its convention]; MINN. STAT. ANN. § 204B.04 (subd. 2a) (West 1992 & Supp. 1997) [between major and minor parties only, and only if allowed by state chair of both parties; the law permitting fusion is, on its own terms, effective only while the 8th circuit order in Twin Cities Area New Party v. McKenna, 73 F.3d 196, was in force]; N.Y. ELEC. LAW §§ 6-120 (1), 6-120 (3), 6-120 (4) (McKinney 1978 & Supp. 1996) [only if party committee by majority vote allows non-party member to seek party nomination]; VT. STAT. ANN. tit. 17 § 2474 (1982 & Supp. 1995) [between major and minor parties only]. The statutes of Arkansas are apparently silent on the matter, except to grant the political parties power to impose party affiliation requirements on candidates, and thus apparently allow fusion where the parties consent. See ARK. CODE §§ 7-7-203 (c), 7-7-301 (b) (1993 & Supp. 1995); Baker v. Jacobs, 303 Ark. 460, 798 S.W.2d 63 (1990). Similarly, the statutes of one U.S. territory are apparently silent on the legality of fusion nominations; see AM. SAMOA CODE ANN. tit. 6 (1981). Virginia statutes were apparently silent on the matter in the case where the party chose to nominate by convention rather than by primary, as was its right. Antifusion statutes come in four basic forms: a ban on "partyraiding," a ban on multiple filing for a nomination, a ban on multiple nominations, or a ban on multiple placement on the general election ballot. Anti-partyraiding statutes require either that a candidate for a party nomination in a direct primary be affiliated with that party or else that a candidate not be affiliated with any other party. They can be more or less stringent, imposing affiliation and disaffiliation requirements prospectively, currently, or retrospectively. As of early 1997, the statutes of thirty-nine states, plus those of the District of Columbia and the Commonwealth of Puerto Rico, prohibited party-raiding, either expressly or by reasonable implication. One additional state, New York, formally prohibits party-raiding but as noted above it allows parties to authorize exemptions from the force of the ban; "minor" parties have of course been prominent in New York state and local politics throughout the twentieth century. Four states and one U.S. territory gave power to the political party to decide whether or not it will allow non-members to seek its nominations under at least some circumstances. A second form of antifusion statute is the anti-multi-

ple-filing statute, which forbids a candidate from filing for a nomination in more than one political party in the same direct primary election. Thirteen states expressly forbid multiple filing for nominations; nine of these thirteen also have anti-partyraiding statutes. The final two forms of antifusion statute, identical in ultimate effect, forbid candidates from accepting (as opposed to merely seeking) multiple nominations or forbid the state election officials from recognizing more than one party's nomination of a single candidate on the official ballot. At least twenty states have anti-multiple-nomination or anti-multiple-placement statutes. To some extent such bans overlap anti-partyraiding statutes and anti-multiple-filing statutes, but many states have more than one sort of ban; some states with anti-partyraiding laws extend anti-multiple nomination, anti-multiple-placement, or anti-multiple-filing laws only to the case where a candidate is nominated by a political party and seeks an independent nomination as well.

106. Obviously, this is an oversimplification. No legal barriers prevent the poor or the working classes from pooling their funds, or from using methods of political organization which rely less on the sorts of resources available to the wealthy, such as money and the expensive technologies it can buy, and more on the sorts of resources available equally to the non-wealthy, such as time. However, it is not clear to what extent (under modern circumstances) these are genuine and effective alternatives to the use of organized and concentrated wealth.

107. State of California, Secretary of State, 1994 General Election: Campaign Receipts, Expenditures, Cash on Hand and Debts for State Candidates and Officeholders, at 54–72 (April 1995).

108. Statistical Abstract of the United States 1995, *supra* note 65, at 436 (Table 681) (minimum wage $4.25/hour in 1994); U.S. Department of Commerce, Bureau of the Census, Money Income in the United States: 1995 (Current Population Reports P60-193, 1996), at xiv (Table C) (giving median household income for California in 1994 as $36,332); U.S. Department of Commerce, Bureau of the Census, Income, Poverty, and Valuation of Noncash Benefits: 1994, at A-4 (Table A-2) (Current Population Reports P60-189, 1996) (giving 1994 poverty income for household of three as $11,821).

109. Corey Cook, Campaign Finance Reform at 8 [contributions from personal and family sources], and at 17 [contributions under $100] (California Research Bureau Issue Summary July 1994).

110. Cook, *supra* note 109, at 19.

111. Cook, *supra* note 109, at 11–12 (citing California Common Cause study).

112. See Cook, *supra* note 109, at 5 (Charts 1–2).

113. The relation between expenditures and votes received holds *ceteris paribus* but not absolutely; among the factors that may not be equal are the candidate's name recognition among the electorate, from incumbency or otherwise, and the distribution of long- and short-term party preferences among the voters in a district. See the summary in Mueller, Public Choice II, *supra* note 58, at 209–212.

114. For example, of the 100 members of the U.S. Senate holding office in the middle of the 104th Congress (i.e., incumbents as of February 1996), 89 had outspent their opponents in the immediately preceding election. The median spending by

the 100 winning senatorial candidates was $3,202,389; the median spending by the 96 losing major-party candidates (four senators were elected without major-party opposition) in those elections was about half as great, $1,629,691. (These numbers have been adjusted by the consumer price index for the relevant year to give expenditures in 1996 dollars.) Only seven of the 100 senators had won election by defeating an incumbent in the immediately preceding general election, and four of those had won despite being outspent. But twenty of the 100 had won election to an open seat, and 17 of them (85.0%) had outspent their opponents in the most recent election; 73 were reelected incumbents, of whom 69 (94.5%) had outspent their opponents in the most recent election. Spending in nominal dollars from CONGRESSIONAL QUARTERLY, POLITICS IN AMERICA: THE 104TH CONGRESS, 1996, at 1508–1531 (1995); inflation adjustment using consumer price index, from STATISTICAL ABSTRACT 1995, *supra* note 65, at 491 (Table 760) (giving U.S. consumer price index for 1990–1994), and 82 FED. RESERVE BULL. at A47 (Table 2.15) (October 1996) (giving U.S. consumer price index for July 1996). Campaign spending for U.S. House of Representatives elections shows similar patterns. The average (i.e., mean) amount spent by a major-party candidate running for one of the 91 open seats in the U.S. House in 1992 was $406,611; incumbents spent an average of $571,089, and challengers spent an average of $173,354. See DWIGHT MORRIS AND MURIELLE GAMACHE, HANDBOOK OF CAMPAIGN SPENDING: MONEY IN THE 1992 CONGRESSIONAL RACES, at 11 (Table 1–5) (1994). At least in House elections, increased spending seems to be much more important for challengers than for incumbents; see, e.g., GARY C. JACOBSON, MONEY IN CONGRESSIONAL ELECTIONS, at 157 (1980). Out of all 435 House races in 1992, the winner outspent the loser in 388 (89.2%); even in the 91 elections without incumbents on the ballot, the candidate who spent the most won 69 times (75.8%). The median amount spent by the candidates (57 Democrats and 34 Republicans) winning open-seat elections in 1992 was $449,104; in contrast, the median amount spent by candidates who lost open-seat elections that year was about three-fifths as great, $267,761. (Calculated from data in MORRIS AND GAMACHE, ID.) For the 1994 elections, the candidate who spent the most won 385 out of 435 elections (88.5%), including 36 out of 52 races without incumbents (69.2%). The median amount spent by major-party candidates (13 Democrats and 39 Republicans) winning open-seat elections in 1994 was $587,420; in contrast, the median amount spent by candidates who lost open-seat elections that year was about four-fifths as great, $474,437 (1994 figures calculated from FEC data summarized in POLITICS IN AMERICA, *supra*, at 1508–1531.) Preliminary spending figures for the 1996 congressional election—figures are not yet available for spending during the last twenty days before the election, and some vote totals are not yet final—show that the candidate with the highest spending through mid-October won 386 of the 434 seats decided (88.9%), including 35 out of the 52 open seats decided in the November election (67.3%). The median amount spent by the winners of open-seat races (24 Democrats, 27 Republicans, and one Independent) in 1996 was $527,895 through mid-October; the median amount spent by major-party candidates losing open-seat elections was about three-fifths as high, $337,560 through mid-October. (Calculated from FEC data summary of November 1, 1996, compiled from candidate reports through October 16, 1996, for the general election campaign of November 5, 1996.)

115. In both the 1992 and 1994 general elections for seats in the California assembly, the candidate with the largest expenditures won 73 out of 80 races each time (91.3%). Counting only races without incumbents, the candidate who spent the most money won 21 out of 25 (84.0%) open-seat races for the state assembly in 1992, and 20 out of 23 (87.0%) open-seat races in 1994. In 1992, winners of open seats had median spending of $156,898; losers, $42,021. The spending gap between winners and losers grew wider between 1992 and 1994; winners of the open-seat races in 1994 had median campaign expenditures of $168,997 while losers had median expenditures of $31,089. STATE OF CALIFORNIA, SECRETARY OF STATE, 1992 GENERAL ELECTION: CAMPAIGN RECEIPTS, EXPENDITURES, CASH ON HAND AND DEBTS FOR STATE CANDIDATES AND OFFICEHOLDERS, at 24–37 (March 1993); 1994 GENERAL ELECTION: CAMPAIGN RECEIPTS, EXPENDITURES,..., *supra* note 107, at 54–72.

116. Although undoubtedly there is a (complex) causal connection between the facts that the campaign financing system is so inegalitarian and the existence of large-scale corporate capitalism in the United States. For a general discussion, see, e.g., CHARLES E. LINDBLOM, POLITICS AND MARKETS: THE WORLD'S POLITICAL-ECONOMIC SYSTEMS (1977).

117. Systems of political finance in other democracies are discussed in the various essays in HERBERT E. ALEXANDER, ED., COMPARATIVE POLITICAL FINANCE IN THE 1980S (Advances in Political Science series 1989) and HERBERT E. ALEXANDER AND REI SHIRATORI, EDS., COMPARATIVE POLITICAL FINANCE AMONG THE DEMOCRACIES (1994). For a legal comparison between the mostly private U.S. system and that of Germany, in which political activity is funded by the public to a much greater extent, see, e.g., Casper, Williams v. Rhodes *and Public Financing of Political Parties under the American and German Constitutions*, 1969 THE SUPREME COURT REVIEW at 271 (Philip B. Kurland ed. 1969).

118. Buckley v. Valeo, *supra* note 8. Note that the Supreme Court has explicitly held that state policies allowing or perpetuating the influences of inequalities of wealth, even on the exercise of fundamental rights, do not, *per se*, violate the equal protection clause of § 1 of the Fourteenth Amendment; see San Antonio Independent School District v. Rodriguez, 411 U.S. 1 (1973). On the other hand, despite the Buckley decision and its progeny, there is a line of cases suggesting the contrary with respect to voting rights; see, for example, Harper v. Virginia State Board of Elections, *supra* note 35 (striking down, as violating the equal protection clause, a poll tax requirement for voting in state and local elections), Turner v. Fouche, 396 U.S. 346 (1970) (striking down requirement that office-holding be restricted to owners of real property in the state), and Lubin v. Panish, 415 U.S. 709 (1974) (striking down requirement that candidate pay filing fee in order to appear on primary ballot, if no reasonable alternatives for indigent candidates available). The role of the private system of campaign financing as a screen or filter is discussed at a popular level in JAMIN B. RASKIN AND JOHN BONIFAZ, THE WEALTH PRIMARY: CAMPAIGN FUNDRAISING AND THE CONSTITUTION (1994); Raskin, *Campaign Finance on Trial:*

Challenging the 'Wealth Primary', 259 THE NATION at 609 (November 21, 1994); other popular discussions of the legal issues are in Ackerman, *Crediting the Voters: A New Beginning for Campaign Finance*, 13 AMER. PROSPECT at 71 (Spring 1993); Dworkin, *The Curse of American Politics*, 43 N.Y. REV. BOOKS 19 (October 17, 1996). For more technical discussions from a legal perspective, see also Nicholson, *Campaign Financing and Equal Protection*, 26 STAN. L. REV. 815 (1974); Hamilton, *State Campaign Finance Schemes and Equal Protection*, 61 IND. L. J. 251 (1986); Raskin and Bonifaz, *Equal Protection and the Wealth Primary*, 11 YALE L. & POL'Y REV. 273 (1993); Jezer, Kehler, and Senturia, *A Proposal for Democratically Financed Congressional Elections*, 11 YALE L. & POL'Y REV. 333 (1993); *Symposium on Campaign Finance Reform*, 94 COLUM. L. REV. 1125 (1994). That modern electoral politics on the national level requires gigantic sums of money in order to be successful—or even competitive—is widely acknowledged. Preliminary figures for the 1996 congressional elections showed that spending for the general election totaled at least $468.9 million (excluding money spent in the last twenty days before the election), and that the total spending in congressional races, for the general election alone, would probably equal $600 million. Spending on all federal offices, primaries and general elections combined, was estimated to reach as much as $1.6 billion for 1996. See Federal Election Commission, *Congressional Spending for '96 Election Reaches $469 Million* (Press Release, November 1, 1996); *Special Report—Finances Take Priority in This Year's Races*. 54 CONG. Q. WEEKLY REP. 3081 (October 26, 1996) (citing estimate of $1.6 billion in private spending on federal offices for 1996 election); Los Angeles Times, October 18, 1996, § A, p. 15, at col. 1; New York Times, October 13, 1996, § A, p. 17, at col. 4. For the 1992 election, candidates for the U.S. House reported spending a total of $407.6 million; of this total, over 99% was spent by Democratic or Republican candidates; about 48% was spent by incumbents, 27% by challengers, and 25% by candidates running for open seats without incumbents. See Federal Election Commission, *1991–92 Congressional Spending Soars to $680 Million* (Press Release, January 1994). A general discussion of research findings on the effects of campaign donations and expenditures is in Beitz, *Political Finance in the United States: A Survey of Research*, 95 ETHICS 129 (1984); early discussions by political scientists are LOUISE OVERACKER, MONEY IN ELECTIONS (1932) and ALEXANDER HEARD, THE COSTS OF DEMOCRACY: FINANCING AMERICAN POLITICAL CAMPAIGNS (1960).

119. First National Bank of Boston v. Bellotti, 435 U.S. 765 (1978). But see Austin v. Michigan Chamber of Commerce, 494 U.S. 652 (1990), and Federal Election Commission v. Colorado Republican Federal Campaign Committee, —U.S.—, 121 S. Ct. 2351 (2001). It is well recognized that incumbent candidates have significant fund-raising (and therefore spending) advantages; for the 1992 election, 379 incumbents in the U.S. House and Senate spent $305.4 million, while 800 challengers spent $123.2 million (primary and general elections combined). There are also some partisan differences in fundraising and spending; for the 1992 election, Democratic Party committees at all levels spent $171.9 million while their Republican counterparts spent $256.1 million. If we add together spending by party committees and spending by each party's individual general election candidates for federal office, for the 1992 election Republicans spent $494.5 million

while Democrats spent $457.4 million. These are very large sums of money indeed. An analysis of incumbent members of the 103rd Congress (elected in 1992) showed that from 1987 through 1993 House incumbents had received $131.5 million in campaign contributions from political action committees (PACs) sponsored by business corporations and $62.5 million from PACs sponsored by labor unions. Democratic representatives had received $72.7 million from business PACs and $57.5 million from labor PACs, while Republican representatives had received $58.8 million from business PACs and $4.8 million from labor PACs. In U.S. Senate elections, business PACs gave incumbent Republicans $39.8 million over this period, and incumbent Democrats $32.2 million; labor PACs gave incumbent Republicans $1.5 million and incumbent Democrats $15.2 million. Overall, the members of the 103rd Congress, House and Senate, had received about two and a half times more from business PACs ($203.5 million) than from labor PACs ($79.2 million). On party differences in spending for the 1992 election, see Federal Election Commission, *Democrats Increase Spending by 89% in the '92 Cycle* (Press Release, January 1994), and FEC, *1991–92 Congressional Spending*, *supra* note 118; on the contributions by business and labor PACs, see Common Cause News, *Business PACs Gave $203 Million to Current Members of Congress* (Press Release, August 4, 1994).

120. But as Justice Stevens has noted, "Money is property; it is not speech." Nixon v. Shrink Missouri Government PAC, 528 U.S. 377 at 398 (2000) (concurring opinion). It might be noted, incidentally, that a very large percentage of campaign expenditures go to activities that are only remotely connected to political speech. According to one study, in 1992 only 47.4% of incumbents' expenditures went to advertising or other campaign activities; the remainder went to overhead, fundraising, polling, constituent gifts, donations, or was unitemized. Challengers and those running for open seats spent about three-fifths of their total expenditures on advertising and campaign activities (62.5% of challengers' spending and 64.4% of open-seat spending). Nonetheless, *all* spending, whether for advertising and other more-or-less traditional campaign activities or not, is protected speech under the First Amendment, according to Buckley v. Valeo, *supra* note 8, and its progeny, whose total may not be limited consistent with the Constitution. See MORRIS AND GAMACHE, HANDBOOK OF CAMPAIGN SPENDING, *supra* note 114, at 12 (Table 1–6).

121. See especially Nicholson, *Buckley v.Valeo:The Constitutionality of the Federal Election Campaign Act Amendments of 1974*, 1977 WISC. L. REV. 323; Wright, *Politics and the Constitution: Is Money Speech?* 85 YALE L. J. 1001 (1976); and Wright, *Money and the Pollution of Politics: Is the First Amendment an Obstacle to Political Equality?* 82 COLUM. L. REV. 609(1982). Judge Wright was on the panel of judges from the United States Court of Appeals for the District of Columbia Circuit which originally heard the appeal in the Buckley case. See Buckley v. Valeo, 519 F.2d 821 (D.C. Cir., 1975) (per curiam).

122. See Buckley v. Valeo, *supra* note 8, 424 U.S. at 98–104.

123. The law governing the public campaign finance system is the Presidential Election Campaign Fund Act, originally passed in the wake of the Watergate scandals in 1974 and whose main provisions, as currently amended, are codified in 26 U.S.C.

§ 9001 *et seq.*(1993). Under the current law, the general election campaign for president of the two major parties is fully funded by public money (totaling $61.82 million to each party's candidate in 1996, plus $12.5 million to subsidize each major party's national convention). See 22 FEDERAL ELECTION COMMISSION RECORD at 3 (October 1996). A party receiving at least five% of the popular vote is eligible for retroactive funding, though in a smaller amount, and for funding in the following presidential race. The campaigns for the presidential nominations of the two major parties are partially funded by federal money on a matching basis; this system thus allows public subsidies to candidates who satisfy a minimal threshold (of at least $5000 in contributions under $250 from each of at least 20 states) of private fundraising. In effect the federal statute subsidizes "serious" candidates, but "seriousness" is determined initially not by the intrinsic merit of their platforms or by the actual or potential popularity of their candidacies with the electorate, but by the popularity of their candidacies with people who are willing to give money to a campaign, by their ability to raise sufficient funds to qualify for matching funds. This statutory mechanism thus takes for granted much of the private system of political financing, and in fact uses that system to screen candidates' access to the public system of political financing, and once granted, public subsidies for the presidential primaries are awarded only to those who are able to raise private funds as well (the subsidies match the private funds one-for-one). Presumably this system gives a certain advantage to whichever candidates favor those policies which are also supported by those people who can afford to give $250 contributions to their campaigns. For purposes of comparison, $250 was nearly six days' entire income for a family of four at the poverty line in 1995. See U.S. DEPARTMENT OF COMMERCE, BUREAU OF THE CENSUS, POVERTY IN THE UNITED STATES: 1995 (Current Population Reports P60-194, 1996), at A-3 (Table A-1) (giving poverty threshold of $15,569 income for family of four in 1995) This statutory scheme is set up by the Presidential Primary Matching Payment Account Act, established by the Federal Election Campaign Act Amendments of 1974, *supra* note 78; for details on its administration since 1976, see FEDERAL ELECTION COMMISSION, THE PRESIDENTIAL PUBLIC FUNDING PROGRAM, esp. at 71 (Appendix 3) (1993). As the major-party presidential nominations are presently structured, a candidate for a nomination must participate in presidential primaries first; the last nominee *not* to do so was Vice President Humphrey in 1968. In 1996, for example, nearly 70% of the delegates to the Democratic National Convention, and over 75% of the delegates to the Republican National Convention, were chosen in primary elections or bound by primary results; even caucuses are now the subject of full-scale (and expensive) personal campaigning by candidates. See *Steps to the Nomination—Special Report: A State-By-State Guide to the Process of Choosing Presidential Candidates*, in 53 CONG. Q. WEEKLY REP. at 2477 ff. (August 19, 1995) (giving each party's 1996 delegate selection methods in each state). Given this, even the full public funding of the major party's presidential candidates in the general election therefore piggybacks on the financial screening mechanism of the presidential primaries. The Supreme Court, however, rejected the claim that this system operated as official discrimination on grounds of wealth in Buckley v. Valeo, *supra* note 8, 424 U.S. at 107–108, apparently since it merely replicated, with little or no further exaggeration, the distribution of wealth and income in the private economy. For the 1994 poverty line, see BUREAU OF THE CENSUS, INCOME, POVERTY...: 1994, *supra* note 108.

124. Some empirical evidence suggests that *negative* advertising, at least, has the effect of reducing overall voter turnout, perhaps by as much as 5%. See STEPHEN ANSOLABEHERE AND SHANTO IYENGAR, GOING NEGATIVE: HOW POLITICAL ADVERTISEMENTS SHRINK & POLARIZE THE ELECTORATE at 99–114 (1995); Ansolabehere, Iyengar, Simon, and Valentino, *Does Attack Advertising Demobilize the Electorate?* 88 AMER. POL. SCI. REV. 829 (1994).

125. When John Kennedy was elected to the presidency in 1960, some 63% of the voting-age population voted. More than 60% of the electorate turned out for the presidential election of 1968. But over time, rates of voting have dropped, so that by the time Bill Clinton was reelected to the presidency in 1996, less than 50% turned out to vote. Between the 1960 and 1996 presidential elections, in other words, the equivalent of more than a fifth of the then-active electorate (proportionally) became inactive in Presidential elections. Turnout in the ten presidential elections from 1932 through 1968 averaged 58.3% of the voting-age population; the average in the seven from 1972 through 1996 was 53.2%, a decline of nearly 9%. Total votes cast for president and vice president in 1996 were 96,389,818; the Census Bureau's estimate of the civilian, noninstitutional voting-age population was 196,509,000, for a turnout of 49.1%; as a share of the citizen voting-age population, 1996 turnout was about 53.2% (of an eligible citizen population of about 181.2 million). In the extremely close presidential election of 2000, turnout was about 51.3% of the civilian voting-age population (105,594,024 votes cast from a voting-age population of 205,814,000). Similarly, participation in congressional elections has declined since 1960 from over 58% of the voting-age population to about 46% in 1996. In so-called off-year elections, after exceeding 40% in each election from 1950 through 1970, turnout has declined from about 45% of the electorate in 1962 and 1966 to 36% in 1994. Turnout in presidential-year congressional elections averaged about 54.4% over the ten elections 1932–1968, but only 48.1% in the seven elections 1972–1996, a decline of about 12%. Turnout in off-year congressional elections averaged 41.3% in the nine elections 1934–1966, but only 36.5% in the seven elections 1970–1994, also a decline of about 12%. Calculations for 1932–1994 based on figures in STATISTICAL ABSTRACT OF THE UNITED STATES 1996, *supra* note 65, at 290 (Table 461). For votes cast in 1996, see U.S. HOUSE, CLERK, STATISTICS OF THE...ELECTION OF...1996, *supra* note 64, at 78–82; for voting-age population, see U.S. DEPARTMENT OF COMMERCE, BUREAU OF THE CENSUS, ELECTION '96—COUNTING THE AMERICAN ELECTORATE (Statistical Brief SB/96-2, April 1996). Prior to 1996, voter turnout had not dropped below half of the voting-age population in a presidential election since the first two elections after woman suffrage became law nationwide, in 1920 and 1924; before that, voter turnout had not been less than half of the sex- and race-eligible voting-age population in a presidential election since 1824. To take one example, New York state's turnout for the Clinton-Dole election in 1996 (6,316,129) was less than half (46.5 %) of the voting-age population (estimated at 13,579,000), the

lowest percentage since 1924 and a decline of nearly a third since 1960 (when turnout was 67% of the voting-age population). The turnout of the citizens of voting age was the third lowest in the state since the Census Bureau began counting the citizen electorate in 1870 (the only two lower were the presidential elections of 1980 and 1988); since 1960 the citizen turnout has declined by nearly a fourth, from 70.6 % to 54.0 %.. Estimates of turnout calculated in terms of the sex- and race-eligible *citizen* population of voting age for presidential elections from 1824 through 1968 are given in U.S. DEPARTMENT OF COMMERCE, BUREAU OF THE CENSUS, HISTORICAL STATISTICS OF THE UNITED STATES: COLONIAL TIMES TO 1970, pt. 2, at 1071–1072 (Series Y27–78) (Bicentennial ed. 1975), with introductory remarks by Walter Dean Burnham at 1067–1069; estimates for presidential elections from 1932 through 1992, calculated in terms of the resident voting-age population, including both citizens and aliens, are given in STATISTICAL ABSTRACT, *supra* note 65, at 287 (Table 458). Votes cast for president in New York state in 1996 are in NEW YORK STATE BOARD OF ELECTIONS, 1996 GENERAL ELECTION VOTE (1996).

126. See Ex parte Yarbrough, *supra* note 8, 4 S.Ct. 152 at 159–160.

127. Voting Rights Act Amendments of 1982, currently codified at 42 U.S.C. § 1973 (b) (1993), *supra* note 62.

San Francisco State University Series in Philosophy

This series is designed to encourage philosophers to explore new directions of research in philosophy. The underlying premise of the series is that contemporary philosophical research is impeded by an understanding of the intellectual division of labor according to which philosophy is conceived of as separate from the natural and social sciences, the arts and humanistic disciplines. Science is impoverished by the neglect of immediate attention to the metaphysical and moral questions posed by scientific developments. The arts and humanistic disciplines are also impoverished by a lack of sufficient attention to the philosophical implication of innovation in each of these areas. Philosophy for its part is in danger of grinding away on outdated problems posed by the scientific and artistic developments of past centuries. The usual remedy for this situation, inter-disciplinary work, typically falls far short of the needed re-integration of philosophy, the sciences, the arts and humanistic disciplines. The pressing problems of contemporary civilization, particularly the problems that concern the relationship between science, technology and ethical and political values, we believe, can only be adequately explored by a re-integration of philosophy with other fields. Our series seeks to call attention to itself by meeting high standards of scholarship and producing work of unquestionable merit. Works in our series should contribute to the re-integration of philosophy with the natural and social sciences, technology, the arts or humanities by challenging philosophical preconceptions that block the re-integration of philosophy with other disciplines.

For more information about this series, please contact:

Anatole Anton
Dept. of Philosophy
San Francisco State University
1600 Holloway Avenue
San Francisco, CA 94132
(415) 338-1596

To order other books in this series, please contact our Customer Service Department at:

800-770-LANG (within the U.S.)
(212) 647-7706 (outside the U.S.)
(212) 647-7707 FAX

or browse online by series at:

www.peterlangusa.com